Washington, D.C.
Ghosts, Legends, & Lore

E. Ashley Rooney
and
Betsy Johnston

Schiffer Publishing Ltd

4880 Lower Valley Road, Atglen, Pennsylvania 19310

Schiffer Books are available at special discounts for bulk purchases for sales promotions or premiums. Special editions, including personalized covers, corporate imprints, and excerpts can be created in large quantities for special needs. For more information contact the publisher:

Published by Schiffer Publishing Ltd.
4880 Lower Valley Road
Atglen, PA 19310
Phone: (610) 593-1777; Fax: (610) 593-2002
E-mail: Info@schifferbooks.com

This book may be purchased from the publisher.
Include $3.95 for shipping.
Please try your bookstore first.
You may write for a free catalog.

In Europe, Schiffer books are distributed by
Bushwood Books
6 Marksbury Ave.
Kew Gardens
Surrey TW9 4JF England
Phone: 44 (0) 20 8392-8585; Fax: 44 (0) 20 8392-9876
E-mail: info@bushwoodbooks.co.uk
Website: www.bushwoodbooks.co.uk
Free postage in the U.K., Europe; air mail at cost.

For the largest selection of fine reference books on this and related subjects, please visit our web site at **www.schifferbooks.com**
We are always looking for people to write books on new and related subjects. If you have an idea for a book please contact us at the above address.

Back cover image: Two bronze lions, designed by Dutch sculptor Paul Koning, guard the plaza steps in front of The Netherlands Carillon. *Courtesy of D. Peter Lund*

Title page image: Open to the public in 1888, the marble Washington Monument, honoring America's first president, was the world's tallest structure until the Eiffel Tower was completed. It is the tallest structure in the nation's Capitol and will remain so by law. *Courtesy of D. Peter Lund*

Maryland State Flag image background: © Martin Bangemann. Image from BigStockPhoto.com.

Copyright © 2008 by E. Ashley Rooney and Betsy Johnston
Library of Congress Control Number: 2008920789

Designed by Stephanie Daugherty
Type set in Burton's Nightmare 2000/NewBskvll BT

ISBN: 978-0-7643-2961-6
Printed in China

Acknowledgments

M any of us don't quite understand ghosts. In this book, we have told or retold these stories from a fictional perspective, trying from our comfortable place in the twenty-first century to make sense of the past. Their lost voices must continue to be heard; their untold stories must continue to be recounted—for they represent the ones who didn't live to tell their stories themselves. Throughout our work, we have tried to be as true to historical fact as possible.

Hunting for ghosts and the legends of the past is an interesting challenge. We have to thank our families and friends for their tolerance as we talked about the ghosts we found and the history we uncovered. The photographs of D. Peter Lund and Michael Lodico, Jr. were great assets to our work.

Contents

The Iwo Jima Memorial, which depicts one of the most famous incidents of World War II, is dedicated to all Marines who have given their lives in defense of the United States since 1775. *Courtesy of D. Peter Lund*

GHOSTS

Washington D.C. celebrates many famous heroes, both known and unknown. Statues of them can be found throughout the city. In some cases, their ghosts wander about the city too. Sometimes the stories of these ghosts are not known. Often their stories *are* known, however. Some may still hope to change the face of history. Others are looking to recapture that special moment. These ghostly tales endeavor to give these spirits a past and perhaps even a future.

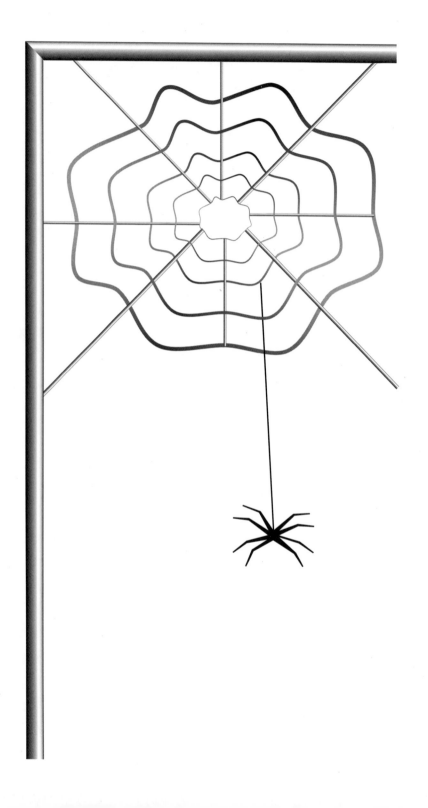

OLD STONE HOUSE

In Washington, D.C., a city of grand memorials, stands an unassuming building commemorating the daily lives of ordinary Americans who made this city, and this nation, unique. The Old Stone House, the oldest known structure remaining in the nation's capital, is a simple eighteenth century dwelling built and inhabited by common people. Today, several ghosts inhabit it.

Christopher Lehmann was hunched over his ledger, working by the light of two precious candles. Rachel, sitting by the fire, redarning one of his old socks, glanced over at her husband from time to time. His occasional grunt or sigh worried her. Gentle and kind as a rule, Christopher lately had worn a frown more often than not and was clearly distracted.

Finally, he slammed his quill pen down on the table and walked over to stand by the fire. Rachel stole a sideways glance at him. The firm set of his jaw and his pinched lips did nothing to assuage the tension Rachel felt. She wished he would speak; his silence was painful to her. Rachel set her darning in her lap and wiped her hands on her white apron. She reached up to tuck her errant blond curls discreetly under the simple white cotton cap that she wore.

Rachel's movement caught her husband's eye. The gesture that he had seen so many times touched a chord of tenderness in his heart, and his face softened as he watched her slender hands run through the tendrils at the back of her neck. Suddenly, he longed to touch that white neck and kiss her delicate ears and smooth, soft lips. He wanted to hold her and take comfort in her warmth and her scent.

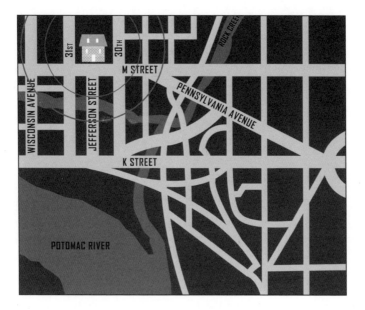

"My dear," he cleared his throat to bring himself back to the task at hand. "I have come to a decision."

"Yes, husband." Rachel lifted her blue eyes to her husband's face. Her eyes were the soft shade of blue so common to the Germanic stock from which she came. Her face was not beautiful, but it was as fresh and open as when they were married twelve years earlier.

"I am not a farmer. For too many years, I have labored at a job for which I have no talent. I cannot compete with our neighbors who, it would seem, have the soil in their blood." Rachel waited silently to see where this thought was going.

"What I love, what I want to do, is to work with wood. It is what I am good at." He walked over to the table where he had been sitting and gently ran his hand across the smooth pine. Christopher felt immense pride because he found no flaw in his workmanship as his fingers, sensitive as a surgeon's, caressed every facet of his masterpiece. Indeed, he had crafted every piece of furniture in their small house. He had created their bed as a wedding present for Rachel. As the boys came along, he lovingly built a bed for each of them.

Rachel sat very still despite the emotion that she was feeling. She was the daughter of a farmer. In fact, farming was the only occupation she had ever known. She naturally assumed that her husband would always be a farmer just like her father and his father. True, she did love it when Christopher would return from his workshop with a chair or bench or chest that he had created to fill in the empty spaces in their little house. She could not imagine, however, that he would give up farming for cabinetmaking, nor how they would survive.

The needle in her hand flew as she pulled the edges of the woolen heel back together. She stabbed the needle in and drew it back out. *Has the man taken leave of his senses,* she wondered. *What can he be thinking? We cannot just up and change the course of our lives. Here we sit on all these acres of rich soil, and he is going to let it lie fallow while he makes chairs! Everyone else is prospering. We can too.*

"I have read about the rich port in Maryland, called George Town." Christopher continued, apparently unaware of her agitation. "I am thinking we should move there. There are ships coming and going all the time with all the materials I would ever need, and they could sell my goods all over the world."

Her darning needle pricked her finger; she yelped. Now he was proposing they leave their home! Although she respected her husband's authority as head of his household, this newest revelation was more than she could stand. Sticking her finger in her mouth to stop the bleeding, she attempted to choose her words wisely. "Dear husband, this is so sudden. I am quite taken aback by this news. Are we not comfortable and happy here? You are proposing we leave our *home*? Everything is here: our families, our house, our land, and our church! Our boys are growing up big and strong here on the farm."

"There will be better opportunities for them in a port town," Christopher said firmly.

"But what do we know about this George Town? We will know no one. We will have to start all over again," she wailed.

"My dear, you must trust me. Have I not seen to the welfare of our family? I do believe I know what is best for our future and us. Be calm and cease this fretting! Everything will work out well."

"But to move and start all over again…"

"My plan is to go to Maryland and buy some land closely situated to the Port. There I will build a house for us, and then I will return for you and Kurt and Hans. In the meantime, you will be well looked after here by Hermann. He will see to the farm and to your needs while I am away, and your parents are nearby."

"And what about them? You are proposing we move far away from my parents…the boys' grandparents."

"Your parents are more capable of this life than I. They are well and strong and besides, your brother George is there."

Yes, but what about me? Rachel was thinking. Christopher's arguments did little to console her. She was appalled at his selfishness and upset by the rashness of his ideas. Each new revelation by her husband led to a new set of anxieties.

Rachel knew she was quite capable of coping in his absence. After all, farming was what she *did* know. And she was quite used to running the house, making their clothes, preparing their food, and healing their ills. She was also accustomed to having her husband make the major decisions in their lives, but never had he suggested anything as drastic as this. He also had never left her for an extended period of time, and she was wondering how well she would handle a long separation from him. As angry as she was now, she knew she would be so lonely without him. Married at seventeen, she had moved from the adoring arms of her parents into those of her husband; she had never been alone. She looked up at Christopher wonderingly. Could he not sense her concern? Did he not care what she wanted? But the look on his face confirmed for her that he had made up his mind.

Without further ado, she rose from her chair, set down her darning, and walked out of the room. Perhaps now he would take notice of her and her feelings.

She waited, sleepless, for hours in their bed, certain that Christopher would come to her. Praying he would see the folly of his idea, hoping he would come and wrap her in the comforting strength of his arms, she willed him to tell her that he had changed his mind. She reasoned to herself that he would forget this foolhardy idea, seeing that it caused her so much distress.

She awoke at dawn. Her husband was beside her in the bed he had created with his own skillful hands, but his back was to her. Rachel felt very alone.

The weeks before Christopher Lehmann left Pennsylvania for his destination in George Town were busy ones. He laid in all the stores he felt his family would need in his absence. With the help of his farm laborer, Hermann, he patched the roof of his house, checked all the fences and the barn, replacing loose planks and missing nails, planted the crops, and tended to the livestock. In addition to the two horses, that did double duty as plow animals and cart-pullers, there were chickens, ducks, goats, and a lovely jersey cow that kept the family supplied with her rich milk and cream.

Rachel's emotions continued to run wild. She loved her husband deeply, but she still was angry with him over a decision she considered impetuous. She poured most of her attention onto her two young sons, making certain not to infect them with her concerns. "Schlaf, kindlein, schlaf," she sang to them when she tucked them in their cots at night. The lullaby soothed Rachel as well.

Christopher treated Rachel gently, but was unwavering in his resolve. "Please, my dear wife," he would coax, "trust me. I will take care of us. Everything will be fine." Rachel could not resist his tender concern, and, for a time, she would be calm and loving again.

"I am going to ride Old Bob," Christopher had told Rachel. She would be left with one horse to pull the plow and the wagon. Neither of their horses was young, but they were of strong stock and had always been well cared for.

"He will get you to George Town safely, I am sure. He's a good horse." However, she did not like his traveling alone. "Is there no one else who may be going to George Town as well?" she asked him.

"Many people, I understand, are going to seek their fortunes near these large ports. I am assured that I will find other travelers along the way with whom I can ride."

The day dawned when Christopher was set to leave. In spite of herself, Rachel was unable to contain her tears. Christopher held her closely, kissing her cheeks and then her lips and whispering soft words of reassurance in her ear. He lifted each of his sons so that he could look directly in their eyes. He told them to take care of their mother and the farm and that he would return soon to take them to their new home.

Going Away

It was well past dark, two days later, when Christopher finally arrived in George Town. Thankfully, he had met up with others traveling in the same direction, and one of them, a fellow German named Jacob, had actually made the trip previously.

He was happy to direct Christopher on the long journey. The men found a tavern with rooms above for travelers such as themselves. After settling Old Bob in a nearby stall with sweet hay and a good ration of oats, Christopher was ready for the tall lager he ordered in the tavern below his room. Jacob joined him. "Ah, it is good to sit and rest a spell, eh Chris?"

"Yes, indeed. Plenty to do tomorrow, but for now, this is all I could wish for." As he said this, Christopher mentally retracted the statement. Goodness knows, he certainly wished Rachel and his sons were here with him. However, with all the uncertainties facing him, he did feel a certain relief in knowing they were safely at home on the farm. He chuckled to himself at the irony of that thought....No, *this* is home now!

It was just dawn when Christopher roused himself, uncertain initially as to his whereabouts. He dressed quickly, washing with water from the pitcher that had been placed on the dresser the night before. He was bursting with anticipation and was eager to see his surroundings in the light of day. As he stepped into the warmth of the June morning, the soft summer sunlight pierced its way through the tree branches and cast its pinky golden spell over all who were awake to see it. Birds were singing their full-throated morning greeting. The town was already bustling. Horses were pulling wagons along Bridge Street that ran in front of his lodging.

Christopher knew that he could follow them to the river port where the ships came and went bearing their precious wares. Christopher was eager to see the port and set off down the long, steep hill to the river. As he neared the wharf, he could see that there were several ships tied up, their rigging slapping and clacking against the huge spars. The sight of an approaching ship in the distance, its large square sails close hauled—sails so white against the blue of this hot and humid summer's day—brought memories flooding back to Christopher of stories his Grandmother would tell him.

"My parents came to this country on a ship across the huge ocean. The ship had enormous sails that would catch the wind that pushed them across the sea all the way to the new world."

As Christopher got older, his Grandmother would tell him more and more detail. "Mama and Papa came, as so many did, in search of a better life. They heard that they could have their own land and do with it what they wished; and that they could pray as they wanted to pray; and that in this new world they would prosper. My father and mother could not resist such promises, but poor Papa was never to see this land or benefit from its freedoms. As you know, dear Christopher, your great-grandpapa died of the fever way out in the ocean. I never even knew my own father."

Christopher Lehmann heard this and many other stories as he was growing up. He learned that his great-grandparents and Rachel's had come to Philadelphia on the same ship in 1683 with the first large group of German immigrants, and that many passengers on those early ships had perished from the dreaded typhus. Christopher's great-grandfather was among those casualties. His grandmother was born only weeks after the ship arrived in Philadelphia.

As she was widowed with no means of support, Christopher's great-grandmother saw no option other than indentured servitude to support herself and her only child. As it turned out, this circumstance had its advantages. Mother and child were assimilated into the new American culture much more quickly than if they had remained with their German community. They learned English and the ways of the New World; consequently, Christopher appeared more American than German.

Christopher and Rachel had essentially grown up together. The hardship of the voyage to America had drawn their families close. That closeness had been maintained through the generations, culminating in Rachel's marriage to Christopher. As Christopher Lehmann shook himself from his reverie, he became suddenly aware of the similarities in his great-grandparents' story and his own. They thought it a good idea to seek their fortunes in the colonies, just as he was searching for a better way of life in George Town. This knowledge jolted him into an appreciation for Rachel's moodiness before he left. His great-grandfather had not been able to live his dream, and the hardships suffered by his wife and daughter were well known to both Rachel and him. He must write Rachel a long letter of reassurance as soon as he concluded his business here. He would tell her how strong and healthy he was and how he would let no harm come to his family.

Christopher knew that meeting people was critical to gaining information that would help him accomplish his goals. He walked around the bustling dock. Ships were unloading and loading; tradespeople were making deals; and townspeople were strolling about enjoying the sight of these large ships with their sails flapping in the breeze. Above them all, a flock of seagulls wheeled, hoping for scraps. He spoke to them all—from the men in crisp laundered linen to the small traders smelling of stale sweat.

"George Town is, first and foremost, a tobacco port," he was told. As the region was about as far up the Potomac River as ships could navigate before reaching the falls, it was the natural place to establish a port that tobacco farmers in Maryland were able to journey to easily. "The town has grown in this immediate area around the port. Just a short way up there," this new friend said, pointing north, "is all farmland."

"And where do most of these ships hail from?" Christopher asked.

"Many are from England, but we are a prime location for trade with New York, Boston, Philadelphia, and Baltimore. Every kind of merchandise is imported from those large cities." Christopher could see a prime opportunity for the export of his furniture.

Gradually, he gleaned the information he needed about getting started in George Town. He met a coach maker who had an establishment there. Christopher struck up a conversation with him over a beer in the tavern one evening.

"Have you been here long?" Christopher asked Charles, his new acquaintance.

"Coming on five years now, I guess. And you?"

"Actually, I have just arrived. I am a cabinetmaker by trade, and I heard that George Town would be a good place to set up my business. I want to build a house and bring my family here, but first I must find a temporary place to work."

After a few more beers and genial conversation, Charles apparently decided that Christopher was a good sort and offered him the use of a corner of his shop until Christopher had built his own.

"I actually am very much in need of a sturdy table. If you make me one, that will secure at least your first month's rent."

They shook hands to seal their agreement. Christopher was elated. Although he had been able to save enough money to leave with Rachel for his absence as well as what he himself needed to get to George Town and pay his expenses for a short while, he knew he must build some furniture and sell it quickly to stay solvent. Once he got going, he was sure that he would make enough to buy some land and build his house.

Never afraid of a challenge, Christopher quickly acquired the basic tools and materials he needed and set to his craft. In a matter of days, he had turned out two lovely tables, one of which went immediately to Charles. His friend Jacob was impressed. "Oh, Chris, you are a fine craftsman. You will have no trouble selling here, for certain." Word quickly spread among the more established inhabitants of the town that a new craftsman was available to make beautiful furniture, and visitors to the coach maker could see his skill as he worked. He was well situated for success.

Suddenly, Christopher had many orders for tables, chests, and chairs. Although he routinely used pine for furniture for his own home, when he saw the chance to construct a higher grade of furniture, he selected the best woods he could find: walnut, cherry, oak, and the occasional piece of mahogany. The men and the women of the town came to his shop in the coach maker's establishment to run their hands over the silken sheen of his pieces and to dream about which one to buy.

Within a few months, Christopher had a pocketful of English currency. He set about his next goal: acquiring some land. During his evenings at the tavern, and as he mingled among the people at the wharf, he had been learning some of the history of this place in which he had chosen to live.

The town had begun as a small settlement in 1696. In 1747, following years of poor prices for Maryland tobacco and numerous complaints from merchants concerning its quality, the General Assembly established a formal system of tobacco inspection and quality control. No longer could planters sell their tobacco directly to tobacco merchants. Instead, they first had to bring it in to public tobacco warehouses for inspection and grading. Gordon's tobacco warehouse was located a short distance down Bridge Street from the tavern. There, after inspection, the hogsheads were stored and then loaded on ships for export. It was crucial to keeping the prices high that only the highest grade of tobacco be exported.

George Town was fast becoming one of the most important tobacco ports along the Atlantic seaboard. In recognition of its significance, landowners petitioned the Maryland Assembly to recognize the area as "George Town," named after the reigning king of England, in 1751. The town was incorporated as part of the British Colony of Maryland.

In due course, the new town commissioners set aside sixty acres, divided it into eighty parcels, and required purchasers of lots to improve the land by building thereon "one good and substantial House."

On June 11, 1764, Christopher put down one pound, ten shillings, for Lot No. 3, a deep, narrow piece of land that had sixty-seven feet of frontage on Bridge Street, and extended just under four hundred feet in length. Then he set about building a house in the manner of Pennsylvania dwellings he had known.

Christopher wrote to Rachel with the exciting news. "My dear wife, I have been successful in procuring for us some land on which I mean to build our house. If I set the house on the street, we will have more than enough room in back for a garden and some fruit trees and livestock to support our needs. There is stone, bluestone from the river, right here in great abundance. It will make a good, strong house for us. I made and sold some tables, that allowed me to purchase the land, and with enough left over to begin acquiring the materials I will need. I hope you and the boys are well. It will not be long now before I come to fetch you. I had told our neighbors that I would probably sell our farm. Now, there is no doubt. If you would tell them that now it is definite, if they want to add to their land, I will make them a fair bargain. I am eager to have my family here with me. When I come for you, we want to have our affairs in order so that we can leave in short order. Your devoted husband."

Rachel's initial fears had abated as she received reassuring letters from Christopher. She had no trouble keeping her mind and body occupied. Aside from the usual chores of keeping her house and caring for the boys, she would knit, sew and pick herbs, and hang them in bunches in her kitchen for drying; she was so fond of their tantalizing scents. She would take her sons in the cart behind Ben and go to visit her parents, or the neighbors. There was no end of things to keep her busy, and though she longed to be with Christopher, she was not unhappy.

First, always, were her sons. Kurt and Hans were growing tall and sturdy like their father. At nine and eleven, they were taking pride in what they saw as caring for their mother and taking over their father's responsibilities in his absence. Hans, the younger, was content to work in the fields with Hermann all day. He asked endless questions. "Why doesn't the horse's hooves trample the shoots? When will the corn be ready to pick?" And on and on.

Kurt stayed closer to his mother. He enjoyed working with the livestock, collecting eggs from the chickens and geese, feeding the pigs, horse, and the fowl, and milking the cow. He would bring his mother the eggs he had collected, put the milk in the icehouse, and take and fetch as his mother needed. He would even help her peg up the laundry, enjoying an easy conversation with his lovely, gentle mother. "Are you going to miss all this when Papa comes to take us to George Town?" she would ask.

"Will it be so very different?"

"Well," she said, "Papa says that there is a busy street right in front of where he is building our house. There are pigs and chickens running around in the road as well as big wagons hauling tobacco and other things that will go on the ships that are down on the river. The river is huge, Papa says, with big ships coming and going, bringing things from across the ocean and taking things back across that we are selling."

"That sounds exciting."

"There are people all around, people selling things, people doing business. It is a far cry from the peace and solitude that we have here, but, yes, it does sound exciting."

Christopher had also written that Jacob was helping him to clear the massive trees off his plot of land. Jacob was not married and only had to keep food in his stomach and a roof over his head. He was quite content, apparently, to cast his lot with Christopher, who was able to pay Jacob enough to fulfill his needs. Christopher also was happy with this arrangement. "Jacob is strong as an ox," Christopher wrote to Rachel. "He is willing as long as he can go to the tavern in the evening with enough in his pocket to buy a plate of stew and a few beers."

Christopher had been mentally planning his house for so long that as soon as he had purchased his land, cleared the necessary trees, and bought the first materials, he was prepared to start building. As necessary, he would create a beautiful chest, chair, bedstead, or table that he would easily sell to replenish his funds so that he could purchase the Potomac-quarried bluestone, the wood for the beams, the nails, the wooden shingles for the roof, and the other requisite supplies.

With Jacob's help, Christopher laid the walls two and one-half feet thick with the blue stone that was hauled by wagon arduously up the steep hill from the river. Christopher's deed had stipulated "one good and substantial house," and he was a literal person. Good and substantial it would definitely be. Day after day, the two men worked side by side, their massive hands rough and torn from handling the huge stones, their backs and shoulders increasing from their already considerable breadth as they toiled, straining and hauling each rock into place. Slowly, the walls grew toward the sky. They employed every tool and bit of ingenuity that either of them possessed to accomplish the engineering feat they had undertaken.

Into the west end wall, he and Jacob constructed a massive chimney, which would be the heart and soul of the structure and of his family's life. From here would come the warmth and the food that they would need to survive. Around this fire, the four of them would congregate to work, talk, eat, and pray. The thought of his family in front of this fireplace kept Christopher going through the pain, exhaustion, blood, and sweat that the building extracted from him on a daily basis.

Occasionally, Christopher would take a respite from his labors on the house. Some days he was so exhausted and sore that he could work no more. On those days, he found his rest and relaxation at the wharf. He enjoyed watching the ships, rocking and creaking, as men scurried on and off, loading cargo that was waiting in huge carts at the river's edge. He would talk to these men when their work was done and question them about their journeys across the ocean. He hoped one day to be able to take his family across that vast body of water to visit their homeland. He would watch and dream, talk, and question. Then he would go back home to move his dream to the next stage.

At last, the house was close enough to completion that Christopher set out to get his family. He longed to see them after almost a year's absence. He had hoped to finish the house sooner, but the winter had been rough. Bad weather had significantly delayed progress. First, it was snow, ice, and terrible cold; then the cool constant rains of spring that slowed his pace to a crawl. Now, though it was not yet totally complete, he was very proud of his work. His house was one of the first on Bridge Street. Details of the house—the roofline, the stonework, the brick gable on the east side, and chimney on the west—resembled the style brought to the colonies by his European forebears. Wooden shingles covered the roof. He found the house to be handsome, and he was excited about showing it to Rachel.

"Jacob," said Christopher, "I can wait no longer. I am off to bring my family here. Can I rely on you to work on some of the details in my absence?" Jacob and Christopher had learned to depend on each other. Jacob would not let Christopher go faster or do more than he did, even though he had no stake in the outcome. In return, Christopher took the place of the family that Jacob did not have. Each evening they would meet at the tavern and share a supper of meat pudding made from the left over meat from lunch, a roast potato, and a beer. They would drink and talk over the events of the day and the goings on in this busy port city.

"Of course, go on with you now. I am eager to meet Rachel and my 'nephews.'" Jacob felt he knew Rachel and the boys for Christopher spoke of them constantly. "Safe journey to all of you and hurry back. If you are gone too long, I might just move into this fine house myself!" He gave Christopher a good-natured slap on the back.

Going Home

Christopher had written Rachel that he was coming home. Her anticipation was such that it seemed to take forever for him to actually get back to the farm. She happily packed their few belongings. There was not much: their clothes and furniture, the tools that Christopher had not been able to take with him, a small amount of pottery and cutlery, and a few cherished items were all they had. The farm wagon had more than enough room for these. She had been busily sewing new breeches for the boys and for Christopher out of fabric she had been saving. She fashioned a blue dress for herself and, even though the linen was coarse, the color was lovely and flattering. She did want them all to be as fashionable as she could make them for their arrival in George Town.

Rachel no longer doubted this move. She was desperate to be with her husband. Through his descriptive letters, she had become quite intrigued with the thoughts of her new life in the 'city.' She related all she knew to her sons and worked to build their enthusiasm so that by the time Christopher came for them they would all be eager for this change.

One afternoon, Rachel was quickly pulling the laundry off the line, trying to beat the rain that was certainly on the way. Her senses had been on alert ever since she knew Christopher was coming. She often imagined the sound of Old Bob clopping down the lane only to find that it was all in her head. Sometimes she would weep from the sheer weight of her loneliness and the anticipation of his homecoming. She had managed well for the most part during this long separation, but she would be happy to have her husband make the decisions once again and carry the responsibilities on his ample shoulders. She longed to have him to talk to, to share in the upbringing and joy of their growing sons, and to be by her side every night.

As she grabbed her basket, she heard the sound of hooves in the distance. This time it was unmistakable; there was a horse coming down the lane at a quick pace. She dropped the basket and ran towards the lane, peering into the distance. She was so afraid that once again she might be disappointed. It could just be one of their neighbors who had been stopping by frequently to check on her, but at last she could make out the distinctive mass and gray coat of Old Bob.

Suddenly self-conscious, Rachel tugged at her skirt and straightened her apron, smoothing it down the front. She felt her curls and tucked some stray ends under her cap, pinched her cheeks, and licked her lips. Her joy quickly overcame her shyness, and she ran with total abandon toward her husband. Christopher pulled the horse up with a jerk of the reins and leaped off. He was filthy with the dust and grime of days of riding, but in Rachel's eyes he had never looked so handsome. She fell into his embrace and melted into the safety of his huge chest. Without yet saying a word, he held her for long minutes and then raised her lips to his and kissed her more soundly than ever before as the promised rain fell softly over them.

Home Sweet Home

Christopher was able to conclude his business in Pennsylvania with some ease. Their neighbors on the south side of the farm were prospering and had a large family. They were happy to purchase the Lehmann farm in anticipation of marriages to come and expansion of the family farming business. The farm tools and most of the livestock stayed with the farm. The two families struck a fair deal that pleased each of them.

When the day came that the wagon was completely loaded and Christopher and Hermann were hitching up Old Bob and Ben, Rachel walked one last time through her little house. This house and farm were all she had ever known, except her parents' farm where she was born and raised. This was the only life she had ever known, but she was no longer afraid. Her life had come back together with the reuniting of the four of them. She had probably never been quite as content as she was right now, but she did feel as if she were losing an old and dear friend. This house where she had given birth to Kurt and Hans was as familiar as their dear faces. She sent up a little prayer that their life in this new place would be as happy and comforting as it had been here.

Saying good-bye to Hermann was hard for everyone. He was a faithful friend and hard worker. Hans could not prevent the tears from falling as he bid him good-bye. They had become so close while Christopher was away. "Don't you worry none, Hans. Old Hermann, he'll be right here when you come back to visit. Now you go on and see your new home and send me a letter telling me all about it." Of course, Hermann could not read, but he would love to get a letter nonetheless.

The journey was not an easy one. The old cart creaked and swayed and jolted over the rough road. A summer shower, often cooling, but adding to the misery of the little entourage would frequently punctuate hours of choking dust. The boys were so enthralled with this adventure that they were not so affected by the discomforts. Rachel, however, was weary and sore from the constant jostling and the long days, offset only slightly by short overnight respites in roadside inns. Christopher had planned the trip carefully, noting the locations of available rooms along the route he had taken home.

The renewed love that Rachel felt for Christopher since his return, however, overshadowed a lot of her pain. Indeed, she almost felt like a newlywed, so silly they were with one another, laughing, joking, and planning as they rumbled along the road to George Town. Christopher's success in selling his lovingly created furniture had eased Rachel's anxieties as to their future well-being. She looked forward to having only a small garden instead of a large farm. She happily anticipated living in a house built by her own husband. Life looked very rosy to Rachel, and she was filled with optimism about the future.

Rachel could tell when they were nearing their destination. Roads went off in all directions. There were buildings, houses, wagons, and riders on horseback, people leading livestock, and chickens and geese flapping about in their hurry to get out of the way of the traffic. Never had she or Kurt and Hans seen anything like this. The most people they had ever seen in any one place was at church and that was maybe thirty people. They had never experienced this vibrant activity, but they were instantly attracted by the excitement of it. "Look there, Mama," yelled Hans, pointing out a four-horse team pulling a wagon filled with produce.

"Yes, they are going to market, Hans," Christopher told him. "See that over there…that wagon is full of hogsheads of tobacco on their way to the tobacco inspection warehouse that's just west of Water Street. That is very close to our house! We are almost there now."

"I don't see any hog's heads. Those are just big barrels. Where's any tobacco?" The boys were overwhelmed with all the new and unfamiliar sights.

"Hogshead is what they call those barrels they use to ship the tobacco to England. Each barrel holds about fifteen hundred pounds."

Christopher had pulled the horse up in front of a stone house on the edge of the road. "Oh, Christopher!" Rachel exclaimed when she confirmed that it was indeed their house.

Today, several ghosts inhabit The Old Stone House, the oldest known structure remaining in the nation's capital. *Courtesy of Betsy Johnston*

"It is beautiful! Look boys, our new house that Papa has built for us. Isn't it wonderful?" Rachel was incredulous. Here, on this bustling street, she was going to live in a fine house with a lovely bit of land behind it. Her heart was pounding with gratitude to God who had bestowed such blessings on her and her family.

Christopher could hear Jacob on the second floor of the house and called out a greeting to him. Rachel liked Jacob immediately. He was a huge man, with coloring similar to Christopher's, but he was not nearly as handsome. He warmly welcomed her and the boys; in turn, she expressed her gratitude to him for his assistance to Christopher.

As weary as they all were, they nonetheless wanted to get settled as quickly as possible. They also had to unload the wagon so that the horses could be unhitched, stabled, and fed. The needs of their faithful steeds usually came before their own. So Jacob and Christopher together carried in the largest pieces of furniture while the boys made many trips with the smaller items. Rachel twirled around the rooms in disbelief. On the lower floor was Christopher's woodworking shop with the saws, chisels, and clamps he had already amassed as well as a supply of pine planks and a blanket chest that he had been working on. At the other end of this room was the family's gathering space with its huge fireplace. Upstairs was a bedroom for Rachel and Christopher and one for their two sons.

"The house is not quite finished," Christopher confessed. "I was so eager to have you here that I completed the first floor and hoped we could make do while the upstairs is being finalized."

Life Changes

After his family arrived, Christopher continued his practice of spending any spare time down at the pier. He loved to take his sons there and point out the intriguing goods that arrived from foreign lands and instruct them in the products that the colonies were shipping. By far, the largest and most valuable export was tobacco. One day, having finished the chest that he had been working on, Christopher begged Rachel to join them.

"My dear, you have been working too hard. Do come with us to the river. Surely you can spare the time for a stroll, and there is so much to be seen."

"Not today, Christopher. I am so close to finishing these curtains I have been sewing. I have wash to bring in, and then I must go to the butcher's for a leg of mutton."

"If you come with us, we can purchase a nice fish instead. It will do you good. Do come!"

"Yes, a fish would be nice. Do bring me one, but I must finish this work."

So, Christopher and his sons set off for the wharf with not a care in the world nor an inkling of what fate had in store for them. They wiled away several hours, milling among the booths that merchants would set up daily to exhibit their wares, before looking in at the fishmonger to find the perfect selection for Rachel.

There was everything one could desire, from copperware for cooking to fabrics imported from Europe. A new ship was arriving, and Christopher and his sons watched in awe at the skill and speed with which the seamen lowered the snowy white squares of sail while oared craft went out to meet the ship to guide her into port. The sailors then hitched their ship to the pier using heavy coils of rope and set up a gangplank that the passengers and crew used to disembark. The rigging slapped against the now naked masts, and the ship rocked, creaking her discontent at being confined. As was his custom, Christopher sought out some of those on board to talk to, to glean news of the passage and from whence they had come. He was unsuccessful in finding someone eager to converse, but from the crew he learned that it had been a long and rough passage; many had become ill.

Full of information they wanted to share with Rachel as well as a nice fresh fish, the threesome hurried home. In spite of her protests, Rachel felt left out of the day's adventure. She scolded herself for always putting work before pleasure, but she couldn't shake her ill humor, and later in the evening she showed her impatience with the boys' endless chatter. "Off to bed with you now! You have had a full day, but there will be many chores to see to in the morning. The garden needs work, and there are still trees to be taken down in the back so that your father can build the shed for the horses. We cannot afford to board them forever."

Christopher understood his wife well enough to know that she was miffed. He decided that it was best to leave her be, certain that her usual good nature would return by morning.

Work progressed on the little house and the land behind it over the next days. Rachel hung her pretty new curtains and continued to plant her garden as she found the right herbs and vegetables at the market. There were so many different and intriguing varieties available here.

The boys worked side by side with Christopher. They were learning and thriving in their new environment. Rachel thought she had never been so content. Her happiness was to be short-lived, however. In the middle of the night, about ten days later, Rachel awoke to find her husband tossing and turning next to her. She could feel the heat radiating from his body. When she reached out and touched his brow, she found it to be very hot. She quickly got out of bed and lit the candle on her nightstand. "Chris, Chris, what is it?"

Only barely coherent, he just moaned in response. She soaked a cloth in the pitcher's cool liquid, rolled it up, and laid it gently on her husband's forehead. "Ohhhhhhhh," he moaned, but he stopped his thrashing.

"Mama," called Hans. "Mama, I'm so hot! Please, Mama, come here." Rachel hurried into the boys' room to find them also burning with fever. She filled three cups with water that had been brought in from the well the evening before. She lifted Christopher's head and coaxed him to take some sips. Then she ran back to the boys, did the same, and then made cool cloths for their brows. Her mind raced to imagine what could have made them so ill. Then she remembered the day they had gone to the port and their tales of the new ship that had come in.

Rachel dared not leave the house to go in search of a doctor. She prayed that it would not be long before Jacob would come so that she could send him for help. In the meantime, she dashed from bed to bed, administering liquid, and changing the now-warm cloths for cool ones. Her work had little effect however, and by dawn, she was exhausted and frantic.

When Jacob knocked at the door, Rachel leapt to open it. The look on his face made Rachel realize that she was standing before him in only her nightdress, her long blond hair hanging to her waist. Blushing hotly, she snatched up a shawl and quickly drew it around her while explaining the situation to Jacob. After a quick look at Christopher, he hurried off for the doctor.

By the time Jacob returned with the physician, Rachel had thrown on her clothes and hastily pinned her hair under a cap. She had laid fresh sheets over the feverish bodies of her husband and sons and once again replaced the damp cloths, wiping their cheeks and necks and brushing their wet hair away from their brows.

The doctor examined each of the three in turn, shaking his head as he listened to their hearts and looked into their eyes. Turning to Rachel, he asked: "Who have they been with recently?"

"They went to the port about ten days ago. They saw all sorts of people that day. They bought me a fish, sold a walnut chest, and got other supplies."

"Did they tell you anything else?"

"They told me about a ship that had just come in. Many people on it were sick. Some even died."

"This is a very serious fever. I will give you the medicine I have. You must keep cooling them, and you must keep them away from others. I will come back later today and bring you more medicine."

"This is very serious then?"

"Yes. Do you have any food? You must not go out on the streets. Nor can your friend here." The doctor pointed at Jacob. "Either one of you may become ill yourself very soon, and we cannot start an epidemic here."

As Jacob too was now a prisoner of the house, he helped Rachel immensely. He brought fresh, cool water from the well. He collected eggs from the chickens and cooked them in the huge fireplace he had helped Christopher to build. He administered water and medicine to his friend while Rachel tended the boys, and then they reversed the procedure. When he saw Rachel nearing exhaustion, Jacob would force her to rest in a chair as all the beds were taken. And he would watch over all of them when she finally slept.

Jacob was afraid. He had seen deadly disease before. Everyone he cared about was in this room, and his friend and his sons were terribly ill. He feared that Rachel would succumb to this fever. Jacob had never spent much time in prayer, but he prayed now and he prayed hard. He begged the good Lord to spare his friends.

Nine days after the fever's onset, Kurt and Hans appeared to be recovering, but Christopher was no better. He was probably worse. Delirious most of the time, he would thrash and moan. Both Jacob and Rachel had to hold him still long enough to pour the medicine down his throat. Rachel was so weak and exhausted the doctor feared that she was near collapse. The doctor had brought some food, but Jacob was giving it all to Rachel, and he too, strong as he was, was showing the effects of malnutrition and fatigue.

That evening Rachel was sitting by Christopher's side holding his hand in hers. Jacob was not sure if she was asleep or just resting, but he was aware of a difference in Christopher. His half-open eyes were glassy, and his breathing was slow and irregular. Jacob moved quietly to the side of the bed opposite Rachel and studied his friend's labored breathing for several minutes. Suddenly, Rachel's eyelids fluttered. For a moment, she looked directly into Jacob's eyes, and then with terror at her husband whose body had gone limp, his chest still, his lips slack. "Oh no, oh no, dear God, no!" Rachel laid her head on her dead husband's chest and wept bitter tears of grief. Silent tears slid down Jacob's cheeks as he tried to hold himself in check. Kurt and Hans slept soundly. The trial of their illness had passed, but it had left them extremely weak and tired.

Rachel was so overcome with despair and exhaustion that she was unable to leave her bed even for Christopher's burial, which took place behind their little house, under a great oak tree. Jacob feared that Rachel had contracted the deadly disease that took her Christopher, but, gradually, her love for her sons drew her back among the living.

Through Christopher's illness and death, Jacob had never left Rachel and the boys. Although the quarantine was lifted, he still remained. He took over all of the work that Christopher did, except the cabinetmaking, a skill he did not possess. However, he continued to put the finishing touches on Christopher's house, kept up the garden and tended the livestock as well. He kept the boys occupied and told them stories about his life.

Jacob tried to console Rachel though he, too, felt a huge void in his life. Together, they searched for answers. "Why did Christopher have to die?" they would ask each other. She would wail, "He worked so hard and so long to make a life for us, and he had almost succeeded. And now he's gone." Life went on in a gray dull way. But some days were darker than others, "Why, dear God, did you take my husband? Why did you take my children's father, just when you had given us so much to be happy for?" Rachel often wondered what would have happened if she had accompanied them to the port on that fateful day. She asked the same questions day after day and served the same tasteless cornmeal gruel every night.

As the months passed, Rachel regained enough of her equilibrium to face the fact that she no longer had any money to live on. Jacob had labored, unpaid, but with winter coming and the garden no longer producing, food was scarce. He took on jobs elsewhere, but he continued, in what spare time he had, to watch over his friend's family and do the hard work that Rachel and her sons couldn't.

"Dear Jacob," Rachel said one evening when he had come by. "I must sell some of our furniture if we are going to survive." The flatness to her voice betrayed the hopelessness that she felt.

"Do not sell the furniture, Rachel. I have been thinking too. There is a market for Christopher's fine tools. I will find a buyer for the tools and make an advantageous deal, if you will let me."

"Oh Jacob, I feel so guilty about having to sell anything of Christopher's." She sank into a chair miserably. "Those tools still have his sweat on them; the furniture is his creation. I have been searching for another solution. I thought about taking in a boarder…"

"But the tools are worth good money," he argued. Jacob was not to be distracted.

"I can hardly bear to part with anything that his hands touched. Oh God, is there no other way?" She buried her head in her apron and broke down in sobs. Over the winter, Jacob would surreptitiously sell tools here and there, and buy food and supplies as carefully as he could. Rachel knew, but she chose not to acknowledge the source of the family's livelihood.

The following spring, however, the two friends had to sit down again to assess the situation. The boys were adolescents now, wanting good hearty meals. They earned what they could by working as farm laborers and handymen, but they didn't earn enough to support themselves. As they sat at the dining table that bore Christopher's signature, Jacob took Rachel's hands in his. His calloused, muscled hands reminded Rachel so much of Christopher that she cried. As the tears coursed down her thin face, Jacob gently asked her to marry him. She agreed. Rachel was very fond of Jacob and the boys adored him. Their life didn't change much, however. Although he was a hard worker, Jacob had no particular skill to rely on, and his earnings did not go far.

Together they tried to hold onto the house, but they soon knew that they would have to sell Christopher's furniture. First, they sold the cherry table on which they ate supper every night. The gathering room looked empty without the table that she served all their meals on. The person who bought it wanted to buy the matching chairs too, but Rachel waited until she absolutely needed the money. When her hope chest went, Rachel fell to the floor sobbing in despair. Again, Jacob made the most propitious deals he was able, and the family was able to survive until 1767.

Just two short years after Christopher's death, when nothing of value was left to them, Rachel knew that she would have to sell the house. Long before, Rachel had ceased to pray, feeling that God was no longer listening. The healthy, robust young woman, so full of love and hope and goodness, was all but gone. Rachel had become frail, her eyes dull and underlain with dark circles, her once round, pink cheeks now sunken and sallow, her full, voluptuous figure now as forgotten as the passion that it had bestowed. Rachel felt the all-consuming pain of failure. She had not saved her husband, and now she couldn't even hold on to his work. Rachel wandered the empty rooms, touching the walls and running her fingers over the smooth, polished wood of the floors. Her Christopher had been so talented, and now nothing was left of his except for the house. He had died before realizing his success. Without him, Rachel was lost, although Jacob was good to her.

On June 9, 1767, Rachel sold the house to Robert Peter, George Town's leading businessman. That day Rachel walked out of her beloved house for the last time. As she stepped out of the doorway, she turned slightly, placing her hand gently on the rough bluestone which had been placed there by Christopher's own hands. She stood motionless for several minutes. Then, she dropped her hand and stepped out into the street where she was absorbed by the traffic, never to be seen again.

Postlude

Peter had come from Scotland as agent or factor of Glassford & Co., which commanded a large share of the tobacco trade. He bought the house for his companion, Cassandra Chew. Peter acquired land, became a commissioner of George Town, and in 1789, its first mayor.

Mrs. Chew built a wing in the rear of the original house. She eventually moved to larger quarters, but her two daughters owned and either lived in or rented out the premises well into the nineteenth century. The Chew family's arrival ushered in an era of relative ease in the Old Stone House. They listed slaves among their possessions.

George Town meanwhile was growing rapidly. It had become a lively place with horse races, concerts, fairs, and the new Jesuit College (now Georgetown University). Wartime had slowed commerce, but after the Revolution, a surge of trade brought prosperity as never before. American merchants shipped barrels of flour along with tobacco. Bridge Street (now M Street) was a main thoroughfare for road traffic from the Western frontier into George Town. The town attracted travelers who found lodging and entertainment at inns and taverns. In 1790, the town fathers banned free-running pigs and chickens from the streets. By then, citizens were caught up in the ferment of speculation over the choice of land for the nation's capital.

Author's Note

The Old Stone House has been used throughout its history as a residence or residence/shop, until the U.S. Government purchased it in 1953. The National Park Service has administered it since that time. Although there have been attempts to prove that the house was either George Washington's Engineering Headquarters and/or Suters Tavern, neither theory has been substantiated.

A good surviving example of pre-Revolutionary American architecture and the oldest remaining structure in Washington D.C., the Old Stone House is a testament to Christopher Lehmann's planning, talent, and ability. It is also is haunted by a particularly unfriendly male spirit who has scared a number of people with his angry visits. We know that the majority of ghosts are the troubled souls of people who left unfinished business on earth. Certainly, this would describe Christopher Lehmann who had worked so tirelessly to build a comfortable life for his family and was wrenched from life at the very moment that he seemed to have found success. Perhaps he is still angry about this outcome to his life. Perhaps that is why he rattles around the house and causes doors to slam and items to fall off of shelves for no apparent reason.

Other ghosts also live in that house. Surely one is Rachel who feels cheated out of her happiness. Maybe she feels that if she makes enough noise and commotion he will return and make her happy once again. Then there are her two sons who lost their dad and their happy mother. And maybe another is Jacob, who did everything possible for Rachel, but still she loved Christopher better.

Visitor Information: The Old Stone House, administered by the National Park Service and located at 3501 M St., NW, is open to groups of ten or more by appointment: 202-895-6070, and to the general public, Saturday and Sunday, Noon-6:00 pm Free admission.

THE GIRL WHO NEVER LEFT

In the middle of Washington is a grand Federal mansion, which had many roles during its long, illustrious life. By the late 1880s, it became neglected and forlorn. Many people said they heard and saw ghosts wandering about. There were the usual chilly drafts, foot tracks in the dust, midnight screams, and people in 1800s' dress. More sinister were the stories about two daughters, but the family records say they are just stories, and all the children are accounted for. Who knows?

My father, John Blake, III, was born in 1771—the only son in a family of fourteen. He had eleven sisters who cared for him, who yearned for his attention, and doted on him whenever possible. That made him accustomed to getting his own way. A Southern man, he affirmed his honor through business and his elegant home and family. Many respected him and went to him for counsel and advice.

Father was the master of the house. He and Mother, Matilda Hoge, followed the pattern established by his family. They had thirteen children, and eight of us were girls. We had beauty, they say, and we had wealth, and certainly Mother was doing her best to teach us how to make the most of our charms, but we didn't always have happiness. Certainly, my sister didn't, but I am getting to that.

Originally, we lived in our VERY distinguished ancestral home in Virginia. The King of England had granted the land to transplanted English gentlemen who had come to make their fortunes by growing tobacco. Luckily, my father had slaves who planted and weeded, pulled suckers, topped plants, and harvested the crop.

Our home, which is called Five Fields, is a grand house. A long tree-lined drive approaches it. On one side there is a gigantic lawn covered with cedars, pines, magnolias, and other trees arranged in groves. On the other side is the river, where all the produce of the place is shipped and where we receive anything we need. Mother always says that we have to behave well because we live in this wonderful house, although I don't know why we have to behave in a certain way because of a house. It's just a bunch of rooms and chimneys, after all. In turn, she says I shouldn't ask questions, but simply accept that this is the way it is. I get very tired of accepting things the way they are. Anyway, she says my grandfather selected the high land, one mile from the original house, for his permanent home, which he called Five Fields. But my grandfather couldn't have been thinking straight for then he leveled the hill (can you imagine how many slaves that must have taken!) over an area of six acres! Then they constructed terraced lawns that look toward the river. Instead of using brick like everyone else, he had the native stone quarried. Completed in the 1700s, Five Fields is rather like a great English house. People say the house is unique because everything else in Virginia is built in red brick. But, obviously, my grandfather marched to his own tune.

They say I am like him. I would rather march to my own tune, any day, even if it were out of tune, than march to someone else's idea of a song.

I really liked Five Fields. The furniture is old but good quality as my Grandmamma would say. A large collection of gilt-framed family portraits, painted by such people as Gilbert Stuart, Thomas Sully, Thomas Hudson, and John Wollaston, line the walls. A harpsichord bought for my mother and a mirror stove are in the front hall. In the dining room stand two cherry dining room tables, twenty-six cane bottom chairs, and a great-carved cabinet. Father even maintains a deer park and a band of musicians among his servants. As Mother says, we weren't lacking in the finer things of life—if you think deer are among the finer things!

As children, we had a wonderful time at Five Fields. The grounds were massive, the woods great fun to play in. We rode horses, swam in the river, rowed, and played battledore in the garden in summer. We checked out the dairy, the poultry yard, and the aromatic orangery. Although my older sister, Abigail, and I lived in a world dominated by our father and brothers, we were good friends with our older sisters and brothers. The younger ones stayed with the servants, while we gallivanted all over the landscape.

In those years, Virginia had few towns. Towns were unnecessary because our plantations were quite self-sufficient. Our slave craftsmen included carpenters, blacksmiths, shoemakers, weavers, distillers, coopers, tanners, and so forth. They could produce the food, clothing, tools, and specialty items that we might need. We had medicines, although the omnipresent Blue Mass was guaranteed to treat dysentery, constipation, syphilis, malaria, gonorrhea, melancholia, worms, tuberculosis, toothache, and more. We also had quinine, alcohol, camphors of various sorts, soda, alum, calomel, and brandy, of course. If we really needed something, the ships that carried our tobacco to England would deliver our desires, whether they were bolts of fabric or new books, to our wharf. Although Mother would tell Father what she wanted, he was the one to do the purchasing and to make the final decision about what we would get. He selected the furniture, carpets, wallpaper, and other furnishings for the house. We had almost everything we needed right at the plantation, including a family burial spot and an orangery where we made our own version of cointreau!

Mother was always worrying about the cooking and serving of food and arranging for supplies whether they came from the smokehouse or the dairy. Our Negro cook and his helpers prepared our meals in an outside kitchen. Breakfast consisted of cold meats, fowl, game, hominy, and hot breads like Sally Lunn and biscuits. Dinner was at 2 pm. It often included several kinds of fish and crab, ham, and vegetables fresh from the garden, which were all placed on the table at once. We drank homemade beer and cider, while Father and his friends enjoyed claret and Madeira.

Although we had many guests—because as Mother said we Virginians were known for our hospitality—we were dependent on each other for entertainment. Sometimes after dinner Mother would sit at the harpsichord and dash off some music. Then we would play our cornets, harps, violins, and guitars. Sometimes we would play whist or backgammon. Other nights, my brothers played chess, while my sisters and I played with our toy theater. We owned many tiny dolls with various costumes and a great number of scenes—castles, abbeys, and hunting lodges. I wrote plays about the beautiful princess who fell in love with the handsome prince—much to her downfall—and we would act them out with the dolls. We also read aloud from popular plays and novels.

When we had guests, we might dance or bowl on the green. When the weather was bad, we acted out our own version of Shakespeare's plays. We liked the ones with lots of swordplay and plenty of blood and thunder. Of course, we studied the classics, drawing, and writing, and our mother and her widowed aunt prepared us to converse on an array of interesting topics, but I preferred to be outdoors. My sisters and I were also supposed to be learning how to embroider, and each of us worked on our sampler while our brothers were learning how to fence. Frankly, fencing appeared to be much more fun than needlework.

We were not indulged. Duty was the key word. Our parents gave us a strict upbringing, enforcing obedience to their commands, and emphasizing that we should remain respectfully subordinate to them throughout their lives. Our Father was intelligent, self-contained, steady as a rock. He made us feel safe, secure, and protected. Mother would tell my sisters and me, "Let your mind receive useful and pleasing lessons, and your hands and feet be employed in the pleasing task of not only serving yourself, but your parents, your brothers, and sisters."

Frankly, I did not think that pleasing my parents was interesting at all. I was tired of hearing about my graceless walk, my slovenly hairdo, or my raised voice. Father would tell us to copy our dear mother in modesty and industry. "Modesty adds a certain allure to your loveliness," he would proclaim. He would also lay down general rules of behavior, such as "Strive not with your Superiors in argument but always submit your judgment to others with modesty."

He said that I did too much questioning of the rules. Mother had told me, "You must wear your hat outside because the sun will make you very brown and ugly. Then we will not love you as much." In turn, I asked her whether it made a difference if we had blond or brown hair—if one color was more lovable than another. She sent me to my father, who looked at me with narrowed eyes, his mouth set in a grim line. He told me that as long as I was a good girl, he would dearly love me. That led me to wondering what would happen if I wasn't a good girl. A muscle twitched in his eyebrow, and his voice lowered. He prophesied that while I was modest and delicate that I would be loved and cherished. That if I wasn't, I would be shunned.

The Country Mice

Abigail and I shared the same room. She was seventeen, three years older than I, blonder and blue-eyed. Small waisted, she looked delicate, but she was always one of the first to be picked to dance. The boy would stand in front of her, nervously twisting his hands, rather red faced and stuttering somewhat as he asked her to dance. She would graciously extend her hand, stand, adjust her skirts, and off they would go. "Think, Deborah," she would whisper late at night. "Soon, I can put my hair in an up-do and make my formal debut. It will be so wonderful not to be a child anymore."

"But then you will go away and leave us," I would grimly point out.

"I'll never leave you."

My heart jumped. Abigail's friendship was very important to me. My mother might talk about the sweetness of domestic comfort, and I might laugh at that, but I knew the significance of having a strong supportive relationship with my sister.

She continued. "Besides, you can come visit. Once I'm married, I will have my own home."

I giggled. "Then you will be a Sedate Matron."

"Maybe. But first I have to make the right choice. I cannot give my hand if I can't give my heart first."

"Oh, I agree. Marriage without love would be terrible."

"I thought you didn't believe in marriage," Abigail said.

"No, I don't believe in it for me. I would be a poor obedient companion and not very good at managing my husband's house. I'm going to write romances instead and submit them to a magazine. And you will tell all your friends that your sister is a great writer."

"You do that, while I become a mother and a gracious hostess like Mother always talks about. When I am married, I will have no other concern but to please my husband."

"Oh, you sound just like Mother."

"I'm a good student," she smiled. "Before I get married, I will get to go to all those balls and parties so I can find a husband."

"Once you do, he will whisk you away from here."

"We'll see," she smiled sweetly. "I love my family, and I never want to leave the area. I just have to find the right man."

Marriage meant that we had to take a leap of trust. We had to go from our familiar home into a future that we knew little about. It could mean our future happiness or abysmal suffering. We had heard the whispers about unhappy marriages. We knew that as women we were dependent on our spouse, whether he was a good husband or not—which is why I did not intend to marry.

To protect us from making a mistake in the choice of a husband, our parents had established strict rules of behavior for us. We weren't just beautiful feminine baubles for our parents to display. Our family's wealth and gentility were evident in how we looked, sang, danced, and played our carefully-chosen musical instruments. A favorable marital alliance would enhance our family's honor and prestige. It might even facilitate the development of some beneficial personal and business allegiances for Father and provide financial security and social status for us.

Mother taught us that we were to listen and to be agreeable. "Since God told that sinner Eve that Adam should rule over her, we need to accept your father's and then your husband's approval as the proper standard for your behavior."

With many interests, my parents had little time for us. There were fifteen of us after all! Mother emphasized that men were daring and confident while a woman was modest, gentle, and unassuming. Once I heard her say that, I was careful not to let her catch me dueling with my brother Samuel. According to Mother, we women were not merely social ornaments but individuals capable of shaping the family's status through our appearance, accomplishments, social ties, and ultimately our marriage. Fencing was not considered one of the necessary accomplishments!

Father was concerned about the financial status of any possible suitors. He also would tell us about being an American and how important that was. He would ask questions about the Bill of Rights and expect my brothers to have the answers. I often knew the answers too, but he never asked the girls. Even though Father had been educated in England—at very good schools, mother would add—he always wanted us to remember that we were Americans. A firm patriot and a staunch supporter of President Washington, he did not even want us to be friends with our English neighbors. We were to have friendships only with Americans. That didn't really make sense to me because many British people had immigrated to the United States and become Americans. So I figured that what Father was saying was that we couldn't be friends until they had become naturalized citizens. But I didn't say anything to him because we were supposed to respect his opinion. He was our father, and we were never—never—to question his authority.

The City Mice

Although my father had devoted himself to his family, friends, and his farming interests (he was a tobacco planter; he didn't want just the Virginia gentleman's life), he wanted the pleasure and excitements of society and politics. He decided that some town life would spice up the bucolic monotony of country existence. Of course, my mother was thrilled.

"Now, I can see my friends more readily, my dear," she beamed. "There will be parties and balls and dinners. We can find a suitable husband for Abigail and begin to look around for possibilities for the other children."

"I thought I would build a house in Philadelphia. But I am told—by no less of an authority than George Washington—that I should build my house for the winter season in the new Federal City. That one day Washington City will represent the most refined social life and culture of our new country."

"Really?"

"That's right. I have chosen a lot in the open country west of where they are building the President's House."

"Oh," Mother pouted. "Isn't this awfully soon? They are just barely creating a city from a wilderness. I'd rather wait."

"We want to be in the forefront of the new residents in the capital city."

She put down her embroidery. "But, dear, my friend Jane tells me that not much more than one half the city is cleared. The rest is in woods! And there are only about a hundred or so buildings in the whole city."

"It will grow."

"Only about five hundred or so families actually live there now," she pointed out.

"I am not discussing this further." He stood up. One eyelid was twitching. "Our president says that he is planning to construct a beautiful capital, and we will be there from the very beginning."

"Well, dear, as long it is a pleasant environment of attractive homes. ..." Recognizing the obedience she owed him as head of the household, she had pointed out her concerns and accepted his decision.

"Washington City will flourish. Don't you worry."

In 1800, the United States government moved from Philadelphia to Washington City, which was newly laid out on the banks of the Potomac. That November, Congress sat for the first time in the shining white sandstone Capitol, and Mrs. Adams moved into a partly unplastered presidential residence with vacant rooms. She hung the family washing in the East Room, which was designed for ceremonial occasions. The streets were muddy and unimproved. By getting my father to build his house in an area that was still mainly pasture lands and woods, George Washington was one step closer to establishing the capital of the new republic. Meanwhile, my father was demonstrating his confidence in a city that had not yet materialized.

Our new house is known as the Manor House. Mother says it is a beautiful home in what is called the Federal style. Our guests are impressed the minute they step into the circular entrance hall with its large windows, marble floor, apple-green paint, and two stoves. When they see the dramatic curved staircase, they are amazed. And what is really nice is that unlike most American homes at this time, the kitchen is within the house, located in the basement.

At first, Mother complained that Washington City was a city of people who came and went. "People never remain long enough together to become personally acquainted. How can we hold any balls and parties when no one lives here?"

"They will."

"But how long before they move here?"

"They will come," Father said flatly.

She ignored him. " And how will our daughters ever find husbands, if there isn't a large selection of available men?"

She talked about that a lot. My parents considered marriage to be a "holy institution." One night, Father said it was woman's duty to marry and to help swell the population. My brother, Thomas, who had studied biology, snickered, saying, "Don't you mean that women are around to continue the species and to be a pleasure for man." Father laughed.

When our parents weren't home, we created plays on the stairway, even though we were older. We dragged the sheets off our beds and made them into great cloaks that we could use for sweeping into rooms. Abigail was always the heroine because she was the oldest and the prettiest. Plus, she demanded that role. Sometimes, I would play the male role since my brother had taught me how to fence, but usually we could inveigle a brother or two to act out our dramas with us.

One night, I wrote a play called the "Unmarried Sisters," and we put it on one evening for our parents. My heroine was a young maid of desperate expectations who discovered that being unmarried might be preferable to being married to a scoundrel. My mother was not amused.

In Washington, the houses stood so far apart that people identified their residence by the public building nearest them, e.g., "a few blocks from the Capitol." The Capitol was two white stone squares. Cows grazed where one day governmental buildings and majestic avenues would be laid out. Instead of monuments, there were brush piles. Where houses were planned, there were just barren hills. A considerable part of the land was farmed. Pennsylvania Avenue between the Capitol and White House was a continuous mud puddle. There were no fences or gardens and not much business.

Once President Jefferson took office in March 1801, the city began to change. Although he was widowed, he asked Dolley Madison, wife of his Secretary of State, to help him host dinners with numerous offerings of roasted poultry, meats, fish, soup, and vegetables. During congressional sessions, the pace of life quickened. Father and Mother met important people from the military, the diplomatic corps, and Congress members as they attended card parties, salons, receptions, dinners, and balls. Many foreigners visited Washington. Father pooh-poohed them, saying they were just trying to outdo the Americans with their fancy equipages, their extensive mansions, ruffed shirts, silver spurs, and ropes of diamonds. He really didn't like the British, but they were present at many events.

Soon, we were living in the Manor House during the winter social season, usually from November to April, and our parents were holding balls, receptions, and dinner parties. We were more elegant now. A dancing master came to the house, and my brothers had private tutors. The servants preened in their blue Quaker cut coats turned up with red and trimmings of silver lace. Their appearance added to the grandeur of a meal. Men praised my Father's dinners and wines; Mother's friends waxed enthusiastic over the china, silver, and elaborate table appointments. The diplomats brought their ministers and attachés, who were young, curious, and fun. Washington society loved to come to the Manor House.

My mother embarked on her mission: finding Abigail a suitor. She and my aunt devised lists of appropriate suitors for Abigail. They carefully considered a gentleman's background, education, wealth, religion, and character. They ticked off her good qualities: appearance, manners, fashion sense, and social graces. Mother made sure that she exchanged visits or calling cards with the right families. After she made the calls, she waited for an invitation. Abigail's hair was swept into an up-do, and dressmakers were called in. We both got new riding dresses. Abigail had a pale blue riding dress adorned with coral braid. She wore it with a matching hat trimmed with white swans down and white gloves and shoes. I had a green riding dress ornamented with frogs' militaire in front; I wore it with a green velvet hat, trimmed with white fur. We were allowed to ride in the park with our older brothers.

One day, when they had galloped off, we met two of the British attachés in their scarlet uniforms who had attended a ball at our house the week before. We had already been formally introduced. We rode together, laughing and talking. They were really quite fun. Abigail and I decided that we would not mention our accidental meeting at home.

Washington City had many more men than women, which made my mother's task of finding a suitable husband for Abigail easier. More young single men began attending my parents' parties. Father fussed when they weren't Americans, but Mother pointed out that if they were going to entertain diplomats he would have to put up with their attachés. They came in their top hats, cutaway coats, breeches, and riding boots. We heard that the breeches on some were so tight that it was impossible for their wearers to sit down in them. Think they were fated to stand up whenever awake!

When Father and Mother held a ball, they often asked those of us who were old enough to be present. Abigail and I wore rich China taffeta or splendid brocade, which would rustle and trail behind us when we danced. Although my hair was still down, I got to wear satin slippers and participate in the Quadrille, if the square was short a person. I was always part of a side couple, but sometimes Abigail and her soldier friend were the head couple. They looked so magnificent. She would glance sideways at him; he would cock an eyebrow at her. When the dance was over, they would escort us to chairs, where we were supposed to stay. When it was time for refreshments, he would accompany her to the table and carefully hold her plate while she selected delicacies for the two of them. I watched them carefully because I could use their gestures in the plays I was always writing. When I couldn't find them, I would go upstairs and wait in our bedroom for Abigail to come tell me what happened next.

Dinner parties were more political. Father would say that women had no business to concern themselves about the business of running this country but should trust those that know better. I found it difficult not to say anything. Sometimes father, sitting at one end of the long table, would rant and rave about the British and their actions against our ships. If the British officers were there, they would just smile politely. Sometimes the men would talk about the need for expansion into the Northwest Territories, which sounded like such a great adventure. I shocked my sisters by saying I would like to go. Of course, after the Battle of Tippecanoe, Father was ever so proud of America. Mother just nodded, smiling, murmuring, "Yes, dear, yes, dear."

On June 12, 1812, the United States declared war on Great Britain. All the diplomats and the soldiers left. At first, the fighting was at sea and on the Great Lakes. Father was often bad tempered because he said the country was missing both military and civilian leadership. He criticized President Madison a lot, but he stopped grumbling when the *USS Constitution* ("Old Ironsides") defeated the *HMS Guerriere*. That was a glorious day.

Abigail seemed moodier. I often found her staring out the window or writing a letter, but she would never tell me to whom she was writing. She was hiding something, but I was busy— too busy to ask her what was going on—but I did notice that she didn't seem to be as present. She would just stare blankly when we were doing our plays on the stairs; sometimes she would even leave—and she was the heroine! One night after dinner, I couldn't find her, although I never saw her leave the house. Later she came into our bedroom when I was asleep and undressed quietly and quickly. When I asked her where she had been, she just shook her head.

"Don't ask me, Deborah."

"Why not?"

"Because it will just upset you and get me into trouble."

"Oh." I didn't know what she was talking about.

A week went by. She looked paler and very unhappy. Mother talked about giving her a potion for the vapors.

One night I woke up and she wasn't in bed, but I heard angry voices. I went out into the hall and looked down the stairway. Father and she were standing halfway up the stairs, arguing. She had her coat on, and her hair was straggling down her back. Suddenly, I realized that she had been sneaking out at night. That's why I couldn't find her. Father snapped at her, "Where have you been?"

She didn't say anything.

"Have you been sneaking out? Who are you seeing?"

She looked down.

His mouth was a grim line. "Whom have you been with? I know you've been with someone, haven't you?"

"What makes you say that?" she retorted.

"Why else would you be out at night? Who is he?"

From my perspective, it looked like she was looking down at her feet. She backed up against the stair railing.

Father took a step closer. "He's someone I won't approve of, isn't he?"

She still didn't say anything.

He was looming over her. She must have been able to feel his breath. "He's British isn't he?" I gasped. How did he know that? I had just realized it myself. Abigail had been acting peculiarly ever since that ride in the park.

"I won't have you seeing him. You are disobeying my wishes."

"I hope heaven will direct me that I do not disappoint you, but..."

"He's the enemy," he shouted. "This family's principles and interests are on the side of America!"

Abigail backed further up the stairs, leaning into the railing as Father moved even closer. He reached out, and she went over the railing, landing on the floor far below with a thud. The whole house seemed to shudder in anguish. I screamed. Father looked at me, his face was white. He ran down the stairs, crying "Abigail, Abigail." But I knew even before he reached her body that all life was gone. "It's an accident, Deborah, an accident." My mother was there, and she was crying.

Was it an accident? I'll never know. But Abigail was right. She never left the house. To this day, inhabitants of the house talk about seeing a flickering candle shadow moving up the stairs. Then, there's a horrific shriek and a thud at the bottom of the beautiful stairs.

Perhaps it was because the house slaves said she was haunting the house or perhaps he just couldn't stand to be there anymore, but Father moved all of us back home.

The Second Daughter

About four years later, we moved back to Washington. I was almost eighteen. My younger sisters and brothers were no longer amusing playthings. They were beginning to be viewed as adults-in-the-making who needed to trained and shaped. That meant that I as an older sister was approaching marriageable age.

Not that I wanted to be on that particular brink. Ever since Abigail's death, I had lost my place in the universe. Everyone else appeared to be neatly slotted for life, while I remained in my memories. I didn't know that it was possible to be this lost.

Some days I would forget that she was dead. I'd think, oh, I must tell Abigail about this, and then I'd realize that she wasn't there anymore. That she had died in a heap at the bottom of the stairs. I'd be overwhelmed with the horror of it all over again. The shock was even worse because I'd remember how she died all over again, too.

Coming back to Washington was hard. Abigail had died here—and I certainly couldn't forget that final thud. I didn't want to go, but Mother and Father decreed that there wasn't a choice. The Manor House was planned to accommodate a large family, staff, and an active social life, and I, as a daughter of the house, would participate.

"You will have a good time there."

"I don't think so. I'd rather stay at Five Fields."

"We won't permit that. You all are older now. You can participate in rounds of visiting; you can go to the parties; you can meet new people."

"I just want to be stay here. Besides, I have a new friend Nancy, who you said is just what a woman ought to be: sensible, modest, and polite." I didn't tell her that Nancy had a wicked sense of humor and also read Jane Austen. She would accuse her of fanciful ideas and being precocious too.

"That isn't to be. You are a beautiful young woman who is eligible for marriage now."

The War of 1812 was over; Napoleon was gone for sure; and the world was very different. Thanks to Schiller's play, which we were just seeing and reading, Mary Queen of Scots dominated the thoughts of the dress designers. No longer did we wear the low-cut dresses that we wore before the war. Instead, dresses rose to the throat, terminating in lace frills, and we wore long white gloves to cover our arms. We also wore rustling petticoats, which made our skirts voluminous. At some houses, two women couldn't get through the same doorway. The belles of Washington City glittered in a galaxy of pearls, diamonds, gold, and sapphires. I really didn't care what I wore. I just wanted to write.

My mother was a great believer in George Washington's "Rules of Civility and Decent Behavior in Company and Conversation." According to her, these maxims had been in use in France and England for over one hundred years before they were set as a task for young George Washington. "And we all know," she would say, "that his consideration for others, his fineness of character, and his powerful influence were shaped by these common practices in decent society. I expect my daughters to be polite and to remember 'Every Action done in Company, ought to be with Some Sign of Respect, to those that are Present.'"

"Yes, Mother." Mother could be very tedious.

She declared that I had to guard against being considered "clever." "Marriage," she said, "means exchanging the authority of a father for that of a husband. And no suitor would think that you respect his authority when you ask those questions of yours. You don't even respect your father's wishes these days. He knows what's best for us."

"How could he know what's best for me? He's not a woman. He's not young."

She drew herself up. "He's your father, Deborah, and the head of this household. He knows what's right for you and me. And it is not appropriate for you to pass judgment upon what he decides for you. "

"Well, maybe I have chosen to forgo marriage."

"You may not have any choice, Deborah, if you continue in this manner. Your mind is not amiable. And then you will have nothing."

She infuriated me. "It's not marriage that makes a person special, but the way they choose to live their life," I retorted.

"Given the way you express yourself, you may not have any suitors anyway."

"Good," I snapped. "I don't want to be a mealy-mouthed, tea-pouring, sweetly singing woman."

"Well, you may not want to be, but you will end up becoming the spinster aunt—who all your brothers and sisters will call on for help. You will get to take care of the sick child or the ailing parent; you will be asked to act as secretary or housekeeper, while they are having a grand old time."

She certainly made my future sound grim. Stubbornly, I shook my head. "I don't have to be that person. I'll write plays and be famous."

She laughed. "Women are rarely famous. That's not our role. Our natural destiny is to be a wife and mother. Our husband's affection depends in a great degree on our conduct."

"That does not appeal to me, Mother."

"Don't you want to have a household?"

"Not particularly. I'd rather write. Like Jane Austen."

"Who hasn't married, I believe," she retorted.

"And that's just fine with me. I'm going to be the first great woman author from the United States."

"Think of what you'll miss. The joy of having children, for one. A woman's pleasures are entirely concentrated in her family." She paused, "Not that you're giving me much pleasure at the moment."

Why would I want to be a mother? I have fourteen siblings, after all. I have heard my mother scream when the baby was coming. I have seen the little coffins when a baby didn't survive. I know how hard motherhood can be.

She continued, "Without a husband, we have nothing. No household, no position. Women are responsible for maintaining the home and children. Without a husband, you will be the 'Old Maid' because you won't have a position in society. You will just be a perpetual dependent in the homes of your brothers or sisters, helping out with the nursing and childcare in exchange for room and board."

Of course, the last thing we wanted to be was an "old maid." Unlike those thin, pinch-faced, unmarried New England women we heard so much about, unmarried Southern women were considered a failure to be shipped from family to family. Their only job was to act as a nursemaid or a housekeeper for they were the dreaded "Spinsters."

I went upstairs to my room and threw myself on the bed. I so missed Abigail. She would have understood.

Soon after we returned, Mother refurbished the house. On the stairway landing, she placed marble statues in the tall niches. She replaced the high-backed stuffed chairs with the easy elegant curves of Grecian chairs and couch in the drawing room. The dining room now had substantial mahogany chairs, table, and sideboard. The curtains in the downstairs rooms were burgundy. Father selected different pictures and busts, bought large mirrors, and fitted the candlesticks with chimneys and glass prisms that hung from the rim of the sockets. They reflected the light and enhanced its effect. The atmosphere was very elegant—and quite similar to what Dolley Madison had done in the Presidential House before it had burned.

Mother and Father entertained frequently and in fine style. They hosted, dinners, teas, and balls. With so many people crowded into entertaining rooms, women as well as men stood, which meant we enjoyed more ease and freedom than was possible if we were sitting and waiting for gentlemen to approach.

These days twenty or more people attended dinners. To feed these people, Mother had at least forty plates and not less than fifty knives and forks for dinner and dessert, tumblers, wine, and champagne glasses. The dressmaker came and fitted me for two new evening gowns: one in bright purple satin with a high lace collar and the other in crimson velvet with a tasseled fringe decorating the hemline, sleeves, and neckline. My slippers were satin, and my hair twisted into ringlets. As one brother said, I looked quite smashing.

But, oh, I was bored.

Mother would reprimand me for scowling or yawning at these events. "You will never meet anyone," she said. "Not the way you act! You must omit that spirit of contradiction, which is highly disagreeable to everyone. And you are to be sure that your countenance always displays sweetness and modesty and cheerfulness."

But of course I didn't want to meet anyone. I just wanted to be left alone to write my stories.

I was miserable. Mother was scolding me for being difficult. Father ignored me. And I had to put on a "sweet" face and go to all these parties where I was surrounded by giggling single women looking to meet eligible males.

One bright blustery blue day, we boarded carriages and drove out to the countryside. We disembarked at the falls of the Potomac, gathered wildflowers that were bobbing in the brisk breeze, and then arrived at our picnic site where we had a sumptuous collation and sparkling champagne. I wandered away from the happily chattering group in search of greener and quieter surroundings and went to the edge of the river. I stood there staring down at the mirror-smooth silver-flowing river. Somehow the sound of the river reminded me of Abigail, although why I remembered her then I don't know. Suddenly, someone grabbed my elbow.

"You are getting too close to the edge, you know." It was a nephew of the Tottens, who had attended several recent parties. My parents had summarily dismissed him when his name came up for their next party. "He has nothing," my mother had declared.

"Yes, I guess I am."

"Don't guess. You are. And think how cold that water is."

I don't know why I said what I said then, but Abigail was really on my mind. "My sister got too close to the edge of the stairway, and she fell you know. She died."

"I heard about it." He nodded gravely, still holding my arm. "I lost my brother when we were skating on thin ice in Massachusetts. He was my best friend. We were very close."

"So you know what it feels like?"

"To lose a sibling? Yes."

The memories flooded in. I shivered. *I can handle anything that life throws at me. I may not be able to handle it well, or correctly, or gracefully, or with finesse, or expediently, but I can handle it,* I told myself. His eyes were as blue as the sky. Abigail was there for sharing, joking, crying, and just being. It was so much more meaningful with Abigail than it was now.

Without her, I am so alone, I thought. "I lost the only person who understood me," I said. Why was I saying these things to this stranger?

He nodded sadly. "It does feel like that, but one day you will find someone else who understands. One way of dealing with losing someone important to you is to open yourself up to your sorrow."

"What do you mean?"

"Well, to love people and the world more than ever because you know how short life is and how precious. Life may not be the picnic we hoped for, but while we are here we might as well enjoy it."

I had never heard anyone talk about death this way. In my family, we didn't talk about Abigail at all. She had been there, and then she was gone. She was like all those other sisters and brothers who never made it past infancy. It was as if she had never been. If I had known that night would have been my last chance to see Abigail, I would have hugged her a little longer, a little tighter and kissed her on the cheek. Maybe I would have told her that I loved her. If I had known it was her last night on earth, I would have reminded her of how much she meant to me, and what an important part of my life she was. But I didn't, and so life goes on in its drably dreary way. We don't get any lessons in dealing with death, even though it happens to everyone.

He let go of my elbow. "Now that I know that you're not going to fall, tell me about yourself."

His eyes were sparkling. He really seemed interested. "There's not much to tell except that I want to be a writer, and my parents want me to be married."

"And are you a good writer?"

"Oh yes."

"And what do you write about?"

"People and how they live and feel. I want to understand society better." I was a little embarrassed by this question. I had some ludicrous attempts at poetry, and a few satiric short stories, which I was thinking of submitting to *Lady's Magazine*, an *Entertaining Companion for the Fair Sex, Appropriated Solely to Their Use and Amusement*. "It's your turn. What do you do?"

"I am a poor painter from Massachusetts. I am visiting my favorite aunt and uncle this month."

"What do you paint?"

"The sea. The sea fascinates me. But no one buys my paintings so I am a poor painter of the sea." He laughed. "Someone's calling you. It must be time to leave. Perhaps we could meet in the park and go for a walk."

Never shy, I said, "That sounds lovely. When?"

The next day, I slipped out of the house to meet Edward in the park. I noticed with amusement that my mouth went dry when I saw him standing there waiting for me. His clothes drew attention to his slim waist and accented the muscles of his chest and shoulders. He was a good-looking man, I noted happily. Bees swarmed. They say that to everything there is a season. Perhaps it was my season to fall in love. Perhaps my time has come, although I had not expected it nor wanted it.

We had a wonderful walk, and I cannot remember anything we talked about. When we left each other, I found myself aware of his warm blue eyes, of his strength, of the smile that promised joy. When I came in, my sister Amelia looked at me and asked what had I been doing. "Why?" I asked her.

"Because you are glowing," she said. Mother looked suspiciously at me but didn't say anything.

I knew Edward would be at the ball the next night. I felt so nervous. Even though I said I didn't care and I had said I didn't want to be a tea-pouring wife, I chose my dress carefully. The would-be great American woman author, who said she cared nothing about clothes, wore a peach blossom Egyptian robe, shot with silver threads, silver shoes, and a silver armlet and earrings.

The room was surrounded by light. Candles blazed in the windows, and the musicians played gently. One room was crowded with people in rainbow colors and silver and gold. The crystal chandeliers dazzled, glittered, and shone over all the people. I pushed through them, waving indiscriminately at friends, looking for Edward. When I saw him, a surge of joy rushed through me. I was elated—I had thought that almost all was lost and now I knew that it wasn't—it wasn't at all! He reached his arms out as if to hug me when he spied me. My heart jumped up to meet his smile. Our faces were just inches away. He put his right hand up slowly and touched his index finger to my shoulder blade. He slid the finger down my arm; I did not move, but all my nerve endings did. We danced several times. Our unspoken words hung between us, shimmering in the candlelight. I leaned my body against his and felt his desire rising to meet my own.

After our third dance, Father came over and said he must speak to me. "I notice you are dancing a lot with Edward Bosworth."

"Yes."

"We don't think he is suitable for you."

"Why not," I snapped.

"Because he's a poor painter from the North and without much family. We expect more for you."

"But I like him."

"There will be others," he shrugged and walked away.

How dare my father tell me what I could or could not do? I wanted to be with Edward, to listen to his voice, to laugh with him, to hold him. I saw him standing at the window, looking around at the crowd. I slipped back in. Defiantly, I danced two more times with Edward.

That night I dreamed of Abigail. She was holding her arms out to me. The skies wept, and the next day dawned with a pale rinsed sky. The trees dripped the storm remnants into the grass.

Mother came into my room. "Your father is very displeased with your behavior with the Totten's nephew. You will have a bad reputation."

"I don't care. I like him. I love him."

She snorted. "Love, phooey! You don't even know what the word means. You will behave yourself and do as we tell you." She walked out of the room.

The day was hot and steamy. I left the house, but Edward wasn't in the park, and I didn't know where else to find him. That evening there was a "crush" at a friend of the Tottens. I knew he would be there. When I saw him, I took his arm and we went outside. The thunder rumbled in the distance. I could smell the electricity in the air. All my nerve endings were trembling. When he raised his eyes to meet mine, I felt the same tingling sensation in my face. He groaned, "Deborah. Your father called on my aunt and complained about my behavior with you."

"What?" How could father have done such a thing?

"She told me that he said I was unwelcome here in Washington."

"Untrue." I said indignantly.

He laughed. "Maybe, if I am so fortunate, that it is untrue for you, but not for him."

"You are—we are—fortunate." I mouthed.

"Do you want to be the wife of a poor painter in Massachusetts? Do you want to give all this up?"

"For you, of course."

His hand reached out for mine. We stood quietly, hand in hand, as the lightning cracked around us. "Well then," Edward said. "Why don't you go home, get your belongings, and we will leave." The rain began to pelt on us. We ran for the drawing room. We stayed at the crush until late.

When I came home, the candles were out, and the house dark. I slipped in quietly, taking off my slippers. When I was halfway up the stairway, my father called me from the dark above. "Deborah, you're late."

"Yes."

"You stayed there with that Bosworth fellow."

"Yes."

"I told you that he's not suitable for you."

"I disagree."

He loomed in front of me. I backed up against the railing. "You will not disagree with me. I am your father—the head of this household!"

"I am in love with Edward."

"Too bad." He came closer. I backed away. "You are my daughter. He is unsuitable, and your conduct is unacceptable."

"But he suits me!"

"You have been told since you were a child that you should respect your father. Obviously, you don't." His breath was hot, furious.

I was silent. He was right of course.

"I won't have a child that disrespects me." A muscle was twitching in his cheek.

"I'm going to marry him." I shouted, and suddenly I was hurdling over the railing. Abigail reached out for me, but it was all over.

History repeats itself, they say. Odd, don't you think, that two sisters fell over that railing? But we are together again and we both haunt the Manor House.

Our father also haunts it for he is filled with regrets. He lost two daughters, and he will never be sure whether he lost them in an accident or an act of violence.

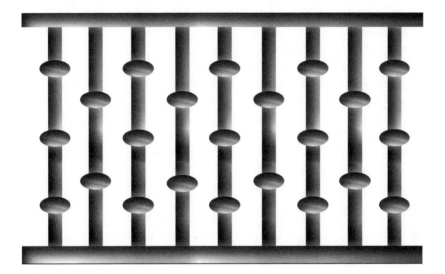

PURSUIT OF GLORY

Situated at 1610 H Street, NW, and located across from the White House, Decatur House is one of the oldest surviving homes in Washington, D.C. Completed in 1818 for naval hero Stephen Decatur and his wife Susan, it is one of the capital's most sought-after addresses. Benjamin Henry Latrobe, considered by many to be the father of American architecture, designed this excellent example of neoclassical architecture.

For decades, people have said that this National Trust Historic Site is haunted. When you visit the Stephen Decatur House, you may happen to see a shadowy figure gazing out of the second floor window or stealthily leaving the house from the back door; this is the ghost of Stephen Decatur. He still returns, hoping to continue to change the face of history for the United States. Meanwhile, his wife Susan wanders its halls, weeping.

I was known as a sophisticated woman and a "good catch" as they say. My Father, the seventy-third mayor of Norfolk, had done a good job of spoiling me to expect the better things in life. People have always said that my mother—whoever she was—was a mulatto. I was well educated, well read, and musically talented. People liked me, and I was in great demand—and not just for my skill at playing the harp. Aaron Burr had come courting and so did Jerome Bonaparte, brother of Napoleon. But one had a bad reputation, and the other had a brother who controlled the world. When I finally settled down at age thirty, I picked a man three years younger who loved the sea and his honor as much as he loved me.

I grew up during the years when pirates from the Barbary States of North Africa (the Sultanate of Morocco and the three

Regencies of Algiers, Tunis, and Tripoli) preyed on merchant ships sailing in the Mediterranean, seizing their crews and cargoes, and holding them for ransom. Many European nations annually paid tribute or protection money to keep their vessels free from attack. Prior to the Revolutionary War, the British navy had protected the United States and its ships, but after the war, the new republic had no navy and no way to combat the pirates, so it too paid tribute. By 1792, Congress voted to appropriate monies to purchase peace and to pay an annual tribute. By 1800, payments in ransom and tribute to the privateering states amounted to twenty percent of United States government annual revenues.

Public opinion urged the building of a naval force so that the country could develop its commerce and defend its right to trade. The first three men-of-war in the United States were the *United States*, the *Constitution*, and the *Constellation*. Those names are still famous today.

My husband, I like to think, was America' first great naval hero—after John Paul Jones, of course. At age nineteen, Stephen Decatur sailed as a midshipman aboard the new frigate *United States*. I can see him now in his brand new midshipman's uniform. His hair would be waving in the sea breeze; his large dark eyes would be sweeping the horizon, looking for the enemy. Shipboard rules and duties wouldn't intimidate him because he had been reared in the traditions of the sea—his father was a successful American Revolution privateer, and he knew other officers on the ship: Charles Stewart and Richard Somers.

When Stephen was a young sailor, he met third lieutenant James Barron, who killed him many years later. But when Stephen was only a young midshipman, he truly respected James Barron because of something that happened on that trip. On October 19, 1798, the *United States* ran into a violent gale with thirty-foot waves and raging winds. Stephen said the fierce wind and high seas went on day after day. The wind was so strong that the masts began to shift in place. Just as the ship seemed ready to founder, Lieutenant Barron volunteered to lead a team in fastening new lines to the masts to save them from certain peril. Stephen told me that Barron and his men saved the ship and their lives. At age twenty-nine, Barron was a hero. Stephen told me much later how he fully respected Barron after that feat. And maybe that act was the catalyst for Stephen's continued courage throughout his life.

The War with Tripoli

As our country's naval power increased, political leaders began to realize that the United States could refuse to pay tribute. Finally, when Thomas Jefferson became president, he stopped the payments. In turn, Tripoli declared war on the United States in May 1801, and Jefferson sent a group of frigates to defend American interests in the Mediterranean. My Stephen was right at the forefront. Daring and heedless of personal danger, he was ready to become known for his heroic deeds on the quarterdeck.

On February 16, 1804, as a mere lieutenant, he took ten U.S. sailors and conducted a night raid right under the enemy's guns. The disguised *Intrepid* glided into Tripoli's harbor, where Stephen and his crew set fire to the captured U.S. frigate *Philadelphia*, preventing her use by the enemy. Everyone throughout the world applauded his audacious destruction of the *Philadelphia* in order to keep it out of the hands of the barbarians. Lord Nelson, England's greatest naval hero, supposedly proclaimed his feat to be "the most bold and daring act of the age."

Stephen's heroic act changed his life forever. Everyone knew who he was—even schoolchildren. Little boys would reenact the burning of the *Philadelphia* and argue about who would play the role of Decatur. At age twenty-five, Stephen was promoted to captain.

His courageous conduct during the August 3, 1804, bombardment of Tripoli added even more bronze to his heroic stature. Learning that his brother James had been killed through Tripolotan treachery, Stephen led his men in hand-to-hand fighting while boarding and capturing a Turkish gunboat. Stephen and the much larger Turk captain were fighting each other. When the latter turned Stephen over like his morning toast and was about to kill him with his knife, Stephen seized the hand that gripped the knife and pulled out a loaded pistol with his other hand. Reaching around the huge Turk, he pressed the muzzle in his back and fired directly downward. Stephen wasn't a man who was going to sit around and think about things; he was a man of action. And all Americans knew that he was a hero.

He made port in Hampton Roads, Virginia. Everyone in Norfolk was talking about him and his passenger, the emissary from the Bey of Tunis, who had brought four Arabian thoroughbreds as a present for Washington officials. After all, not many of us have met anyone from Tunis—much less someone accompanied by the hero that everyone was talking about. My father, the mayor of Norfolk, organized a boating party and arranged it so that we anchored near Stephen's ship.

I wore my newest dress with small covered buttons and the sleeves halfway above the elbow. My new kid shoes had small silver clasps, which made my feet look remarkably small and neat. And my bonnet was open on top so my hair passed through it. He wasn't there, but the officer of the deck invited us aboard so we could see the horses and other gifts brought from Tunis. I was looking about when I spied a beautiful Italian miniature of the glamorous hero. He was really handsome and had great personal magnetism. The next day at the municipal reception, I met him in person. Now, I could study him more closely and he me.

And we both liked what we saw. The miniature was very nice, but he was so much more. His whole person—especially when in full uniform with its gold lace and braid—radiated strength. Not just physical strength but strength of character. We met again that night where there was a "great showing of ladies and gentlemen," but he concentrated on me. And perhaps I was tired of the dances, assemblies, musical concerts, amateur theatricals, and the afternoon calls; perhaps I was ready to fall in love.

Ours was a true affair of the heart. Stephen was smitten, calling me his paragon. I was smitten too, but he was going to have to learn new skills and develop more polish to make the next career step forward. His father's friend, Dr. Rush, gave him a list of books to read, which he proceeded to do. Handsome, courageous, and ambitious, he inspired awe in the public, was worshipped by his crews, and lionized by presidents and diplomats. No wonder I fell in love with him! Together, we would go to the very top.

We had what they term a whirlwind courtship. On March 8, 1806, four months later, we married in Norfolk. I knew when I married Stephen that he personified Lovelace's lines: "I could not love thee dear, so much, Loved I not honor more."

During this period, many people arranged elegant and sumptuous dinners in honor of Stephen. At one, there were thirteen toasts. About one hundred of his former schoolmates and friends arranged another event. That was the night of sixteen toasts. If I hadn't loved Stephen, if I were a fellow captain, I might have been very envious of him. The world was his. He was a fundamentally noble man who embodied the ideals of chivalry and patriotism. He received many rewards, which I certainly enjoyed sharing. But if I were a man, I might have been very jealous of Stephen.

The *Chesapeake* Incident

In the early 1800s, British military ships began stopping American trade ships and forcing sailors to work on their ships. In our eyes, they were kidnapping our American sailors. On June 22, 1807, the British frigate, HMS *Leopard* cornered the U.S. Navy ship, the *Chesapeake*, under Commodore James Barron and demanded to search for British navy deserters. Barron refused, although the *Chesapeake* was ill prepared to put up a fight. Some of her forty cannons were not properly mounted, gear and supplies were unstowed, and most of the crew did not know where their battle stations were. Moments later, to the horrified astonishment of the Americans, the *Leopard* fired on the defenseless *Chesapeake*. As the Americans frantically prepared to respond, the *Leopard* fired a second time and then a third. By this time, the British had killed four (one of them died in a hospital) and wounded eighteen sailors. Realizing that his ship was poorly prepared for battle, Barron finally lowered his flag in surrender. The British removed four supposed deserters.

The next day, Stephen went down to visit the *Chesapeake*. Although he had once admired James Barron, who saved his life years ago, he was furious that a Navy officer had allowed his ship to surrender. Stephen declared that Barron's inaction was the fault. That it was dishonorable that he hadn't fought. Most Americans saw the incident as proof of the Royal Navy's arrogance. But then most Americans were not heroes like my Stephen.

In October, an official court of inquiry into the causes of the *Chesapeake*'s surrender was held. The board concluded that Baron had shown great indecision and a disposition to negotiate rather than determination to defend his ship. Consequently, President Jefferson had to order a general court martial. Stephen was ordered to serve on the court, but he tried to beg off.

The Secretary of the Navy rejected Stephen's request, saying that court martial of Commodore James Barron, one of most senior Navy officers, would be precedent setting for our young nation. His peers had to judge him. On February 8, 1808, the court found Barron guilty, but because of mitigating circumstances they only suspended him from all command in the U.S. Navy for five years. Convinced of his innocence, Barron was shocked at the sentence and outraged that Stephen, his old friend, had agreed to the verdict. My Stephen considered the sentence lenient, but then my Stephen is a warrior and Barron is a seaman.

My Stephen also has very high expectations of others. I told him later after several wines and a good dinner, "My dear. You may be a hero, but not everyone is. You expect too much." He just laughed and patted my hand. Despite his inability to tolerate or be tactful about the failings of others, he was a man who believed that everyone had the same standards of honor as he. He also had the ability to inspire his crews with that love of the Navy, which he himself felt. They obeyed because they not only liked their gallant captain, but they had confidence in his leadership.

The War of 1812

Over the next eight years, Steve commanded several frigates. In 1808, he was in charge of a squadron patrolling the eastern seaboard from Maine to Virginia. He was bored with the job, but he did like the courtesy rank of commodore that he received. He also got to hoist his pennant on the main of his flagship. Like any of us, he was very flattered to have the accouterments of rank and prestige. In 1809, Stephen was appointed commander of the *United States*, his very first ship. Stephen drilled and trained his crew for battle while those of us at home anxiously waited for another war.

In June 1812, the United States declared war on Great Britain because of the continuing British acts of aggression against American ships. Stephen put his ship, the *United States*, to sea immediately. Several months later, his crew spotted HMS *Macedonian*, at dawn on October 25, five hundred miles south of the Azores. Two years earlier, when the two vessels were tied up next to one another in Norfolk, Virginia, the British captain wagered a beaver hat that if the two ever met in battle, the *Macedonian* would emerge victorious. But if that story is right, he was wrong! The *United States* transformed the *Macedonian* into a dismasted wreck, and Stephen took it as a prize. He then refitted it so it could travel back across the Atlantic where he would benefit from the sale of its cargo.

The British captain went aboard Stephen's ship to give up his sword, but Stephen said that he could not take the sword of a captain who had so bravely defended his ship. He tried to make the captain's surrender as pleasant as possible, assuring him he was not the first to surrender a ship and generally trying to raise his spirits. When the *United States* sailed into New York harbor with its prize, they were greeted with great acclaim. Every boat on the western side of the East River carried passengers across to see her. By the time her sails were secured, spectators swarmed on the Navy Yard and the surrounding area. During the next several weeks, balls and banquets were held with the "best of liquors and the choicest wines" and many nautical decorations. Someone even wrote a song.

Then quickly met our nation's eyes
The noblest sight in nature—
A first-rate frigate as a prize
Brought home by brave Decatur.

New York's red-carpet welcome climaxed in January with a parade of some four hundred officers and seaman marching to the beat of the French band Stephen had freed from the *Macedonian.* Cheering crowds, feasting, drinking, and patriotic oratory—what more could we ask for? Honors poured in. Maryland, Massachusetts, New York, Pennsylvania, and Virginia thanked him officially. Pennsylvania and Virginia awarded him a sword. Congress awarded him a beautiful gold medal. Officers and crew shared in the prize money.

By late spring of 1813, Britain had blockaded all the important ports from New York to the Southern states. Stephen was stymied in New London, Connecticut. My husband who liked the freedom of roaming the seas was reduced to waiting for the enemy. In early 1815, he daringly attempted to run the blockade with the *USS President,* but his famous luck ran out when the British West Indies Squadron began to pursue him. After a fierce fight, he managed to disable a British frigate, but two other British ships overhauled him. With his ship crippled, twenty-four men killed, fifty-five wounded including himself, and a major adversarial force, he "deemed it his duty to surrender."

Stephen blamed himself, which he shouldn't have—as everyone knows. He is too hard on himself, I tell him, but he doesn't listen to me. He does not tolerate weakness in anyone—much less himself. He has these standards. He and his men were transported as prisoners to Bermuda and paroled in late December.

The War with Algiers

During the War of 1812, the Barbary pirates captured a Yankee sailing brig off the North African coast, enslaving eleven American soldiers. President James Madison first tried to resolve the issue through diplomatic means, but our country was not in a position to demand justice until the end of the War of 1812. Once the Peace of Ghent was ratified in February 1815, President James Madison asked Congress to declare war upon the Algerians. On May 20, 1815, the most powerful fleet ever assembled by the young nation set sail for North Africa under Commodores Stephen Decatur, Jr. and William Bainbridge. Yes, Stephen was promoted to Commodore, the highest naval rank.

With ten ships under his command, Stephen set sail before Bainbridge and steered for Algiers hoping to secure the Algeria flotilla before it reached homeport. He captured the Algerian fleet flagship *Mashouda* as well as the Algerian brig *Estedio* in route to Algeria, which gave him significant bargaining power. Wearing a full dress uniform complete with tight pantaloons and long boots bound at top with gold lace, Stephen refused to negotiate, saying instead that the treaty was "dictated at the mouth of our cannon." Perhaps he was the one who initiated the term Gunboat Diplomacy because he merged his demands for compensation with threats of annihilation. The Bey of Algiers agreed to a treaty that granted the United States most-favored-nation status, ended the payment of tribute, and freed all prisoners without ransom.

After resolving the disputes in Algiers, Decatur sailed his squadron to Tunis and Tripoli to extract similar concessions. His overwhelmingly successful campaign earned him the nickname "the Conqueror of the Barbary Pirates." Finally, he met up with Bainbridge who seemed most out of sorts. From that day on, he refused to speak to or acknowledge Stephen's existence. I think it was because he was jealous. Everyone was talking about what Stephen had done. He was the hero. Bainbridge was the clean-up crew. He couldn't have liked that.

I found it harder and harder to have Stephen gone on these long trips. We had no children, and I worried so about the perils of the Navy life. When Stephen arrived home, we were entertained at a series of celebratory dinners and presented with gifts. He was a hero at the top of his profession. Everyone admired him. Even he agreed that he had regained his honor after the loss of the *President*. He was just thirty-six. I was so happy. He loved me passionately, and his honor and his country just as much.

His exploits earned him a great deal of money. With this prize money in hand, and with his appointment as a Commodore who would serve on the Navy Board of Commissioners, Stephen and I came to Washington in 1816. During his tenure as a Commissioner, Stephen became active in the Washington social scene. At one of his social gatherings, Stephen uttered an after-dinner toast that would become famous: "Our Country! In her intercourse with foreign nations may she always be in the right; but right or wrong, our country!" My Stephen had changed the face of history by his exploits in all those wars with Tripoli and Algiers and the War of 1812. He made the U.S. Navy a respected force. He was a great hero. Now, we needed to move on to different areas.

Gallant courage alone did not guarantee us a place at the top of the social and political hierarchy. We needed a fine house to exhibit our status and prestige. In 1819, using Stephen's prize money from the captured ships, we bought eleven lots on the northwest corner of Lafayette Square, commonly known as the President's Square, near the newly constructed Presidential House. We requested that Benjamin H. Latrobe, architect of the Capitol, build us a house suitable for entertaining significant and important people. He built a nearly cubic three-story town house, constructed with red brick in the austere Federal fashion of the day. In January 1819, we moved our portraits, furniture, my books, my harp, and the customary household items, Stephen's naval trophies, swords, and testimonial silver services; and those various foreign objects captured through fighting the Barbary pirates.

We intended Decatur House to be a focal point for Washington society. Its carefully selected furnishings and manicured gardens would guarantee us a place in the highest Washington social circles. There, we could mingle with cabinet-rank officials and their families, along with the diplomatic corps and other high-ranking officials. After all, Stephen was so beloved he could easily become President of the United States! And it was my role—just like Godey's *Lady Book* said—to fortify Stephen's sense of duty and direct his ambition.

Our guests would arrive at our three-story brick house with its four great chimneys and step into a center hall with a geometrically patterned floor and a vaulted ceiling. On this level we had a suite of rooms for entertaining. Their long windows opened onto wrought iron balconies—very useful during Washington's summers—overlooking President's Square. When large numbers of guests were invited, we could throw open several rooms because of the sliding doors connecting them. Guests would help themselves to refreshments set out on tables, and servants would carry trays loaded with other delectables and beverages. My pianoforte and harp were on this floor. The servants had their quarters in the attic and tended a garden at the rear of the house. There was a carriage house and stables.

The Duel

Almost broke and age fifty, James Barron, who had commanded the *Chesapeake*, returned to the United States from abroad. Stephen told me he had spent most of this time in Copenhagen trying to make living as a merchant skipper. Although Barron wanted to be reinstated, Stephen, a member of the Navy Commission, announced that Barron did not deserve to return to the Navy. "It is a naval officer's first duty to fight, not to sail ships," he declared. He said there was no place in the Navy, which now stood high in the public esteem, for a man who had struck his colors without a fight. He was quite vocal about his feelings that Barron had proved himself a coward.

In 1819, Barron accused Stephen of destroying his career. Stephen wrote him back, refuting his charges. Later, I found there were thirteen letters exchanged. My Stephen was as harsh and sarcastic as Barron. The only way they could settle their differences was through a duel.

His fellow naval commissioners refused to act as Stephen's seconds, saying he did not need to fight the duel to preserve his honor. But Commodore William Bainbridge, who hadn't spoken to Stephen for all these years, suddenly offered his services as his second. I thought that rather odd. Why would Bainbridge suddenly change his tune about Algiers and act as if their friendship was now restored?

Stephen didn't tell me anything; he just seemed more solemn than before and whenever I looked up, his eyes were upon me. I was all involved in preparing for the ball that we were giving in honor of the marriage of President James Monroe's daughter, Maria. It was the first in a round of festivities in honor of the bride, and I wanted it to be particularly special.

On the morning of March 22, 1820, Stephen left the house and met Barron in Bladensburg, Maryland. Although dueling was outlawed in Washington, D.C., an unofficial "dueling ground" existed there. On March 22, 1820, Commodore Stephen Decatur and Commodore James Barron met on that field.

The seconds, Elliott and Bainbridge, both enemies of Stephen Decatur, had agreed to the use of pistols at a distance of eight paces. Before they commenced the duel, Barron said to Stephen, "I hope, sir, that when we meet in another world, we shall be better friends than we have been in this."

"I have never been your enemy, sir!" replied Stephen. After a challenge to a duel has been accepted, the opponents can not speak or acknowledge each other until ordered to fire upon each other according to the etiquette of dueling. The seconds could have stopped the duel because of this conversation, but neither did so.

Stephen and Barron paced off eight steps and turned. The two men fired; both fell to the ground, Barron had been struck in the hip, which deflected the bullet down into his thigh. Stephen was struck in the hip as well, but the bullet had gone upward into his abdomen, slashing several blood vessels. He was in agonizing pain and was dying. When they brought him back to the house, he refused to see me, because he couldn't bear to witness my suffering. As the hours dragged

A National Trust Historic Site, Decatur House is an outstanding example of neoclassical architecture. *Courtesy of D. Peter Lund*

by, he remarked he did not think it possible to bear so much pain. Friends came to see him, and he expressed his thanks for their concern. He signed his will. Later, he said he would not mind death if it had come on the quarterdeck. "If it were the cause of my country, it would be nothing." Weakly, he thanked the friends who anxiously waited around him, but told my father, whom he had summoned earlier in the week, "You can do me no service; go to my wife and do what you can to console her."

After twelve hours of suffering, my husband, Stephen Decatur, Jr., an American hero, died on March 22, 1820, at age forty-one. He had defended his honor by entering into a duel, and he had died for that. People throughout the country wept for him; no charges were pressed; no questions were asked. They tell me that ten thousand persons attended his funeral: officers of the United States Navy and Marine Corps of the United States, Commodore Rogers and Commodore Porter, President James Monroe, former President James Madison, the Cabinet, members of the Senate, House, Supreme Court, Foreign ministers, consuls of foreign powers, citizens, family, men who had served under him, and me, the one who loved him most. A poor sailor as he wept over him exclaimed that "the Navy had lost her mainmast." With me it is far worse; I am a total wreck.

We had just danced at John Quincy Adams' home the night before. He came to the house when he heard that Stephen was dying. He said in his eulogy that the United States had lost one of its heroes: "one who has illuminated its history and has given grace and dignity to its character in the eyes of the world."

When he died, his career was far from over, and there were many paths he might have followed. As Stephen's good friend Washington Irving once said: "A gallanter fellow never stepped a quarter deck...God bless him." We had even thought he might become our first Naval President, but a bullet prevented that dream. No wonder, I walk halls of this house. I'll never stop haunting it.

Postlude

I lived for another forty years. I never remarried because I never got over the shock of losing Stephen.

When he died, he left an estate worth one hundred thousand dollars and our lovely house, which we had lived in for just fourteen months. I found it hard to make ends meet, something that was quite a change from the days of fancy parties and high ambitions. When I appealed to Andrew Jackson for help, he purchased some of my French china and silver serving dishes. But I needed more. I was forced to move to Georgetown and rent out my beautiful house, where I thought we would be so happy, to a series of Washington officials. Over the years, the ambassadors of France, Russia, Britain, and U.S. Secretaries of State Henry Clay, Martin Van Buren, and Edward Livingston rented it.

I sold Decatur House in 1836. I turned to Catholicism and even lived in a convent for some time until I found a tiny house in Georgetown. I never stopped writing letters in praise of my husband. I'll never stop my weeping for my Stephen. If you listen carefully, you can hear me in the hours just before dawn.

Author's Note.

Susan died in July 1860. James Barron recovered and was reinstated to Naval Service in 1824. Susan never forgave the seconds, Bainbridge and Elliott, and refused to socialize with them. She watched as Bainbridge wallowed in serious drug addiction until his death in 1833, and Elliott, revenged, but never respected, died a bitter man.

Over the years, the house went through a number of owners, until Marie Beale bequeathed it to the National Trust for Historic Preservation in 1956.

Visitor Information: Decatur House is one block north of the White House on Lafayette Square, on the corner of H Street and Jackson Place. The museum entrance is located at 1610 H Street, NW. House tour hours: Tuesday - Saturday: 10 am - 5 pm; Sunday: Noon - 4 pm.

STRANGERS IN AN UNKNOWN WORLD

Researchers have estimated that approximately fifteen million Africans were transported to the Americas between 1540 and 1850. In the seventeenth century, a trader could purchase a slave in Africa for about $25 and sell him in America for $150 or more. To maximize their profits, slave traders jammed as many slaves as possible into their ships' holds, where the slaves had no room to move. Their hands and feet were chained or tied together. Researchers estimate that approximately fifty percent of the slaves died on shipboard from self-starvation, smallpox, and dysentery.

Alexandria, which was part of Washington, D.C., was home to Franklin & Armfield Slave Market, one of the largest slave-trading companies in the country, from 1828 to 1836. By the 1830s, the company was sending more than 1,000 slaves annually to Natchez, Mississippi, and New Orleans markets. As the possibility of outlawing slavery in Washington, D.C. became more definite, Alexandria's citizens began to worry about their economy. Without slavery, they believed their economy would suffer greatly. In 1846, its citizens voted to ask Congress to retrocede Alexandria back to the state of Virginia. Congress agreed to do so on July 9 of that year.

During the first half of the nineteenth century, the nation's capital was a center of the slave trade. In the shadow of the nation's Capitol—right along the Mall—stood the Robey and Williams slave pens. One slave pen, Robey's Pen, was just seven blocks from the Capitol on 7th Street. The Compromise of 1850, a series of laws that attempted to resolve the territorial and slavery controversies, outlawed slave trade, though not slavery, in the capital.

Although the city has changed and the Federal Aviation Administration building on Independence Avenue between 7th and 9th Streets, S.W., now stands on the site of the Robey slave pen, if you listen carefully on quiet moonless nights, you can hear the clang of *chains and the deep moans of anguish from those nineteenth century inhabitants of Washington's slave pens. Those men and women had survived a horrific journey from West Africa to the United States. They had lost their families, their friends, and their way of life. The number of Africans who survived or perished can never be counted correctly, but we can still hear their cries from the grave.*

Yaisa was only twelve—an ugly twelve, unfortunately, with bad teeth and protruding eyes. But her mother had told her that her looks would keep her safe from those men who had a wandering eye. As Yaisa thought of her mother, she saw the bright red bandana wrapped around her head and the tiny twigs made from a special bark that she kept in her teeth. She smelled the aroma of roasted peanuts and the greens that her mother was so frequently cooking in her pot. She saw their hut and felt the warm sun on her body. She promised herself that she would return one day to the sight of the rolling sandy plains of the western Sahel rising to the foothills in the southeast.

Yaisa recalled heading toward the center of the grove. The soft mossy earth felt good under her feet. She could smell the perfumes of wild flowers and an odd musty odor, which she couldn't identify. She was looking for herbs for her mother. They had gathered oranges and other fruit that morning. Now she needed some herbs. As she bent over a likely looking root, she heard the sharp crack of a twig, followed quickly by the squawk of a bird overhead. She turned toward the sound of heavy feet behind her. She saw a yellow face, a head without hair, and an upraised club. Then something hard and heavy struck her shoulder. Shrieking, she spun on her foot and turned to run, but the club hit her head, rocking her with such pain that she cried out. Everything went black.

She remembered being gagged and bound at the wrist and hobbled at the ankles. Someone made her stand up and forced her to walk by poking her with sharp sticks. Other women and men were also bound and gagged. If someone stopped or fell, the guards beat them until they stood again. This morning, one woman just lay there while they whipped her. Her eyes were dull with pain as Yaisa stared at her, willing her to get up again. But the woman just shrugged and put her head down as the whip snapped greedily at her body. Blood appeared and then gushed.

The Trek

Terror clawed at Yaisa. She could be beaten like that woman. Sobbing quietly, she kept stumbling on the road with her bruised feet and parched lips. There was little food and less water. Some had bleeding ulcers; others just looked at the ground. She and an old woman were tied together. If one of them stumbled, they were both knocked off stride and fell into a clump on the side of the path. At night, one of the guards roped her to a tree with three other girls. Not a word was spoken. They were too tired, too scared. On the tenth morning, the girl with the big distended belly passed a mass of writhing intestinal worms. Then she lay in the dirt panting. The rest of the captives stepped over her.

On the twentieth day after they had left the swamps, they reached a vast savanna covered with rust, golden, and red grasses. Huddling together, they trod past the anthills and acacia trees. That night the stern-eyed guard efficiently roped the group to one of the thorny acacia trees. One young mother held her baby to her shriveled empty breasts, but the child was too puny to nurse and the mother too weak to assist her. Flies crawled into their eyes and nostrils. The mother stared blankly at the horizon; her eyes were almost colorless. Yaisa sat besides her, taking her hand in hers. "You must eat," she said. The woman's hand was cold, she stared straight ahead as tears ran down her face. Yaisa's eyes followed hers, traveling the length of the horizon, searching for that familiar anchor of home.

Whenever they stopped, guards surrounded them, snapping their whips or waving their cudgels. Bruises and cuts covered the captives' arms and legs. Their ropes rubbed their necks, wrists and ankles raw. Crusted blood coated one man's head. His eyes were dazed. When another man refused to eat, the bald trader signaled to a guard, who led the captive to a log and made him kneel with his arms stretched out. The trader strode over and cut off his index finger. The captive ate his rice.

Soon, they no longer looked at each other. Flies crawled and feasted on their wounds and abrasions. Dust clung to their hair and coated their tongues. Many had died: some from the guards' cruelty, some from the lack of food, some from illness. They were so sick and weak that they could barely stand. They began to realize that they had seen their home for the last time. They were alone.

At last, an escarpment of hills appeared on the horizon. They climbed up the rocky pathway to a small clearing. Her muscles knotted with fear. When the bald African trader yanked one of the men forward, he resisted, and a guard whipped him to his knees. A white man, smoking a large cigar, stepped forward, spread the slave's lips and inspected his teeth. He then explored his arms, his chest, and his belly. Using their whips, the other guards forced him to bend over a log, where they spread his buttocks apart. After the white man inspected the five men, he started on the girls. The first one bit his hand when he opened her mouth. He sideswiped her with his massive fist. Eyes popping, she spat at him. The bald African trader stepped in and began lashing her across her bare breasts. The women were shrieking; the guards were cursing, but the girl being beaten didn't say a thing. Finally, the guards threw her to the side. The white man walked over to her and held the lit end of his cigar to her breast.

The guards turned to the next girl. Cowering, she dropped to her knees. They turned her over the log, and the two men checked her private parts as she wailed. Reaching around to her chest, the last guard twisted her nipple. She dropped to the ground, screaming. The next girl began to wail before they even finished.

Yaisa was number four. When it was Yaisa's turn, she shut her eyes and remembered her mother's hut. She remembered the life-giving rain that made every plant grow. She remembered the warmth of the sun. She said to herself that this coarse hand

Enslavement and bondage have existed for generations. African tribes enslaved each other and were enslaved by others long before the coming of Europeans to Africa. Many African societies kept slaves. Sometimes the slaves worked in the homes of the wealthy; sometimes they became soldiers or sex slaves. Some villages became known for marketing slaves.

Once the Europeans came, the slave market became more lucrative. Slave traders used the rivers to penetrate deep into the county. After kidnapping potential slaves, they forced them to walk in slave caravans to great warehouses along the rivers. From there, they would be shipped downriver to European coastal forts. Shackled and underfed, only half the people survived these death marches. Those too sick or weary to keep up were often killed or left to die. Researchers suggest that approximately 50,000,000 Africans were enslaved. Once they reached the African coast, they were transported across the Atlantic to the United States and the Caribbean to be sold. Less than 10,000,000 survived the journey.

Most of the Western European maritime countries were involved with the enslavement and transportation of West Africans. Although Portugal was the first to become involved, the King of England established the Royal African Company in 1672, and by 1698 Parliament ruled that any British subject could trade in slaves. During the first-half of the eighteenth century, British ships increased their transport of enslaved Africans to British colonies from 5,000 to 45,000 a year. By 1760, Great Britain had become the number one slave-trading state.

with the prickly black hairs was like a stick that she might put in her mouth. The fingers poking her breasts and her belly were branches in the forest that reached out and snagged her as she ran through the beautiful flowers. But when the man turned her over the log and touched her private parts, she no longer could recall home.

The bald African trader and the white man went to the edge of the clearing. The white man pointed at all the men, the first girl whom he had burnt with his cigar, and Yaisa. Girls two and three were left behind. Yaisa felt like she was losing her family again, although they had barely talked. She wondered what would happen to them, but she didn't really want to know. The African trader shook his head angrily; their angry voices rose. Finally, the white man wrote something on a piece of paper, reached into a sack for a bottle of brown liquid, and gave both to the trader who took them, grinning happily.

Within a short time, the guards chained Yaisa and the others together and led them away. The white man and the guards marched her group along the path until they were loaded into canoes to travel downriver. They knelt on the floor of the rough wooden canoes, still chained, with the sun burning down on their heads. The flies followed the boat, crazed by the smell of their sweat and the open sores. The guards paddled the canoes past the thorn bush, the stark plains, and the thickly wooded banks.

On the fifth day at dusk, they reached a large building that loomed over them. It looked like a castle with little slits for windows. She could see the bats beginning to flit out of their roosts. The guards called it a barracoon. The white man separated the women and men. They poked and prodded them downstairs into a massive stone chamber without any windows. It reeked of corruption and decay, terror, and rotting filth, but she couldn't see anything. She could only hear soft breaths, bodies stirring, and a child's whimper from above.

They reached a thick door studded with iron. The guards opened the door and pushed them into the darkness. Yaisa felt the rough walls behind her. They were damp, making the room smell dank and dark. She sat on the bare dirt floor with what felt like excrement. The whiskers of a rat brushed against her breast. She wiggled away and hit a large unmoving lump on the floor lying in something wet and putrid. Yaisa realized she was touching a dead person.

By the next day, her eyes had adjusted to the darkness, and the stench no longer made her stomach heave. When the rats climbed over her, she didn't shriek. Flies plagued every moment of the day. She learned to breathe shallowly and that there were worse things than being raped. In the barracoon, time stopped. Yaisa could hear moans and groans from below. Random shrieks pierced her ears. The sky was barely visible so she could not tell when night crossed the sky or when the sun turned the sky a soft glowing pink. Now her only clock was the ring and clank of chains and the snap and crackle of whips.

Time without the sun. Time without days or nights. They were all hungry and thirsty, sick and weak. Some were so emaciated that the guards just shook their heads. Others were badly scarred from being whipped or beaten. Each day, their life force drained from them into small puddles on the dingy floor.

Yaisa stayed at the barracoon for three months. Hands had pinched her thighs and nipped her breasts. She had a cross branded on her breast and was raped twice. A rat had bitten her ankle, which remained swollen and sore. By the end of the three months, she kept her eyes to the ground. She thought about death a lot. She had seen people die from small pox and the bloody flux or dysentery. She had seen them be beaten to death. She had seen them just close their eyes, shut their mouths, and will their death. She realized that each person approaches death in his or her own way. There were many roads arriving at the same destination, she told herself. There are many ways to enter the same village. She wondered how she would approach it.

She thought there were about one hundred women from many different tribes in the slave pen when she was first brought to it. But each day more were added to their number.

The guards gave them a bowlful of rice and some fish each day. They used one barrel for a toilet. They curled up to hide their bodies from their captors' lewd gaze and groping hands. Some just squatted against the walls: others prowled as far as their shackles would permit. Most just withdrew from the outside world and went deep into themselves.

The Middle Passage

One day, the guards came in, snapping their whips enthusiastically. "It's time for you to move on," they announced. They chained them in pairs, shackled wrist to wrist or ankle to ankle. Yaisa felt a stir of excitement. They were going outside. She could smell salty air and see large birds flapping overhead. Clouds of flying insects from the nearby marshes were buzzing about. Everywhere there was noise and confusion. The guards marched them to a dock where boats were waiting. They were put in the boats and rowed out to beyond the breakers where a great ship rode at anchor. Overhead, a flock of seagulls flew about. Many of the slaves began to moan as they realized that this ship wasn't going to take them home. They would never see Africa again.

Their captors pushed and prodded them up the gangplank and then pushed and whipped them down below deck in a space that was about 20 feet wide, 120 feet long and 5 feet high. The guards put the women in the one end of the hold and the men in the other. Yaisa slept spoon fashion between two other women, who were chained to her. When she awoke in the pitch darkness, she bolted upwards, but her forehead hit against the ceiling only about five inches above her. She groaned and tried to twist away, but she couldn't move. Through the sickening stench of bodies, blood, and urine, she heard moaning, shrieking, and chanting. Someone was shrieking that Allah was coming. She smelled vomit and feces.

She could feel someone's shoulders, arms, and legs on her left and her right side. She explored her shackled left wrist with her right hand. Pulling lightly, she realized that her chain was connected to the girl next to her, who moaned steadily. The girl on the other side was shackled to her right wrist. She didn't move when Yaisa pulled the chain. Yaisa wondered if, in turn, she were shackled to another girl on the other side and if that girl were shackled to another girl and if there was a long line of girls linked together by heavy clanking chains. They were all so close that she could smell their breath. She realized that she was semi-naked, chained to other girls who didn't speak to her, or who lay there moaning.

Her head felt ready to explode. *It's like a beehive,* she thought. *Each of us are so many bees packed away, fitted into each other, a living mass.* They remained that way the whole night, for the chains and the number of bodies prevented any movement.

The Middle Passage is the name for the middle leg of the slave runner's three-part voyage. The first leg of the voyage from Europe to Africa, the ship carried goods that usually included cloth, brandy, rum, and guns. Upon landing on Africa's "slave coast," European and Yankee sailors traded their cargo for African men and women who had been transported from the interior to the west coast of Africa. Once fully loaded with its human cargo, the ship set sail for the Americas, where the slaves were exchanged for sugar, tobacco, or some other product. This leg of the journey took approximately eight weeks. The final leg brought the ship back to Europe.

The occasional flicker of light through the deck hatch told her whether it was daytime or night. Their cocoon rocked slowly, and Yaisa pressed her body against her shackle mates. She heard others vomiting and felt the spray of vomit from the woman on her left side. She shut her eyes and dreamed of the smells and sights of her own village. She heard the village's great drum boom and saw the farmers dance out a rhythm to match its beat. They would fling their hoes on one drumbeat and catch it on the next. She saw herself walking with the women who sang as they walked to the field, carrying food for a midday meal in great pots on their heads.

She wanted to cry, but the groans about her overpowered her tears. People were shouting, crying, and praying, "Help me, help me." Although she did not understand all the dialects, she could hear the plea in their voices—their desperation and terror. She could feel the heartbreak of mothers weeping for their children; she could hear the groans of the fathers who had lost their families; and the shrieks of all their breaking hearts.

When the ocean was rough, the water poured into the hold where they lay. The sewage and filth washed around their bodies, which were rubbed raw by the wooden planks on which they lay. After the hatch had opened and closed for two nights, Yaisa knew her left-side mate was very sick, but her vomiting didn't bother her as much as the intense itching of the body lice. Yaisa scratched constantly. A hot, choking stench filled the hold.

Yaisa would dream of the fish leaping from the river near her home, of fat wildebeest haunches roasting, or steaming tea sweetened with honey. She remembered a story that her grandmother had told her about the lion that was caught in a trap. Along came a mouse, which promised to help the lion in return for his freedom. The mouse freed the lion by gnawing through the ropes. The moral of the story, according to her grandmother, was that: *Little friends may prove great friends.*

But Yaisa didn't have any friends. Everyone was a stranger, torn from family, home, and village. Everyone had lost their mothers and their fathers. All had lost their pasts and their futures. They were outsiders in an unknown world.

If she had been at home, she would have been gathering herbs and roots, beans and berries, and pounding millet with her pestle. She would have lived in a hut with her family and others. When the cattle had eaten all the grain in the field, they would move on to another area and begin again.

The immediate horror was that everyone was stuck in this gut-wrenching filth. If the woman next to her was sick, Yaisa not only heard and smelt her vomiting but she could feel it spraying around her—and there was no way she could wipe it off. The girl to her left groaned frequently. Her hand felt hot when Yaisa touched it. Yaisa tried to move her body further away from her, but the shackles constrained her. She kept thinking about dying, but she didn't want to die. She wanted to live and wait for another day.

Ten nights later, the guards came in and released the chains and whipped them up the hatchway. They stumbled in the darkness, trying to avoid the whip. When they reached the top of the hatchway, the glare of the sunlight stung their eyes. They were surrounded by an endless expanse of deep green water. Giant white sails snapped and flapped over them. The gently rolling deck beneath their sore bodies, stiff legs, and manacles made their balance uncertain.

Yaisa was still shackled by her wrists to her right-hand and left-hand mates. They were all naked, crusted with disease and the contents of ruptured bowels. Blinking against the awesome light, she buried her face in her elbow to avoid the tormenting sun. She breathed in the salty air, hearing people vomit around her, whips against flesh, and shrieks of pain. Yaisa turned to look at her left-hand mate—the girl who was always groaning. She was practically hanging by her wrist shackles. Yaisa and the girl on her other side supported most of the weight of her flagging body. A large bumpy rash filled with a thick, opaque fluid covered her limp body. Some bumps had a depression in the center that looked like a bellybutton. Yaisa drew back in horror. A guard looked over and then shouted, "Smallpox." Another guard came over to the two girls. They unshackled the sick girl, rolled her into a slick cloth, and dumped her over the side.

Yaisa gasped, turning away to her right-hand mate—to see that she was the girl who had spat at the guard back in the clearing. She looked awful: skin and bones, knobs of joints, and coated with filth. She had a round burn mark on her breast from the white man's cigar. Her back was oozing. A whip had left a deep festering scar on her gray flesh. She was staring at Yaisa with similar shock. She must look just as awful. Yaisa noticed the guards were staring at their breasts. She tried to cover hers with her shackles.

Then the guards were shoving them toward a group of other guards, who hosed them with salt water and scrubbed them with long-handled brushes. Yaisa screamed as the salt water stung her whip cuts. She shrieked even more when the stiff brushes scraped off her scabs. The water was frothing and pink at her feet.

The guards pointed the hoses at their feet so they began to jump to avoid them. The guards laughed, leering at their nudity. "Jump." said the guards. "Jump." The African men just stood there staring, but then the guards began to whip them, "Jump."

Staring at her solemnly, the other girl pointed at her chest, whispering, "Madi." She repeated the gesture. Yaisa pointed at herself, saying, "Yaisa." The guard snapped his whip. But the two girls smiled at each other. A friend. She had found a friend in the midst of this horror.

Yaisa shivered. Although the sun was strong, her body shook with chills. The crack of a whip hit the deck near her feet. "Start jumping." Like puppets, they began to jump, dragging their chains, around and around the deck. They weren't allowed to talk, but Yaisa knew that Madi was there. They weren't as alone as they had been before. Although they were from different villages, they were together now. When it was mealtime, they sat together—not talking—but together. Yaisa noticed that Madi's eyes were still defiant, even when the guards made her eat some rice filled with wiggling maggots.

As the hot sun dried them, Yaisa searched for lice. She found several still stuck to her skin. She popped them off, crumbling them between her fingers. They exploded in a spit of blood. The ship timbers groaned, the sails billowed overhead, and white gulls swooped overhead.

One slave refused to eat. He kept shaking his head, even when the guards whipped him. One guard forced open his mouth with a strange contraption. They stuffed the food into that to force-feed him. The next day the slave was dead. Some threw themselves into the ocean; others just seemed to will death; still others just died from the trip. Each night the guards locked them into the hold; each morning, more bodies were thrown overboard. When the ocean was rough, the guards closed the hatches, leaving the slaves gasping for breath. The heat was intolerable. Yaisa found it hard to breathe in the hold, which reeked of accumulated vomit, diarrhea, infection and terror. The shelves on which they lay were wet with body fluids, the result of the dysentery. The screams, the crying, the groans of the dying, and the muttered prayers of those who still believed in a God made it a scene of unbelievable horror as the ship rolled on.

The ship sailed on into a deep sullen gray sea often covered by a milky mist. The wind became colder, the sun paler. Often the mist shrouded the ship. More people died. When Yaisa received her saltwater hosing, she watched the guards bring up the bodies of those who died during the night. The guards threw the bodies into the sea. Once she saw a pair of dark fins swimming quickly towards a body. The sea frothed, and the body was gone.

Yaisa began to shriek until Madi shook her head. That was the first day that Madi told her a story. She stretched out her fingers so she could touch Yaisa's arm. "I'm going to tell you how the crocodile got its knobby ugly green skin."

Yaisa looked up. "Really?"

"Yes. Now in the beginning, the crocodile would spend all day in the muddy river waters and only come on the land at sunset. His skin was silky smooth and bright yellow because he was not out in the daylight. When the crocodile came on shore in the evening, other animals would admire his beautiful golden skin in the pale moonlight. He would preen and pose.

"The crocodile began coming on land more frequently so more animals could see him. He so liked their admiration that he began crawling up the riverbank when the sun was just coming up in the morning. Then he would stay there all that day. He decided he was better than the other animals. Certainly, he was more handsome, he told himself. He began bossing them around.

"Now, the giraffe, the hippo, the elephant, and all the other animals did not like to be bossed around by the crocodile. They began ignoring him, and fewer and fewer animals admired his skin. Finally, they weren't even coming to see him. But the crocodile kept crawling up on the riverbank in the daytime, and his skin became covered with thick bumps. Soon his yellow smooth skin had become an ugly green bumpy skin. One lovely morning, the crocodile saw his reflection in the river. He was horrified. So today he disappears from view when others approach; the only thing that anyone sees is his eyes and nostrils above the surface of the water."

"Maybe the crocodile is like the white man. So ugly that we have never seen him before." Yaisa said. She laughed.

She and Madi whispered after their daily hosing. They laughed and cried together. Sometimes they prayed. The guards threw bodies of the dead slaves into the sea every time they were taken to the deck. The darkness became worse: the smells were more intense, the groans louder. The whips snapped less—perhaps because the life juices were going from so many. As more were found to have smallpox, the chief guard would inspect each slave more carefully. If he found any signs of smallpox, he would snap out an order, and the other guards would toss the slave, kicking and screaming, into the dark frothy sea. Sometimes Yaisa saw the black fins swarm around. She wondered idly if a shark could get smallpox. She wondered what it would feel like to be tossed into the ocean. Would it be easier than being on this ship? Every day Yaisa felt a little worse; she began to have stomach pain and diarrhea.

One day the ocean began to change. First, seaweed appeared and then birds. Then Yaisa saw a distant gray line. It was land. The guards were pointing, laughing, and shouting. She and Madi jumped up and down. As the land came closer, Madi told her a story about God and the Earth.

"In the beginning," she said "God was so proud of the humans he had created in his image that he wanted to live as close as possible to them. So he built himself a beautiful home in the blue sky—just above their heads. He was a part of everyone's life. Everyone knew his face and, if people were in need, he would offer to help. It was a lovely arrangement, but after some months, God began to notice that the people were treating him without respect. Sometimes people did not greet him. Sometimes children spat at the sky. Sometimes daughters were rude to their mothers or people would damage the sky. Now God hoped that this disrespect would not last. Then one afternoon, God went to take a nap. One thoughtless woman began to thump grain in a large wooden mortar. Bang, bang, bang. As she thumped her pestle, she hit the sky. BANG. The whole sky shook. Certainly, God couldn't sleep with all this noise going on. As he rose to ask her to be quieter, the woman suddenly jerked her pestle and hit him in the eye with it. God gave a shout of anger. He raised his arms way about his head and pushed the sky upwards, flinging it far into space.

"Once they realized that the sky was no longer part of the earth and that God was no longer one with them, the people became angry with the thoughtless woman. They pestered her to resolve this problem. She collected all the wooden mortars she could find. She stacked these on top of each other until the resulting tower almost reached the sky. She needed only one more to reach the sky. Unthinkingly, she pulled the lowest mortar out from the bottom of the stack and put it on top. Of course, the whole tower came crashing down. Ever since then, God has remained in the sky where we can't approach him as easily as before and where he can't do as much to help us." Madi sighed. "If God were present now, I wonder what he would do?"

"He would stop this from happening to us."

"I hope so. But for now, it is up to us."

The land was very close now. They could see the dock thick with mast and sail. Small boats came and went. The slaves began praying and praising Allah. Chains rattled.

Sails flapped. Yaisa could smell salty air and fried food. She could see faces looking up at them. The ship stopped moving, bumping hard against something solid. It lurched to one side and then to another.

The ship bustled with movement as men hurried to disembark. The guards signaled them to stand. Those who didn't were whipped but more gently than usual. They were pushed and shoved to the gangplank. Many white faces were waiting there. Men were unloading cargoes and piling the boxes onto carts or stacking the great wooden crates along side. Still chained, the slaves walked past a large marketplace stacked with fruits and vegetables. Some Yaisa recognized, some she didn't. She could smell hot metal, baking bread, animal dung, and other scents that she could not name. Animals complained, people laughed, cartwheels creaked, and peddlers called. The white faces stared at them, talking, pointing, and gesticulating. Some rode in two and four-wheeled contraptions pulled by large animals who made clip-clop sounds when they walked. She saw white women dressed in lovely colors and squirmed at her own nakedness. The white women wore bonnets, which were tied under their chins. The men wore dark coats and light trousers. Black people were standing around, waiting behind the white people.

Madi smiled at her, and she smiled back. It would be all right because she and Madi were friends. She was so funny, fearless, and full of life that Yaisa was sure that some of it would rub off on her. They would stick together.

The Slave Pens
Suddenly, they found themselves at the doorway of a large square building. They entered. Their guards locked her wrists and ankles in thick iron cuffs attached to short chains that were bolted to the walls. Yaisa sat. After some time, an unchained black man entered and put down bowls of water and food before each of them. He unlocked their arms so they could eat. Madi signaled her to eat and drink. The food tasted strange, but it was good and she was hungry. She looked around at her

In presenting the Netherlands Carillon "From the People of the Netherlands to the People of the United States" Queen Juliana said, "To achieve real harmony, justice should be done also to the small and tiny voices, which are not supported by the might of their weight. Mankind could learn from this. So many voices in our troubled world are still unheard. Let that be an incentive for all of us when we hear the bells ringing." *Courtesy of D. Peter Lund*

surroundings. The high windows were barred, but she could see the sun through them.

A black man came in with a large basin of water and made gestures that told them they were to wash. A man shaved the male captives and rubbed their skin with oil. Yaisa laughed, "They think they can make us look pretty after all this." Another black man gave them clothing. A hat, coat, shirt, pants, and shoes went to the men; calico dresses and kerchiefs to the women. Madi's dress was too big for her. "You look like a skinny tree in an anthill," Yaisa joked.

One of the guards grabbed her, "Listen here, this is selling season." He took them into a large room in the front part of the building and began pushing them into groups. "Time to get into the coffle." Bound in pairs, along a long chain, the male captives came first. Behind them, but without chains, stood the women lined up by height. Madi and Yaisa were able to remain together at the end of the line of women. After them came the children and behind them came mothers with infants or children in arms.

They were led outside to a platform and made to stand there. Many white people were standing on the ground, talking, and laughing. One woman in a green silk dress, proclaimed, "They are like children, you know."

"Yes," said her escort. "On my plantation, we have to whip them quite frequently."

"They are just like animals of the field," said another woman. "When I hear people talking about ending the slave trade, I wonder how we would live without them to take care of us."

"Who would do the work?" Madi winked at Yaisa.

A man with a big, white hat seemed to be in charge. His face flushed red and shiny as the morning went on. He made the slaves hold up their heads, walk briskly back and forth, while customers would turn them about, make them open their mouths, and show their teeth. People gazed, touched, prodded, and poked. Firm muscles meant production; long fingers agility; clear skin good health. Whip marks meant an unruly character; flat breasts meant infertility; gray hair meant old age and weakness. The white men talked, bantered, and laughed as they ran their hands over breasts and abdomens, probing secret parts of the body. The slaves were stripped, examined, priced, and sold.

One man walked up to Madi, thrusting the butt of his whip against her chest, while groping her breasts, her belly, and her long legs. She spat at him. He took her arm and bent it backward behind her back. Yaisa could see the tears coming to Madi's eyes, but she didn't say anything.

"Young and supple, fresh from Africa," the white-hatted man shouted. The crowd began shouting out numbers. Finally, they stopped, and one man came forward to take Madi's chain.

Yaisa shouted, "Madi," but she was gone. Now it was her turn. The crowd moved around her. They poked at her mouth, prodded at her chest. The tears rolled down her cheeks. She had lost her homeland, her family, and now even her friend. She was a stranger in a strange land.

Visitor Information: Robey's Slave Pen operated where the Federal Aviation Administration building stands on Independence Avenue between 7th and 9th Streets, S.W.

FATHER ABRAHAM

The White House or the Executive Mansion at 1600 Pennsylvania Ave, Washington, D.C., has been home to nearly every President of the United States. Appropriately for the "land of the free," many of the nationalities present in America during that era participated in the building of the President's House. President Washington and French-born city planner Pierre L'Enfant chose the site for the new residence, and the practical and handsome design of Irish-born James Hoban won. Slave labor dug the footings and built the foundations. Scottish immigrants erected the sandstone walls and the floral decorations while Irish and Italian immigrants undertook the brick and plasterwork.

A major symbol of the Presidency, the 132-room White House is open to the public (free of charge!) and is one of the most popular tourist attractions in America. The home is so lovely that some of its residents have remained as ghosts. One of the oldest ghosts is First Lady Abigail Adams who can be seen carrying Presidential laundry to the East Room where she hung it to dry.

But the ghost most often seen is the unhappy spirit of Abraham Lincoln, the sixteenth President of the United States. Residents of the house, visitors, and staff members have heard Lincoln's footsteps on the second floor, seen him donning his boots in the northwest bedroom, lying quietly on his bed, deep in thought, and knocking on bedroom doors late at night. During her husband's administration in the 1920s, First Lady Grace Coolidge saw him in the Oval Office, looking out at the Potomac River. When Queen Wilhelmina of the Netherlands was a White House guest, she claimed to have seen Lincoln's ghost. Many feel that his spirit remains with us because his assassination interrupted his work and prevented him from carrying out his vision for the nation .

Other ghosts have also walked the White House grounds. They include Willie Lincoln (Abe's son who died in the Lincoln Bedroom), John Kennedy, William Henry Harrison, Abigail Adams, Eleanor

Roosevelt, Andrew Jackson, Thomas Jefferson, John Tyler, Frances Cleveland (Grover Cleveland's wife), David Burns (previous owner of the White House land), an unknown British soldier, and a black cat that apparently forewarns of national emergencies. But in this story we are writing about Abraham Lincoln.

> Why if the old Greeks had had this man,
> what trilogies of plays—what epics—
> would have been made out of him! ...
> How quickly that quaint tall form
> would have enter'd into the region
> where men vitalize gods,
> and gods divinify men!
> But Lincoln, his times, his death—
> great as any, any age—
> belong altogether to our own.
>
> "Death of Abraham Lincoln"
> Walt Whitman, 1879

When I told my mama that I was leaving our Illinois farm and accompanying Ward Lamon Hill to Washington, she shook her head. "You can't leave the farm, son. Your brother and father can't take care of all that corn."

"They will have to, Mama. Mr. Lamon says Mr. Lincoln wants him, and he...he wants me! He says it will be handy to have me around—especially if there is to be a war. And I want to work for Mr. Lincoln."

"Working for our new President will be a dangerous job, son. Not everyone likes Mr. Lincoln. They even call him a baboon, and then there are those Secessionists!"

"But, Mama, I can do it. I promise I will be safe. And working for Mr. Lamon and the President would be such an honor. Besides, I can get away and see the world and make some money."

What I didn't tell her was that I hated farming. I was so tired of all that plowing, cultivating, seeding, weeding, watering, and harvesting. If I went to Washington, D.C., I would wear a suit, work with college-educated men, and meet exciting people as our country grew under this new President.

"Maybe it would be an honor, son, but you don't know what might happen. This world is coming apart when brother is talking about fighting brother, and the country is talking about war."

I hate to admit it, but she was right. I guess mothers often are—perhaps because they have seen a lot more than we have. My mama went on to say that everyone knew that Mr. Lincoln was a sad, sad man. First off, she said, he was sad because his mother, Nancy Hanks, died when he was so young—she gratuitously pointed out how sad I would be if she died and I agreed. She said he was sad because he had to work so hard when he was a boy in the western frontier, splitting rails and working on a ferryboat and getting himself an education. It's so strange to think that Illinois was once the western frontier. Then she sighed and said he was just always sad.

I pointed out that he had a keen sense of humor. That he was always joking. Like when he was accused of being two-faced, he replied, "If I had two faces, do you think this is the one I'd be wearing?"

She laughed. "Do you know he also said, 'Tis better to be silent and be thought a fool, than to speak and remove all doubt.'"

"Nope."

"Well, he did. Mr. Lincoln has a great way with words, but I think his style of humor covers up great pain."

"Oh, Ma. You're exaggerating."

"There are stories…" She looked down at the bowl of peas that she was shelling.

"What kind of stories?"

"Well, like his visions." She said reluctantly.

"Tell me."

She put down her bowl and settled back in her chair. I knew that this was a prelude to a story. "You know that he grew up poor, but he always believed that he was destined to rise to a great height…that he would be able to confer lasting benefits on his fellow men."

"I think that's true. I believed it when he said, 'A house divided against itself cannot stand.'"

"He believed also that from a lofty station he would fall," she interrupted. "That's what scares me, son. I don't want you to fall with him."

"I won't Mama. I promise." In retrospect, what did I know? I was only twenty, after all.

"Well," she said, "Everyone in Springfield was so excited the dawn of Election Day 1860. They say that the day began with cannon, music, and great excitement. Mr. Lincoln was the Republican Party candidate, and he spent the day and evening with his friends at a telegraph office. By that night, we all knew that he been elected the sixteenth President of the United States. All night, guns were fired, congratulatory telegraphs received, and such wonderful parties held. It was a great day." She hesitated.

"And so what happened?" I asked.

"The story goes that when Mr. Lincoln finally dragged his tired body home that night, he lay on a sofa, which faced a large bureau with a mirror sitting on top of it. As he stared at his reflection in the glass, he saw a double image of himself. It was as if he had two noses. He could almost measure the distance between one nose and other. Then he noticed that one of the faces had the full glow of health and other was pale and pallid. When he looked more closely, he thought that the mirror portended that something awful was going to happen.

"And?"

"But then his hallucination faded away like dreams do, but every once in awhile he would just get a glimpse of it again—just like you do when you have a bad dream. So he went home and told his wife, Mary. She was a strong believer in the spirit world. But the hallucination never returned." She swallowed hard. "Mrs.

Lincoln, who believes in dreams, said it was 'a sign' that he was to be elected to a second term of office, and that the paleness of one of his faces was an omen that he would die during his second term in office." My mama laughed, cynically. "Mrs. Lincoln certainly wasn't known for her positive attitude."

I hadn't heard that story before, but I didn't really care. I knew I would convince my mama and that I was going to Washington D.C. to guard the President of the United States. What an adventure I was going to have. And it was.

Foreshadowing

And so I left Illinois and went to Washington. As promised, I had a great job with Ward Hill Lamon, who had been Lincoln's law partner and was U.S. Marshall of the District of Columbia. Strong, stout, and six feet high, he could shoot a pistol better than any man I had ever seen and use a knife quite deftly. He saw his job was to keep Mr. Lincoln safe—that the ceaseless and watchful care of the guards around him was essential, and I was one of them. We dressed in plain clothes—really simple frock coats—and followed the President whenever he left the building. It was a dangerous job. People really wanted to kill the President. Before Mr. Lincoln had become President, an Italian barber in Baltimore planned to stab him while he was on his way to Washington. He had so many enemies in the South that it was believed he would be murdered before he could even be sworn in as President. Somebody told me that someone even sent him poisoned preserved fruit. Luckily, the packages were examined first!

By the time of Mr. Lincoln's inauguration in March 1861, seven cotton-growing states (South Carolina, Alabama, Florida, Georgia, Louisiana, Mississippi, and Texas) had seceded from the Union. Despite all the threats and boasts, neither the Union nor the Confederacy was ready for war. The South had no standing army and no ships. Most of the men in the U.S. Army were stationed out west to guard the nation's frontier posts. The U.S. Navy had only about forty boats in commission.

In his Inaugural Address, Mr. Lincoln said, "In your hands, my dissatisfied fellow countrymen, and not in mine, is the

Opened in 1922, The Lincoln Memorial celebrates Abraham Lincoln, the six-teenth president of the United States. In the form of a Greek Doric temple, the building contains a large-seated sculpture of Abraham Lincoln and inscriptions of his Gettysburg address and his second inaugural speech. The memorial has been the site of many famous speeches, including Martin Luther King's "I Have a Dream" speech. It is open twenty-four hours a day. *Courtesy of D. Peter Lund*

momentous issue of civil war. The government will not assail
you.... You have no oath registered in Heaven to destroy the
government, while I shall have the most solemn one to preserve,
protect and defend it." But people didn't listen to him—or
at least the Southerners didn't. When the Confederacy fired
on Fort Sumter and forced its surrender, he called for 75,000
volunteers. In the beginning, they were mostly farm boys eager
to leave the farm and to be on the battlefield full of flags and
bugle calls. If I hadn't gone to Washington with Mr. Lamon, I
would have kissed my mama goodbye and gone off to fight the
Secesh too. I would have done anything to escape that farm.
My mama should be glad I took this job!

Four more states seceded: Arkansas, North Carolina,
Tennessee, and Virginia. The Civil War began on April 12, 1861,
and the sunlight began to glint off the barrels of Springfield
rifles. Mr. Lincoln received so many death threats that the White
House adopted round-the-clock security, but the public wasn't
told. I learned to shadow people and work undercover. My work
was certainly exciting—much better than growing corn.

> *The firing on that fort will inaugurate a
> civil war greater than any the world has yet
> seen...you will lose us every friend at the North.
> You will wantonly strike a hornet's nest which
> extends from mountains to ocean. Legions now
> quiet will swarm out and sting us to death. It
> is unnecessary. It puts us in the wrong. It is
> fatal.*
>
> —Robert Toombs, Confederate
> Secretary of State and Confederate
> Brigadier General

The war, however, was really grim. Lamon talked about his friends who had died. One man he knew lost three sons and two nephews. So many fatalities. Mr. Lincoln looked haggard and his sad face was streaked with depression. Perhaps he knew that when the war was all over, it would be more than six hundred thousand dead. Think of all those people who died—not to mention those who lost a leg or an arm.

People said that Mr. Lincoln had second sight. A chatty woman in the War Department told me that one night, Mr. Lincoln rushed into their telegraph office in a panic. "Contact the Union commanders," he ordered.

"Why?" asked the operator.

"Because the Confederate soldiers are just about to cut through the Federal lines."

"How do you know that?"

And Mr. Lincoln responded, "My god, man! I saw it."

No wonder he always looked grim and sad. Sometimes he told funny stories, but then it was like he would disappear into himself. Sometimes, we would find him leaning back in his chair with his hat tipped over his face, his hands clasped around his knees—the epitome of melancholy. His children made him smile though. Many people send dogs, rabbits, goats, and ponies to the White House because Willie and his brother, Tad, love animals. We had a real menagerie going there. And both boys could be quite mischievous, breaking mirrors, ringing call bells—even going so far as to interrupt Cabinet meetings. They would hook up two goats to carts or kitchen chairs and drive them through the main floor of the White House. But Willie had his serious side. Sometimes, when Mr. Lincoln and we inspected the troops, eleven-year-old Willie came along. I would see the two of them talking very seriously about what was happening.

Everyone loved Willie; most of us thought that he was his father's favorite. He was bright, talented, good tempered, and smart. Even though he talked about being a minister, he was all boy. He and Tad even constructed a fort on the White House roof using a small log for a cannon and several decommissioned rifles. They thought they could scare the Confederate soldiers. I wish that was true.

When Willy "took cold" and died, Mr. Lincoln said, "My poor boy. He was too good for this earth!" His dying just didn't make any sense—not with all those soldiers dying, too. Mr. Lincoln put up a brave front, but he was just devastated. He would go to Willie's tomb and raise the lid of his coffin to gaze on his son's embalmed face. Some say he was suicidal at this point. Supposedly, he had Willie's body twice disinterred just to see him one more time. He withdrew even further into himself.

But then some days he would talk about his dead son as if he were still here, playing on the White House roof. He put Willie's drawings and toys where he could see them. He kept watching the door while he worked, as if expecting Willie would run through it and give him a hug. My lady friend said that because Mr. and Mrs. Lincoln were holding on to the dead boy, that Willie couldn't pass over. He was just staying around. It wasn't right.

Someone introduced Mrs. Lincoln to a medium, who helped her—she said—to pierce the veil that separates us from our dead ones. She would sit in the dark, listening for knocks on the table, scratches on the wall, and footsteps in the silence. She heard messages from Willie in everything. She had already lost one son in infancy and now another was gone. The mediums said they brought back her two dead sons as well as a cousin who had died in battle. Poor lady. She was so depressed.

Mr. Lincoln began to attend séances and meet with mediums in the hopes of contacting his son. They said that he visited one medium whose grand piano rose right off the floor when she was playing it. Mr. Lincoln and Colonel Simon P. Case, of Philadelphia, along with several other gentlemen, climbed onto the piano, only to have it jump and shake so hard that they had to get off. Mr. Lincoln said that the levitation was proof of an "invisible power."

People began to talk. No one really liked the idea of the President of the United States believing in levitation and the spirit world. In England, a publisher printed some music called "The Dark

Séance Polka." On its cover was a caricature of President Lincoln holding a candle while violins and tambourines flew about his head. I was glad that my mama didn't see that!

Mr. Lincoln had a hard time sleeping. Sometimes he would leave his big bed (imagine—it was nine feet long and almost nine feet high), and we would find him walking down the second floor corridor in his nightshirt and slippers. John Hay would tell us how sometimes, at night when he was sound asleep, he would hear someone putting a candlestick down on the edge of his bedside table. As John would open his eyes, he would see the President, who would say, "Don't get up. I hope you don't mind if I read to you for a little while." Then he would read some Shakespeare or a chapter from the Bible, while Hay would lie in bed, listening. After Mr. Lincoln read for some time, he would pick up his candlestick and leave with his short nightshirt barely covering his long legs.

Our worries about the President getting assassinated multiplied. Several months after Willy's death, the White House stables caught fire. Mr. Lincoln ran across the lawn and jumped a boxwood hedge to save the stables, but he was too late. We hurried him back into the White House, afraid that an assassin had started the fire, hoping to lure him out.

The war kept getting worse. To stretch my coffee supply further, I mixed roasted dandelion root with pure coffee, and I gave up on sugar. I found myself taking Lily to church socials because there was little theater and only an occasional musical event. I guess the only good thing right now is Lily. She's blond, blue eyed, and smart, and she thinks I'm wonderful!

In September 1862, General McClellan stopped Robert E. Lee and the Confederate armies at Antietam, Maryland. By nightfall, 26,000 men were dead, wounded, or missing—the bloodiest day in U.S. military history. With Mr. Lincoln riding his horse, we visited the battleground. Maybe hell is like a battlefield. It was a morass of collapsed wagons, screaming horses, clouds of dust, soldiers having legs and arms cut off, and wounded begging for help or water. Blood and body parts were wherever I looked. It was awful to see these men who have lost so much, and they were just about my age. I don't care whose side they were on. Mr. Lincoln just walked, almost stumbling, with tears rolling down his wrinkled face.

Then in December at Fredericksburg, Virginia, the two armies together lost almost 18,000 men. All those wives whose husbands never returned; all those mothers who never saw their sons again; men were just dying and dying. The stonewalls were black with blood. Mr. Lincoln just closed his eyes in pain. My friend, William Crook, said that Mr. Lincoln absorbed the horrors of war into himself. Maybe he did, but then he would say confusing things like, "I have a vision of glory and of blood."

On January 1, 1863, Mr. Lincoln issued the Emancipation Proclamation, which declared that all slaves in the South were free "thenceforward and forever." Now, the war was about restoring the Union and freeing the slaves. People kept coming to see the President. He listened to the mothers, the widows, and the office-seekers.

One February day, he supposedly attended a séance at Mrs. Laurie's home. She told him that a spirit calling himself Dr. Bamford described how bad it was for the Union soldiers. How they didn't have enough food or uniforms. Mrs. Laurie told me later that Mr. Lincoln's head just bowed down as if he were being beaten. She swore his eyes were glistening with tears. Mr. Lincoln asked what he could do to make it better. Dr. Bamford told him that he and Mrs. Lincoln should visit the soldiers at the front and talk to them. This step would rally the men and give them courage to continue fighting for the Union.

I don't know whether I believed in that spirit, but what he said was true. Those soldiers needed some rallying. I accompanied Mr. and Mrs. Lincoln on that trip. We talked to the soldiers, who told me that sometimes the Union and the Confederate soldiers just marched towards each other, shoulder to shoulder. When they opened fire on one another, they would be at a range that was not more than a few hundred yards. When they got really close, they sometimes "clubbed" their muskets, which meant holding the gun by its barrel so that the stock could be used to club farmers, friends, neighbors, clerks, lawyers, college boys, husbands, fathers, and brothers. War can be just one great impersonal killing machine. Maybe that was why Mr. Lincoln has this look of torment about him. He had to send all those boys into battle, when sometimes they didn't have any ammunition or shoes. How could he stand it, all those boys being killed?

The armies fought at Chancellorsville, Virginia, in May. Seventeen thousand Union men were killed, wounded and missing; thirteen thousand Confederates. In four days, our country lost thirty thousand men! By July 1863, the Union forces won at Gettysburg, however, but at the cost of fifty-one thousand casualties over three hot summer days. All those brave young farmers, clerks, salesmen, and laborers were wounded, maimed, crippled, or bloody dust.

The tide of the war did seem to be turning, however. Was it because Mr. Lincoln was listening to the spiritualist, we asked ourselves? No one knew, but something made a difference.

Four Score and Seven Years Ago

There were so many death threats against Mr. Lincoln. Some were more than a threat! The second day of the Gettysburg battle, Mrs. Lincoln rode in their carriage while he rode his horse. When the carriage began to descend a winding hill, the seat came loose, throwing the driver to the ground. Unable to restrain the runaway horses, Mrs. Lincoln tried to leap from the carriage, hitting her head. Later my boss, Mr. Lamon said someone deliberately loosened the seat, hoping to kill the President.

We went to Gettysburg by train. Mr. Lincoln continued to work on the speech he had written in Washington. On the morning of November 19, he got on his big chestnut horse

Opposite: Built almost entirely with donations by former slaves, this bronze statue of Abraham Lincoln, sculpted by Thomas Ball in 1876, resides in Lincoln Park, East Capitol Street between 11th and 13th Streets N.E. in Washington, D.C. It shows him with the Emancipation Proclamation in his right hand and holding his left hand over the head of a liberated slave kneeling at his feet. The park is open daily. Washington, D.C. celebrates April 16 as Emancipation Day. *Courtesy of Michael Lodico, Jr.*

EMANCIPATION

to go out to the Soldiers' National Cemetery [now called the Gettysburg National Cemetery], which was to be dedicated that day. The Marine Band played; many others gave long, sleep-inducing speeches. One man there—I think his name was Everett—spoke for almost two hours. But Mr. Lincoln said it like it was: he summarized the war in ten sentences and in a little less than three hundred words. The older I get, the more I like those short speeches. They say that Mr. Lincoln rededicated the nation to the war effort and to the ideal that no soldier at Gettysburg had died in vain. He said that the Civil War was "A new birth of freedom" that would bring true equality to all of its citizens. We still had a long way to go, however.

We here highly resolve that these dead shall not have died in vain, that this nation, under God, shall have a new birth of freedom and that government of the people, by the people, for the people, shall not perish from the earth.
—Abraham Lincoln, Gettysburg Address 1863

Mr. Lamon often armed himself and slept on the floor outside Lincoln's bedroom door. He kept telling the President that he was in danger. But Mr. Lincoln didn't seem scared. Rather, he seemed preoccupied with death and ignored the threats—much to Mr. Lamon's dismay. He was so worried about Lincoln's apparent lack of concern about the death threats that he threatened to resign time and time again—just like Lily refusing to kiss me when she got mad. But Mr. Lincoln would convince him to stay on, promising to be more careful. Then, having promised, he would sneak out of the White House at night without any bodyguards. Too bad—some of us could have used the extra pay! But more importantly, we might have lost our President.

Many people worried about Mr. Lincoln's safety. The Secretary of War, Edwin Stanton, was very concerned. He made sure that the swarms of people who loitered in the White House halls hoping to get Mr. Lincoln's attention were removed at night. Towards the end of the war, he kept telling Mr. Lincoln not to go out at night in case the agents of the Confederate government would attempt to attack him. He even told him not to go to the theater, which Mrs. Lincoln so loved.

Each time a new death threat was received, Mr. Lamon and we would get all nerved up, but Mr. Lincoln just got quieter. It was as if each day he was moving closer to his fate. Lily told me that during one séance Nettie Maynard supposedly told him, "The shadows others have told of still hang over you." Mr. Lincoln replied that he received letters from spiritualists all over the country that warned him of impending doom. When she was leaving, Mr. Lincoln insisted that she come and visit the following autumn. "I shall come, of course," Nettie answered, "that is... if you are still among us." It was as if she knew that something was going to happen.

It has been almost four years of bloody, maiming war since I left Illinois. Many different generals, hard-fought battles, the defeats, the failures, the confusion, and terror. The dead and dying lay in piles three and four deep. And when we tried to sleep, we couldn't. How could we? Mr. Lincoln paced back and forth, great black rings under his eyes, skin sallow, his head bent forward—like he was listening to another voice.

When we weren't talking about beating the Confederates, we were talking about the possibility of Lincoln's assassination. Someone would hear of another plot in Richmond or Washington. In November 1864, Mr. Lincoln was reelected President. Meanwhile, Sherman was marching through Georgia, ordering his troops to burn crops, kill livestock, consume supplies, and destroy the cotton fields, the pastures, the beautiful big plantations, and the miserable little shanties, and everything that made the world work for the South. It was a frightening time, but the war was coming an end. And we all hungered for that. So much so that by that winter, people in Washington were inclined to eat, drink, and be merry. They stopped talking politics, gave up grumbling, and were more interested in parties, balls, and theaters.

Government of the People, by the People, for the People

By March 4, 1865, Lincoln's second inauguration, everyone knew that the war would end soon. The South was finished, and it was only a matter of time. In his speech, Mr. Lincoln focused on reconciliation: "with malice toward none; with charity for all." Too bad more people don't believe in that.

In mid March 1865, we foiled a kidnap plot when Mr. Lincoln failed to arrive as expected at his summer residence, the Soldiers' Home, on Rock Creek Road, about three miles north of the Capitol. He makes such an easy target because he goes horseback riding alone. Once, as he approached the Soldiers' Home, someone fired a rifle in his direction. Luckily, the bullet missed. His only comment was that he lost his hat getting away.

Although he kept ignoring Lamon's concerns and continued to evade our protection, Mr. Lincoln had many gloomy forebodings about his future. Mr. Lincoln commented once that there were men who wanted to take his life and that he had no doubt they would do it.

People say that our dreams foretell major events in our lives. We all knew that Mr. Lincoln had these dreams. Perhaps these dreams were his way of internalizing the grim realities of

In May of 1864, Arlington Mansion and 200 acres of ground immediately surrounding it were designated officially as a military cemetery. Here lie many veterans and other outstanding citizens from the Revolutionary War to the Civil War to the present. *Courtesy of D. Peter Lund*

the war. One day, he told Lamon, "About ten days ago, I retired late. I soon began to dream. There seemed to be a death-like stillness about me. Then I heard subdued sobs, as if a number of people were weeping. I thought I left my bed and wandered downstairs. There, the same pitiful sobbing broke the silence, but the mourners were invisible. I went from room to room; no living person was in sight, but the same mournful sounds of distress met me as I passed along.

"It was light in all the rooms; every object was familiar to me, but where were all the people who were grieving as if their hearts would break? I was puzzled and alarmed. What could be the meaning of all this? Determined to find the cause of a state of things so mysterious and so shocking, I kept on until I arrived at the East Room, which I entered. Before me was a catafalque, on which rested a corpse wrapped in funeral vestments. Around it were stationed soldiers who were acting as guards; and there was a throng of people, some gazing mournfully upon the corpse, whose face was covered, others weeping pitifully.

"'Who is dead in the White House?' I demanded of one of the soldiers. 'The President,' was his answer. 'He was killed by an assassin.'

"Then came a loud burst of grief from the crowd, which awoke me from my dream. I slept no more that night; and although it was only a dream, I have been strangely annoyed by it ever since."

On April 3, we learned that Richmond had surrendered. That night, eight hundred guns shook the sky, they say. People came out on the street talking, laughing, hugging, and shouting. Bands played, and we all celebrated. Then on April 9, 1865, Robert E. Lee surrendered the Army of Northern Virginia to Ulysses S. Grant at Appomattox. When it was all over, General Lee told his barefoot hungry men that it was time to go home. The Civil War was effectively over. Once again, the bands played, the people cheered, and we celebrated the end of this terrible war that killed so many boys and men outright and left many more with dysentery, amputated limbs, and nightmares forever.

The Union had held, but the war took a terrible toll on the nation and on President Lincoln. Every wrinkle in Lincoln's face showed pain. He had lost his son, Willie. His wife, Mary, was deeply depressed. And he was responsible for sending hundreds of thousands of men to their deaths. Towns and villages were devastated. Widows and orphans had no one to turn to. The burden was intolerable.

On April 11, he spoke to the hundreds of joyous people who were gathered on the White House lawn to celebrate the surrender. They came with their bands, banners, and loud cheers to celebrate the moment. All houses were luminescent with candles. He talked about accepting the Southern states back into the Union and about giving the former slaves the vote. One of his listeners was John Wilkes Booth, who turned to his friend and supposedly said, "That's the last speech he will ever make." By April 14, Union forces reoccupied Fort Sumter and raised the American flag over the place where the war had begun four long years earlier.

Mr. Lincoln had promised to take his wife to *Our American Cousin*, on Good Friday, and they already had the tickets. When they departed for the theater, Mr. Lincoln said "goodbye" to his bodyguard, William Crook, instead of "goodnight." Did he know what was going to happen, I asked myself later?

At 9:30 pm, the President appeared in the flag-draped theater box, the orchestra played "Hail to the Chief," and the almost seventeen hundred members of the audience rose, clapping. The President bowed his acknowledgments. He attended the play with Major Henry Rathbone and his fiancée. Before the last call for the third act of the comedy, which everyone was thoroughly enjoying, John Wilkes Booth walked down the aisle toward the box occupied by the Presidential party, passing the bodyguard, who was watching the play from a seat nearby. Nobody challenged him.

With his derringer in hand, John Wilkes Booth came up behind Mr. Lincoln and shot him in the back of the head at near point-blank range. The bullet entered the head about three inches behind the left ear and traveled into Lincoln's brain. Lincoln's head bowed toward his chest as if he had fallen asleep, and Mrs. Lincoln screamed. Some say Booth yelled, "Sic Semper Tyrannis, " which is Latin for, "Thus always to tyrants." Henry Reed Rathbone started to attack him, but Booth stabbed him in the upper arm, leapt to the stage, catching his right spur in the flag that festooned the box, breaking his left foot just above the instep, and escaped from the theatre.

The doctors tried unsuccessfully to save Mr. Lincoln's life. On April 15, the anniversary of the bombardment on Fort Sumter and the beginning of the Civil War, Mr. Lincoln was pronounced dead. That morning his body was taken to the White House and wrapped in the American flag.

With Malice Towards None; with Charity for All

Lincoln's corpse was placed in a mahogany coffin, covered with black cloth, and lined with lead, the latter also being covered with white satin. A silver plate upon the coffin over the breast bears the following inscription:

ABRAHAM LINCOLN,
SIXTEENTH PRESIDENT
OF THE UNITED STATES,
Born July 12, 1809,
Died April 15, 1865.

On Tuesday morning, April 18, 1865, thousands of people visited the White House to visit him one last time. By Wednesday, April 19, 1865, the day of the funeral, the public buildings of Washington D.C., were draped in black.

The funeral was held in the East Room. Mrs. Lincoln recalled her husband's dream in the days that followed. Many governors, senators, judges, representatives, and other noteworthy men attended his funeral. On April 21, the same locomotive that had pulled Mr. Lincoln's inauguration train to Washington in February 1861, now pulled his funeral train home, retracing the same route Mr. Lincoln took when he accepted the Presidency of the United States. It was as if we had gone full circle, but the world was different now. Slavery was no more; the nation as we knew it was gone; and so many sons, brothers, fathers, and husbands lay in hastily-dug graves.

The train carrying Lincoln's body moved slowly to its destination through the many small cities and towns along its route. Crowds congregated along the train tracks so they could see him.

Every April, on the anniversary of his assassination, a phantom funeral train travels the tracks along the route taken by the official funeral train that bore his body west to Illinois. Some say that the funeral procession is actually two trains; the first steam engine passes, pulling several cars draped in black. One of the cars is a military car, from which the sounds of dirges can be heard being played on black instruments. The second steam engine carries the President's coffin home. Watches and clocks in surrounding areas are said to stop during the ghostly procession, resuming once it passes, and found to be five to eight minutes behind. People have reported seeing Abraham and Willie walking off the train hand-in-hand.

President Lincoln doesn't just appear on that funeral train. Many believe that Ford's Theatre is haunted. Visitors see Mrs. Lincoln leaning out of the box, with ashy cheeks and lips. With an involuntary cry, she points to the retreating figure, "He has killed the President." Lights turn on and off, voices, laughter, a gunshot, a scream—all are heard. Occasionally, his apparition is seen at the Peterson House where he died. Mrs. Lincoln continues to cry, "Oh, why did they not take me. Why did they take him?"

Lincoln's death at the supreme moment of victory—the very week the war was won—assumed symbolic and even mystical importance to many. Perhaps these events were meant to be. Perhaps he was the ultimate sacrifice for all those dead and wounded men, and he knew from his dreams that death was his destiny. And perhaps that is why he is often seen in the White House. President Theodore Roosevelt (1901-1909) said that he "often saw Lincoln's homely figure in the different rooms and in the halls." Many believe that Mr. Lincoln appears during wartime. A young clerk for Franklin Roosevelt claimed to have actually seen the ghost of Lincoln sitting on a bed and pulling off his boots. During Franklin Roosevelt's presidency, First Lady Eleanor Roosevelt used the former Lincoln bedroom as a study. Eleanor spoke of the sense of someone watching her as she worked in the room. "Sometimes when I worked at my desk late at night I'd get a feeling that someone was standing behind me. I'd have to turn around and look." Sometimes Fala, Roosevelt's dog, would bark excitedly for no apparent reason.

Queen Wilhelmina of the Netherlands and Presidents Theodore Roosevelt, Herbert Hoover, and Harry Truman all reported hearing unexplained rappings on their bedroom doors. Psychics believe that President Lincoln has never left the White House, that he remains to complete his abbreviated second term, and to be available in times of crisis. For seventy years, presidents, first ladies, guests, and members of the White House staff have claimed to have either seen Lincoln or felt his presence.

Perhaps the inexplicable knocking and the heavy footsteps are his way of reminding us that our soldiers are dying for us.

Visitor Information: 1600 Pennsylvania Avenue N.W. Washington, D.C. 20500. To request a self-guided public tour for groups of ten or more, write your Member of Congress. These free tours are available from 7:30 am to 12:30 pm Tuesday through Saturday (but not federal holidays). For the most current tour information, please call the 24-hour line at 202-456-7041.

Located at the southeast corner of 15th and E Streets, The White House Visitor Center is open seven days a week from 7:30 am until 4 pm.

THE HAUNTED HAY-ADAMS HOTEL

Located across Lafayette Square from the White House, the Hay-Adams Hotel is known for its distinct personality and signature amenities. Originally designed in the 1920s as a residential hotel, the 145-room Hay-Adams possesses the ambiance of a distinguished private mansion with views overlooking the White House, Lafayette Square, and St. John's Church, the "Church of the President." But the beautiful Hay-Adams Hotel has a resident ghost.

The ghost is Clover Adams, wife of Henry Adams. Clover was one of those dynamic people who everyone listened to and some of us envy. The type of person my mother would have said had IT! She was quick-witted, charismatic, and a dazzling conversationalist. In both Boston and Washington D.C., she presided over a salon, and all the important people and all those who wanted to be important vied for invitations. Clover Adams vetted would-be guests, not according to their reputation or financial status but, by a single criterion: did they amuse?

It seemed like a perfect match. Both Henry and Clover Adams came from privileged wealthy backgrounds and lived in a world of power, privilege, and genius. They were acerbically witty, bright, and had friends. Yet she killed herself and haunts the Hay Adams Hotel to this day. Why?

Descendant of U.S. Presidents John Adams and John Quincy Adams, Henry Adams was immersed in culture and wealth and spent much time in the summers at John Quincy's home. Young Henry engrossed himself in the family library, reading Greek and Roman literature, mathematics, politics, physics, and astronomy. After attending Harvard College, he, like many Boston Brahmins, went on a Grand European tour in 1858. From then until 1870, when he was appointed an assistant professor of history at Harvard

University, he traveled, wrote essays, and was a freelance political journalist for Boston's *Daily* and *The New York Times*.

Marian Hooper was better known as Clover. Her family possessed both wealth and prestige. People looked up to them for their good taste. Mrs. Hooper died when Marian was just five years old. Her widowed father, Dr. Robert William Hooper, and she became devoted friends. Clover rode with him, managed his household in Boston in the winter and Beverly Farms in the summer, and acted as his hostess until she married. Sometimes the two of them would even travel abroad. They were very close.

Privately educated at the school run by Elizabeth and Louis Agassiz in Cambridge, Massachusetts, she volunteered for the Sanitary Commission during the Civil War and then traveled abroad in 1866, where she met Henry Adams in London. He had been serving as a private secretary to his father, Charles Francis Adams, whom President Lincoln had appointed minister to England in 1861. When Henry returned to Cambridge to teach at Harvard College, Clover and he began their relationship. Her highly developed artistic tastes, broad curiosity, and distaste for convention attracted the more proper Henry. Soon, Henry was in love, and love permits us to overlook many warning signs.

Clover's ancestry was impeccable; certainly she was socially acceptable. But her mother's family had a history of emotional and mental instability; one relative had killed herself at age twenty-eight. When Henry's brother Charles heard that Clover was Henry's fiancée, he had exclaimed, "Heavens no—they're all crazy as coots. She'll kill herself just like her Aunt." Others warned Henry about the family's history of emotional instability.

Confident and in love, Henry believed he had rescued Clover from her heritage. They had a small wedding at her father's summer home at Beverly Farms, Massachusetts. During their extended honeymoon, Henry and Clover toured Europe and went on a three-month cruise of the Nile. The latter caused Clover to have serious self doubts. She agonized over her perceived weaknesses, seeing other travelers as more intelligent and enthusiastic than she. Her letters to her father expressed what she called homesickness.

In today's world, people would say that Clover suffered from depression. But in those days one didn't talk about depression or anxiety or panic attacks. People gossiped about many things, but they didn't talk about their feelings any more than they talked about their personal spiritual beliefs. Everyone might know a person's past, but no one talked about his or her pain. If they did, they might very well be sent to a sanatorium for a lengthy stay—if not forever. Instead, if they were depressed, they concealed it. In their eyes, suicide was preferable to insanity.

After the Honeymoon

When the young Adams returned to Boston in August 1873, they set up housekeeping not far from the home of Dr. Hooper, Clover's father. She was close to her father once again. Clover had three roles to play: devoted daughter, wife to a Harvard professor, and daughter-in law. She failed miserably at the last task: the senior Adams complained about her strange ways, her sarcasm, and her unwillingness to spend more time with them. This witty, sharp-tongued woman did not fit into their family.

In 1877, Henry gave up the editorship of the *North American Review* and his Harvard teaching position, and the couple moved to Washington, D.C. He hoped that the move might help her overcome her lack of confidence and that her caustic wit would be less evident. They began spending their winters in their home on Lafayette Square, across from the White House, on the site of the future Hay-Adams Hotel. They emptied all their boxes and trunks of the beautiful things they had collected, unrolling the lovely Bokharas, Kashmirs, and Kurdistans on the shiny floors. They hung all the art from the Rembrandt drawings to the Constable oils.

Still almost every summer, Clover returned to Beverly Farms, Massachusetts, to be with her father. She never separated emotionally from him, despite Henry's love and adoration.

Clover Adams led a life that many would envy. She was known for her witty conversation, while Henry had attained a degree of literary eminence. They rode horseback in the morning—often in

Rock Creek Park—breakfasted at noon, often with guests, and in the early afternoon, he would work on his history of the United States. By five o'clock, he would return for tea, gossipy chatter, satirical comments, and more guests; in the evening they either entertained or dined out. Their home became the gathering place for a lively circle of intellectuals, politicians, and those who aspired to be among the elite. They knew every president from Lincoln to Theodore Roosevelt, Andrew Carnegie, Henry Cabot Lodge, and countless cabinet ministers and diplomats. They knew the writers: Mark Twain, Walt Whitman, Henry James, Edith Wharton, Robert Louis Stevenson, John Ruskin, and Mathew Arnold. They knew the artists: John La Farge, John Singer Sargent; the architects, Henry Hobson Richardson, Stanford White; and sculptor, Augustus Saint-Gaudens.

During the winter of 1880/81, they established a friendship they called the *Five of Hearts*. In addition to themselves, it included John and Clara Stone Hay. John was the private assistant to President Abraham Lincoln, author, journalist, and private secretary and United States Secretary of State under presidents William McKinley and Theodore Roosevelt. His wife, Clara Stone Hay, who had inherited an Ohio industrial fortune, was more interested in children and home. The fifth member of this group of friends was a brilliant geologist, Clarence Hill.

The Adams, John Hay, and Clarence Hill were articulate, clever conversationalists. They talked about art and literature, discussed politics, and enjoyed gossiping about other people and events. Sparkling repartee was their forte. When Henry Adams wrote anonymously, *Democracy, an American Novel*, which became an instant bestseller, they delighted in the national speculation about the author. Their far-ranging and witty discussions of politics, literature, science, and art attracted the era's leading artists, writers, and politicians to the Adams residence, which became the epicenter of polite society. Many Washington residents and visitors enjoyed their sparkling tittle-tattle and biting comments.

Henry and Clover remained childless. In 1884, Clover began concentrating on her photography. She was good, but the camera did not offer sufficient distraction. Both seemed to sense that something—a larger sense of purpose perhaps—was missing. Although Henry and she had similar tastes in art, furnishings, and nature, she was much more dependent than he on others for happiness, yet her sarcastic tendencies caused people to fear rather than like her. Clover often said that she did not find her own company amusing, although she was known for her biting wit.

Taking a break from his history of the United States, Henry wrote *Esther: A Novel* about the tug of war between faith and doubt. It has been suggested that this novel is biographical, and the subject was Clover. He published it under the name Frances Snow Compton in 1884.

In 1884, John Hay and Henry bought adjoining lots at 16th and H Streets. They requested Henry Hobson Richardson, a prominent American architect of the nineteenth century, to design two, adjoining red brick, four-story mansions on the present site of the Hay-Adams Hotel. The Adams house was more modern, with symmetrical windows while the Hays' had turrets, gables, and chimneys and windows set off center. Washington society and political maneuvering revolved around their adjoining houses facing Lafayette Square.

Building the mansions was an expensive endeavor. During the process, Clover's beloved father became seriously ill, and she went home to sit by his side until the end. When he died in 1885, she collapsed, despite all of Henry's love and adoration. Her father had been her main anchor to life. Without him, her sense of worthlessness was overpowering—so much so that she destroyed most photographs of herself and little written material exists about her. Neither religious faith nor social or political interests helped her. Her photography was insufficient. She had no children, and Henry, as loving as he was, was unable to fill the void.

After Dr. Hooper's death, Clover slid deeper into depression. Henry entrusted her recovery to his own tender care and the restorative powers of time. They spent the summer in Beverly Farms, but she remained isolated in an ivory tower of deep melancholy.

That autumn, they returned to Washington, where Clover suffered from her feelings of hopelessness and helplessness. One Sunday morning, while Henry went to see a dentist, forty-two-year-old Clover swallowed potassium cyanide, a deadly chemical she used in retouching her photographs. The *Washing Evening Star* initially called her death a "paralysis of the heart."

To the surprise of family and friends, Henry decided to bury Clover in Rock Creek Church Cemetery, where they had often ridden in search of the first spring wildflowers. He did not bury her with her father in Massachusetts. In death, Henry claimed her as his alone, and he commissioned Augustus Saint-Gaudens to sculpt the brooding bronze figure called Grief that marks her (and his) burial place in Rock Creek Cemetery in Washington. The draped and cowled figure seated on rock leans against a highly polished granite backdrop screened by walls of evergreen in the cemetery.

Characteristically, he was much annoyed when people asked what Saint-Gaudens' seated, hooded figure symbolized. "Every magazine writer wants to label it as some American patent medicine for popular consumption—Grief, Despair, Pear's Soap or Macy's Men's Suits Made to Measure. [It is] meant to ask a question, not to give an answer; and the man who answers will be damned to eternity like the men who answered the Sphinx."

Henry often filled his Richardsonian mansion—completed, after Clover's death—with guests. He enjoyed his nieces and nephews, and played "Uncle Henry" and year-round Santa Claus to other youngsters, especially those of his friend John Hay. His classic autobiography, *The Education of Henry Adams,* was published shortly after his death and won a Pulitzer Prize in 1919. Interestingly, he omits any reference to Clover and their marriage. Although his brother Charles regretted his prophecy about her emotional instability, she was not the only one in her family to have problems. Not only did she kill herself but her oldest sibling, Ellen, killed herself in 1887, and the next oldest, Ned, died in a mental asylum after attempting suicide.

Hay died in 1905. When his wife, Clara, died in 1914, the ownership of his house passed to daughter Alice Wadsworth and her husband, Senator James Wadsworth. After Henry died in 1918, the Wadsworths bought his house, which they leased to the Brazilian Embassy.

Clover and the Hotel

Premier Washington developer Harry Wardman bought and razed both homes in 1927. In their place, he constructed a 138-room Italian Renaissance-style apartment-hotel designed by architect Mirhan Mesrobian, costing $900,000. It featured a dazzling array of architectural elements, including Doric, Ionic, and Corinthian orders, walnut wainscoting and intricate ceiling treatments with Tudor, Elizabethan, and Italian motifs. Wood paneling from the Hay residence found a new home in the grand public space now known as the John Hay Room.

When the Italian Renaissance-style Hay-Adams Hotel opened in 1928, the property retained the glamour of the past. Guests came because of the unparalleled views of the White House, Lafayette Square, and St. John's Church. They reveled in such amenities as its large suites, with marble baths, circulating ice water, and, as of 1930, Washington's first air-conditioned dining room. Charles Lindbergh, Amelia Earhart, Sinclair Lewis, and Ethel Barrymore were among the guests in the hotels early years. To this day, travel writers consistently rank the hotel as one of the best hotels in the world.

Clover Adams still lives at The Hay-Adams Hotel in Washington, D.C. The hotel staff reports that the fourth floor of the Hay-Adams is her favorite place. They agree that she is most active the first two weeks in December, coinciding with the anniversary of her suicide on the fourth floor of the home that Henry and Clover were renting, next door to their new house, which was then under construction. The staff have heard the opening and closing of locked doors of unoccupied rooms when no one was there, clock

The beautiful Hay-Adams Hotel is known for its distinct personality and unique amenities. It also has a resident ghost. *Courtesy of D. Peter Lund*

radios turning off and on, a woman crying softly in a room or a stairwell, and a woman asking a housekeeper tearfully, "What do you want?" when the room appears totally empty. Some housekeepers have been called by name, and others have received a hug while cleaning rooms.

Perhaps what Clover needs is a few hugs herself! It's too bad that neither her husband or her friends encouraged her to get help from a doctor or mental health professional.

Visitor Information: Sixteenth & H Streets, N.W. Washington, D.C. 20006

LEGENDS

L egends are stories that have been passed down for generations. Often, they are presented as history, but they are not necessarily true. They are believable but not necessarily believed. When it comes to legends about the world of ghosts, it is even harder to know what is true or what to believe: are there curses, visions of one's death, or evil spirits? Who knows?

A fountain facing the White House. *Courtesy of D. Peter Lund*

TIPPECANOE AND TECUMSEH TOO

1860 *Abraham Lincoln was elected president of the United States. John Wilkes Booth assassinated him in April 1865.*

1880 *James Garfield was elected to the presidency. He was shot and killed only four months after taking office.*

1900 *William McKinley was elected to his second term as president. On September 6, 1901, McKinley was shot and he died on September 14.*

1920 *Warren G. Harding was elected president. He suffered a stroke and died in 1923.*

1940 *Franklin Roosevelt was elected to his third term as president. He died on April 12, 1945, of a cerebral hemorrhage.*

1960 *John F. Kennedy became the youngest elected president. On November 22, 1963, while riding in a motorcade through Dallas, Kennedy was shot and killed.*

1980 *Ronald Reagan became the oldest man to be elected president. On March 30, 1981, John Hinckley attempted to assassinate Reagan in Washington, D.C. Reagan was shot, but was able to survive with quick medical attention.*

From 1840 to 1960, every president elected in a year ending in zero died in office. Could this be coincidence or might it be the result of a curse? Further, there is always the question of whether those in office have been influenced by the last moment of life—or first moment of death—of the legendary warrior Tecumseh. Was such a curse hurled down from the Great Spirit in his name?

To understand this legend, it is necessary to know the background story—the story of the colonists in the New World moving west in their hunger for more land; how that land was taken from the Native Americans, and how the results of those actions have continued to affect the history of our nation.

In the early 1700s, everything west of the Ohio River Valley was a wilderness, and only fur trappers and mountain men ventured there. The Indians still dominated these lands. In the area north of the Ohio River and around the Great Lakes, the Shawnee were among the dominant tribes. The white men and the Indians were competing for control of this region.

On the evening of March 9, 1768, Pucksinwah, war chief of the Shawnee nation, and his twelve-year-old son, Chiksika, waited impatiently for the sound that would signal the birth of Pucksinwah's third child. His wife, Methotasa, whose name meant "a turtle laying her eggs in the sand" was in labor. Pucksinwah and his family, which also included a daughter, ten-year-old Tecumapease, were among the six hundred Shawnee who, four days ago, had left their village on the Scioto River in Ohio to travel to Chalahgawtha (Chillicothe), the capital city of the Shawnee tribe for a tribal council meeting.

Methotasa had been exhausted from the previous day's fifteen-mile walk. Although she did not complain, Pucksinwah sensed her distress and bundled her up and placed her gently on his horse, which he led. Sending his second in command, Shemeneto, to lead their followers on to Chalagawtha, Pucksinwah quickly built a shelter for Methotasa at the edge of a pool formed by a bubbling spring. Pucksinwah had tried to convince Methotasa to remain at home in the village and not attempt the journey to Chillicothe, but she had been equally determined to attend the council. He watched his son carry armloads of firewood for the women who had stayed behind to help Methotasa. These women were known as the "aunts." Chiksika made many trips with the wood, laying it outside the entrance to the shelter. It was cold, but the spring snow had melted, and the day's sun had brightened Pucksinwah's spirits.

Now, however, the sun had set, and Pucksinwah was beginning to feel concern. This birth was taking longer than Methotasa's first two. Finally, one of the aunts came out of the shelter, but she did not look towards Pucksinwah. She picked up some of the firewood and disappeared once again behind the blanket. Chiksika, who had fallen asleep wrapped in a warm bearskin, awoke and went to his father across the pool. Pucksinwah proudly watched his son as he approached. Chiksika was growing tall and muscular and had been showing signs of leadership in his games with the other young braves.

Pucksinwah motioned for Chiksika to sit beside him. He opened one side of his blanket and pulled the boy close to him, enveloping him in the warmth. "When will the baby come, Father?"

"It will be soon now," Pucksinwah responded with a heartiness that belied his feelings. Chiksika sensed his father's concern and quickly changed the subject.

"How many will there be at the grand council?"

"More than you have ever seen. There will probably be close to three thousand men at the council. With all the women, children, and old people such as ours who have come, along with all those who live at Chalahgawtha, we will have more than twelve thousand."

"That's a very large council."

"Yes."

"Are we going to have a war with the English, Father?"

"They continue to force us in that direction, Chiksika. That is the reason for the council. The Shawnee nation has to decide what to do about the whites who continually cross the eastern mountains and take our land. For all the moons I have spent on earth, my son, always the white man comes, killing us with their guns and their disease, killing the bird and beasts that we depend on for food, cutting down woodlands and laying bare the prairies, damming the streams and building fences, taking the land that the Great Spirit bestowed on *all* men."

Just as he finished speaking, a flash of bright light startled Pucksinwah. Turning his head towards the sky, Pucksinwah heard Chiksika gasp as together they watched a huge meteor streak through the heavens from the north, passing directly over them. The lack of sound made the spectacle even more breathtaking. "It's the Panther, Chiksika," Pucksinwah recalled the stories of the elders. "Every night, so the tale goes, somewhere over the earth, the Panther, a powerful spirit, passes over to the south seeking a hole for sleep. This is a very good sign." No sooner had he finished speaking than an infant's wail broke the silence. Chiksika looked with wonder at his father, but neither moved until one of the aunts appeared, smiling broadly, to tell Pucksinwah that he had a son.

Inside the shelter, Methotasa cradled the infant beside her on a large soft buffalo hide. Pucksinwah laid his hand on his wife's cheek and looked with approval on his newborn, whose skin glistened with the bear oil that the aunts had applied in a protective coating. Seated next to her mother, his daughter, Tecumapease, smiled at her father and older brother. Pucksinwah said, "He is a fine son...so fine that there was a great sign."

Methotasa smiled at the baby. "What was that?"

"Just before we heard his cry, the Panther crossed over us."

Methotasa said, "That certainly is his *unsoma.*" [The Shawnee do not name a male child until ten days after the birth, believing that during that time an *unsoma*, a major event involving an animal, will occur. This event signifies what the Supreme Being, Moneto, wishes the name of the child to be.]

"Now we do not have to wait to name this child. He will be known as 'Panther Passing Across' or 'Tecumseh.'"

Childhood

Tecumseh showed early signs of his brilliance. As a toddler, he played with a tiny bow made of a stick and strand of rawhide and arrows formed from dried reeds. He imitated the actions of the Indian braves as they practiced their hunting skills or went off to combat the white man. By an early age, he was a remarkable marksman.

When Tecumseh was three, Methotasa stunned the tribe by giving birth to boy triplets. Multiple births were not common among the Shawnee, but triplets were unheard of. Pucksinwah enjoyed even greater prestige for having sired triplets, but the foremost prophet and medicine man of the tribe said that their birth was an omen to the tribe. One, two, or even all three of these boys would bring disaster to their people. Some even recommended that the boys be killed during the first ten days of their life while they still had no identity. Pucksinwah, however, resisted all such dire predictions. On the tenth day, he named his sons: the first was called Kumskaka—A Cat That Flies in the Air; the second was Sauwaseekau—A Door Opened; and the smallest, darkest, and least attractive one, and the one who cried the most, was named Lowawluwaysica—He Makes a Loud Noise.

By the time Tecumseh was six, other boys, even older ones, looked to him as their leader in their games and sports and mock-warfare activities. He was an excellent tracker and, through endless practice, he had become extremely skilled in using his small bow. He often returned from a day's hunting trip with buckskin filled with squirrels, rabbits, or quail.

Whenever Pucksinwah and Chiksika were away, Tecumseh would take his bow and buckskin and head off into the woods. Although he knew his father and brother were in danger, he also knew to keep his thoughts to himself. The privilege of never being shielded from reality was balanced by the burden of controlling childish emotion. Each time they returned, Tecumseh was happy, but he would contain his joy as he had his worry. Instead, he would sit with the others by the tent's perpetual fire and listen attentively to his father's tale.

As Tecumseh was completing his fifth winter in that Shawnee village in Ohio, a child was born in the colony of Virginia—a boy whose name would be linked throughout history with that of Tecumseh. William Henry Harrison was born on February 9, 1773, on the Berkeley Plantation, which overlooks the James River in Charles City County, Virginia. His father, Benjamin Harrison V, was also born at Berkeley in the three-story brick mansion built by *his* father in 1726, on the property bought by *his* father, Benjamin Harrison III in 1691.

On December 14, 1619, Captain John Woodlief and thirty-eight colonists had settled this land, which was a grant known as Berkeley Hundred. Some contend that *this* was the site of the first Thanksgiving. That may be debatable, but Berkeley was, without doubt, a center of colonial Virginia's economic, cultural, social, and political life. In fact, Benjamin Harrison V was one of the fifty-five signers of the Declaration of Independence, which proclaimed the freedom of the thirteen colonies from British rule in 1776.

Benjamin Harrison owned many slaves. The field slaves plowed the fields and tended the household vegetable gardening, while the house servants cared for the individual family members, the cleaning, the sewing, and the nursery. All of the meals were produced in a separate cookhouse; the washing and ironing of the clothes, the fine table, and bed linens also took place in an outbuilding. The plantation included stables and barns for the livestock and drying barns for tobacco, the most important crop of the era.

Many gracious parties took place at the beautiful Georgian mansion, with its surrounding lawns and gardens, boxwood-lined paths and its breathtaking view of the James River. Berkeley's hospitality was renown. Its table would be set with the finest imported china, crystal, and silver, and laden with game, fish, fresh vegetables, and sweets of every variety. Of course, the centerpiece of these social occasions was the conversation.

Tutors instructed the children. Not only were they taught about literature, history, and sums, but they also learned about the arts and practiced their penmanship, music, and dancing skills. The young ladies were also expected to become proficient in needlework. The children dressed in the style of the adults: linens, silks, ruffles, laces, silk stockings, and waistcoats, all imported from abroad.

Although the cultures of the Shawnee Indians and the Virginia landed gentry were worlds apart, there were striking similarities in the childhoods of Tecumseh and William Henry.

Their cultures each had three primary tenets: family pride, faith in the land, and religion.

Both boys were expected to learn, early in life, self-control and discipline. In the case of Harrison, these were expressed values of his society. In the case of Tecumseh, these values were a matter of safety and well being as a child's cries might alert the enemy or frighten prey away.

From a young age, both boys were skilled horseback riders. Tecumseh proved early on that he could endure long trips on his pony, in a canoe, or on foot. When the Harrison children were not learning the graces of their culture, they could be found riding their ponies around the plantation, often at breakneck speed, jumping walls and downed trees with alacrity.

The importance of land to each culture was as significant as their differing attitudes towards it. To Harrison, as to all of the landed class, land was the basis of wealth and power. It symbolized all the duties and responsibilities the proper Virginia son would inherit. Tecumseh, on the other hand, believed that the land was a gift of Moneto to all his children. The white man's need to accumulate land for personal use conflicted with the Indians' desire to live in harmony on and with the land, with no individual ownership.

Although the names and practices employed by the two cultures' religions were not related in any recognizable way, their actual beliefs were not so far apart. The Harrisons attended the Episcopal Church and worshipped one God. The Shawnee believed in two superior forces: Moneto was a supreme being who ruled the entire universe and bestowed blessings upon all who earned his favor, and sorrow upon those who merited his disfavor. The Great Spirit, considered the ruler of destinies, was subordinate to Moneto. The Great Spirit was a grandmother who was weaving a net into which she would gather those who had proven themselves worthy and take them to a world of great peace and happiness. Those not gathered suffered a dreadful fate. Both cultures agreed on how man reaches his ultimate destiny: good conduct brings rewards and evil brings misery and sorrow.

Tecumseh and Harrison were both born into an era of political unrest accompanied by the threat of war. With their insatiable appetite for territorial expansion, the colonists rapidly pushed westward, acquiring land and establishing frontier communities. They took saws and axes to the wilderness, cutting down the great forests, planting fields and establishing themselves as farmers on land purchased or taken from the Indians. The Indians were struggling to maintain their freedom from the white man while the colonists were working to achieve their freedom from Britain. The political climate of the day was crucial to both families, and a great deal of time was spent discussing it. Both boys were accustomed to sitting around a fire in the evening, soaking up the teachings of their elders.

Tecumseh was born in a region dominated by fierce battles involving the Indians and both the French and the English. The American phase of the French and Indian War (1754-1763), a worldwide, nine-year-long war fought between France and Great Britain, had begun as a contest for control over the Indians and whether the British or French empires controlled the upper Ohio Valley. Ultimately, by the Treaty of Paris in 1763, the French relinquished all military and political power in North America.

Occasionally, the Shawnee and Virginian colonists were connected by war. In 1774, John Murray Dunmore, the British Royal Governor of Virginia, raised a force of three thousand militiamen to subdue the Shawnee Indians in the Upper Ohio Valley in what was known as Lord Dunmore's War. Dunmore was personally interested in western lands as well as officially concerned with protection of the Virginia frontier to the west.

Only six years old, Tecumseh was aware of the Shawnee reaction to Dunmore's preparations. His father and brother, as well as Chaqui, the husband of Tecumapease, were away more often. Their talk around the fire was angry and ominous. Neighboring tribes were asked to become allies and send warriors to aid the Shawnee. Tecumseh begged, "Please, Father, can I go into battle with you?"

Chiksika and Chaqui laughed, but later, Chiksika remarked, "You know, Chaqui, that Tecumseh might be better than some of the braves from other tribes."

"Yes, one day he will be a fierce warrior."

Pucksinwah said, "The white man is like a worm, which, when cut in half, does not die, but becomes two."

Chiksika and Chaqui nodded agreement.

"The settlers' steady movement into Indian territory is like the flood resulting from a dam being opened," Pucksinwah continued. "But it is better to die fighting for Indian rights and land than to live with the white man's foot on our necks."

"My father is right," Tecumseh said.

The Shawnee scouts told them that one wing of Dunmore's army would be arriving in the Ohio Valley before Dunmore and his troops. Since the Indians were outnumbered three to one, they decided to take on this wing before reinforcements arrived.

The Indians were encamped on the west side of the Spaylaywitheepi (Ohio) River, and the militia was on the east side. When two militiamen spied a line of war-painted Indians crossing the river at dawn, they sent out an alarm and the battle began. Gun smoke and the shrieks and screams of the Shawnee filled the land. The Indians surged forward wielding their war clubs and tomahawks with deadly accuracy. This was the first actual battle that Chiksika and Chaqui had ever been in, but the young Shawnee fought with a skill that belied their inexperience. Chiksika darted through the enemy line, swinging his war club and connecting with limbs, ribs, and skulls with sickening thuds. He felt a tremendous rush of pride when he caught his father's gaze on him and saw approval in his eyes.

The mud turned red with blood as the battle continued that day. The Indians quietly and quickly removed the wounded and the dead from the field and carried them to waiting canoes that transported them back across the river. Among those killed early in the fray was Chaqui, who fought well and hard until he was shot in the stomach.

Just before noon, with the battle still raging furiously, Chiksika happened to be fighting close to his father when a rifle ball struck Pucksinwah in the chest. Chiksika immediately threw his father over his shoulder and stumbled as quickly as he could toward the rear where he found refuge behind a large tree. Gently laying Pucksinwah down, the young Indian began packing the wound with down from his pouch. Pucksinwah opened his eyes and gazed one last time at his son. "You are a good son. Promise me you will take care of Tecumseh. Teach him to be a good warrior...a good man. And take care of the little brothers...." His voice trailed off.

Chiksika cradled his father in his arms, pleading, "Please don't die, Father...please don't die...I promise...anything." But his father was already dead. Chiksika held his father for a long moment before lifting him once again and carrying him to the canoes. He watched sadly as the canoe left the shore, and then returned to the battle with renewed purpose born of grief and hatred.

Ultimately, both sides suffered many losses. To save his people, the Shawnee chief, Cornstalk, agreed to peace. In the treaty, he surrendered the Shawnee claims to lands south of the Ohio River and allowed the Virginians to move into Kentucky. In return, Lord Dunmore acknowledged Indian rights to the country north of the Ohio.

Several moons after their father's death, Chiksika took the heartbroken Tecumseh away from the camp to a solitary place where he could talk to his little brother. Chiksika explained that the white men had agreed to leave their lands according to an agreement signed after Dunmore's War. He told him as well what he had promised Pucksinwah as he lay dying.

Less than two weeks later, Chiksika, as the eldest son, took his entire family to Chief Black Fish in Chillicothe. In accordance with the traditions of the tribe, the care of a fallen battle chief's family always became the responsibility of the second chief of the tribe. Black Fish became their surrogate father. Once the children became his charges, their respect for Black Fish turned into deep devotion. Through his adopted father, Tecumseh learned about tribal lore, personal conduct, and oratory. He grew up with several white foster brothers whom Black Fish had captured. One of these was Daniel Boone, who had been captured in Kentucky. [Boone was able to escape and eventually became one of the most famous frontiersmen of all time.]

Adolescence

When the American Revolution began, Chief Cornstalk decided that the tribe would fight on neither side. But soon afterwards, American settlers murdered Cornstalk and his sons. In retaliation, the bitter Shawnee joined the British in their battle against the American colonists. In August 1780, George Rogers Clark attacked Tecumseh's village, killing many Indians and burning the town. Tecumseh, only twelve, fled with his family. Five months later, British troops went to Berkeley Plantation, removed all of the furniture and clothing from the house, burned it, and stole or shot all of the cows and horses. Fortunately, when the war was going badly for the Americans, Benjamin Harrison had had the forethought to move his family out of their home so they were not there for the raid.

The brave Tecumseh grew into a tall, muscular man with a proud bearing, intent hazel eyes, and light copper coloring. As hostile as he felt towards the white man, Tecumseh evidenced a deep morality. When he was about fourteen, he accompanied Black Fish in combined British and Indian attacks on Americans. During a Shawnee raid on the flatboats that were bringing white settlers down the Ohio River, he witnessed a white man being tied to a stake and burned. Horrified, he so severely reprimanded his fellow tribesmen that they never tortured a prisoner in his presence again. On a later occasion, he denounced and personally subdued his warriors when he caught them slaughtering prisoners.

After the War of Independence, Tecumseh fought the white man in the Northwest and assisted the Cherokees in the South. He saw his brother, Chiksika killed in an unsuccessful raid near Nashville, Tennessee, in 1792. The Shawnee chose the youngest in the band, Tecumseh, as their leader.

At about the same time, at the age of eighteen, William Henry Harrison enlisted in the U. S. Army. Four years earlier, he had entered Hampden-Sydney College, but Benjamin Harrison, who dearly wanted his son to become a doctor, interrupted his college education to apprentice him to a Richmond doctor. During this apprenticeship, Benjamin sensed that his son might be coming under the influence of abolitionists. Since the Harrison wealth was based on land and slaves, Benjamin was not going to see his son involved with a group that threatened the family's very existence. So William Henry soon found himself enrolled in medical school in Philadelphia. Shortly thereafter, however, Benjamin Harrison died. Although young Harrison respected his father, he turned his back on the study of medicine and joined the Army. His officer's commission came from President George Washington himself.

The Crossing of Their Paths

Harrison's first orders were to proceed to Fort Washington (Cincinnati). On the way, at Fort Pitt (Pittsburgh), the soldiers built flatboats to go down the Ohio River. The soldiers loaded the flatboats with themselves, food, gunpowder, weapons, and even livestock. The river ride was more treacherous than the three weeks of marching, but less exhausting. Harrison's men steered the boats with long poles and stayed constantly on the alert for Indians on the banks of the river.

As Harrison's party floated down the Ohio, the twenty-three-year-old Tecumseh and a small scouting party were tracking the Army through the woods north of Fort Washington. General Arthur Saint Clair commanded the American soldiers at the fort. Although sizeable in numbers, these soldiers were unused to the wilderness and had never fought Indians before. Tecumseh and the Indians attacked Saint Clair's army just before dawn, taking them completely by surprise. The wild whoops of the Indians with black- and red-painted faces terrified the young soldiers. Many laid down their arms and ran. The Indians killed more than 600 soldiers that day. Around the campfires that night, the Indians celebrated Tecumseh's bravery in battle.

Harrison had never heard of the Shawnee warrior, Tecumseh, before he was on that flatboat on the Ohio River. He saw the results of Tecumseh's work when he reached Fort Washington, however, and he learned all he needed to know about his adversary from the survivors of the battle. This was the first of many times that Harrison's and Tecumseh's paths would cross.

Saint Clair's defeat convinced Congress to authorize a larger army under the command of General "Mad Anthony" Wayne. Lieutenant Harrison became Wayne's aide-de-camp. As a member of the regiment known as the First Sub-Legion, Harrison was in the company of men such as Meriwether Lewis and William Clark, who later became famous for their exploration of the West.

Harrison lived on the frontier for almost three years, returning to Virginia only briefly when his mother, Elizabeth, died in 1793. His eldest brother, Benjamin VI, now lived at Berkeley, having inherited the plantation after the death of his father. Home seemed very quiet to the young lieutenant, and he eagerly returned to the Army.

Harrison and Tecumseh first opposed one another at the Battle of Fallen Timbers on August 20, 1794, near present-day Maumee, Ohio. As aide-de-camp, Harrison's role was to ride alongside General Wayne and carry his orders to the men. Amazingly, Harrison was not injured during the battle, although he rode back and forth many times and among the troops, encouraging them to fight courageously before he would return to the general to get the next set of orders. Harrison credited this to his stallion, Fearnaught: "My gallant steed bore me onward with such rapidity that I escaped unhurt." Outnumbered and outgunned, the Indians retreated. The general commended Harrison for his bravery.

In 1798, Harrison became Secretary of the Northwest Territory, and the following year, he was appointed territorial delegate to Congress. In May 1800, President John Adams appointed him governor of the newly created Indiana Territory. In 1803, Harrison also began to meet with the Indians "on the subject of boundary or lands." President Thomas Jefferson wanted the United States to extend west all the way to the Mississippi River and instructed Harrison to purchase all the land that he could through treaties. Although these treaties stripped the Indians of millions of acres of land situated in the southern part of the present state of Indiana and portions of the present states of Illinois, Wisconsin, and Missouri, the Americans were proud that they were buying the land—not just taking it by force. By 1808, Harrison had bought nearly all of what is now Illinois and Indiana.

Meanwhile, Tecumseh was working to organize an intertribal confederacy. Although he was a Shawnee, Tecumseh considered himself first an Indian, and he wanted all Indians to have a national, rather than a tribal, consciousness. His hope was to unite them in defense of a common homeland where they might all continue to dwell under their own laws and leadership. A cornerstone of his policy was communal ownership of the land. Tecumseh attacked the "peace" chiefs—the leading chiefs of the old Northwest—who signed away Indian land, land that he contended they did not own.

Later, in 1810, Tecumseh would say in a speech to Harrison, then Governor of the Indiana Territory:

> *No groups among us have a right to sell, even to one another, and surely not to outsiders who want all, and will not do with less. Sell a country! Why not sell the air, the clouds, and the Great Sea, as well as the earth? Did not the Great Good Spirit make them all for the use of his children?*

Tecumseh was such a superb orator that people compared him to the young Henry Clay, a rising political leader in Kentucky. Tecumseh became the spokesman for the Indians in the great councils at Urbana (1799) and Chillicothe (1804) in Ohio that undertook to settle grievances. For a time, he studied treaties, spoke at councils, and lived peacefully in Ohio and Indiana. Then, in 1808, at the behest of his younger brother,

Lowawluwaysica, he settled in Indiana. They built a village in the Wabash Valley, in or near what had been the Old Tippecanoe village, "Keth-tip-pe-can-nunk."

Lowawluwaysica had changed his name to Tenskwatawa, One With Open Mouth, and announced to his people that he was their Prophet, following the death of the old tribal prophet. He had gained tremendous credibility among his tribesmen through his accurate prophesies. In 1805, he convinced them that he had a message from the "Master of Life." When he followed that declaration in 1806 with his precise prediction of a solar eclipse, his influence became immense. Although prone to intemperance, deviousness, and megalomania, Tenskwatawa worshipped Tecumseh. Following Chiksika's death, Tecumseh assumed responsibility for his younger brothers. Tenskwatawa's relationship with Tecumseh further increased his credibility with the Shawnee. He and Tecumseh advocated a return to distinctively Indian ways of life, rejecting white man's ways such as the use of alcohol (particularly whiskey, which was destroying entire tribes), and the wearing of textile clothing rather than animal skins and furs. They eschewed the concept of individual ownership of property and intermarriage with whites. They preached against intertribal wars in favor of unity against the white invader.

With inexhaustible energy, Tecumseh worked to form an Indian confederation to resist white pressure. The tide of settlers had pushed game from the Indians' hunting grounds, destroying the Indian economy. He made long journeys from the Ozarks to New York and from Iowa to Florida, meeting with nearly every tribe east of the Colorado Rockies in an effort to forge the various native tribes into a single military alliance to halt the white expansion into Indian Territory.

The Battle of Tippecanoe

In July 1811, Tecumseh was setting out to meet with General William Henry Harrison, in Vincennes, Indiana, before heading south in his steady quest of tribes to join his confederation. Upon leaving, Tecumseh had spoken sternly with Tenskwatawa. "Everything here is being left in trust with you, brother. It is of the utmost importance that the peace be maintained." Well aware of Tenskwatawa's volatile nature and rash tendencies, Tecumseh reiterated his orders to the entire Village of Tippecanoe. "It is imperative that no open hostilities of any kind break out between us and the whites. Harrison is very shrewd. He will grasp at any excuse to open a war with us. If it is necessary to make concessions in order to maintain the peace, make them!"

The council did not go well. Harrison wanted Tecumseh to turn over the Indians who were guilty of murdering two white men. Tecumseh wanted to convince Harrison of the Indians' sincere desire to maintain peace while addressing the white man's deceit in dividing the tribes and illegally taking their land. Neither side accomplished their goal.

Tecumseh had assessed Harrison's shrewdness correctly. When the council had ended, Harrison wrote to President Jefferson's Secretary of War detailing the problem and his solution. The U.S. policy had been to keep the Indians divided and, by dealing individually with chiefs, to gradually take over their land holdings. Harrison basically asked permission to move on Tippecanoe Village in Tecumseh's absence. "I hope, before his return, that the part of the fabric which he considered complete might be destroyed." The Secretary replied that the President desired that peace be maintained among the Indians, but that Harrison had his trust to do what was necessary.

Harrison moved his troops numbering around a thousand men out of Vincennes towards Tippecanoe. Spies kept Tenskwatawa informed of the movement of the troops, and he called a council of the village. He announced, "If Harrison continues to move his troops toward the village, we will have no choice but to attack them." Loyal to Tecumseh's commands, the villagers opposed him, but Tenskwatawa assured them, "I have received a message from the Great Spirit that the Indians will be protected from the white man's bullets."

Harrison's army continued to move toward Tippecanoe. One night, while the General was camping with his troops near

Completed in 1943, the Thomas Jefferson Memorial is dedicated to Jefferson, an American Founding Father and the third president of the United States. The interior contains a bronze figure of Jefferson and inscriptions of his writings, including excerpts from the Declaration of Independence. *Courtesy of D. Peter Lund*

the brothers' settlement at the juncture of the Tippecanoe and Wabash Rivers, his spies told him what they had seen in the Indian village. Tenskwatawa had come before his followers in elaborate and unusual war paint, dress, and jewelry. He had acted strangely, jerking and shaking as though not in control of his body. Finally, he had appeared to waken from his trance and had commanded his followers to a surprise attack on Harrison's camp before dawn: "We cannot wait. We must attack while it is still dark. White men cannot fight in the dark, but we will be able to see as if under the bright sun."

An alert sentry spied the Indians approaching well before dawn. The two forces fought mainly in the pitch dark. When dawn broke, the light revealed dead Indians all around. Understanding that Tenskwatawa's prophesy of safety was unfounded, the remaining Indians retreated to their village where they took what possessions they could and abandoned the village.

Harrison's army spent the day burying their dead and treating the wounded. On the next day, they burned the now-deserted town of Tippecanoe as well as thousands of bushels of corn and beans.

The Indians wouldn't find shelter or food there anymore. The Battle of Tippecanoe made William Henry Harrison famous. He became known as "Old Tippecanoe," or "Old Tip," and when he ran for President that nickname earned him many votes.

When Tecumseh returned home from the South, he found his village burned, his forces scattered and his dream shattered. He was furious with his brother. "In one day, Tenskwatawa, you have destroyed what I have taken over ten summers to build. In one day you have destroyed the hopes of all Indians. You are a fool filled with the lust for power. You are no longer The Prophet. You are no longer a Shawnee. You are dishonored as no man has ever been dishonored. From this day forward, you will live with scorn and disgust, you will be without family and friends, and when at last death does come for you, no one will mourn." Tecumseh cast his brother away.

Tecumseh knew he must now work even harder to accomplish his goal of a united Indian nation. His opportunity arose on June 18, 1812, with the U.S. declaration of war against the British. Tecumseh decided to throw in his lot with the British. He assembled his remaining followers, joined the British forces on the Canadian side of the Detroit River, crossed the river and surrounded Detroit. Fort Detroit surrendered quickly. Fired with his success, Tecumseh departed on another long journey to arouse the tribes before returning north to join the British invasion of Ohio.

A few months after the War of 1812 broke out, Harrison was made a brigadier general and placed in command of all federal forces in the Northwest Territory. His orders were to protect the frontier, win Detroit back, and invade Canada.

In July 1813, Tecumseh prepared his warriors for the attack on Fort Meigs on the Maumee River above Toledo, which was held by Harrison. Tecumseh predicted his own death and disclosed his ultimate goal, "What we begin now is the beginning of the end. At the end of this war, I will leave you forever, as it is the intention of the Great Spirit to grasp me in Her net. It is my hope that before the end, that I may personally kill him who has been, and remains, our greatest enemy, William Henry Harrison."

Tecumseh and the British troops besieged Fort Meigs. Although Tecumseh did intercept and destroy a Kentucky brigade that was coming to Harrison's relief, the British and Indians were unsuccessful in capturing the fort. (When the British and Indian forces then moved on another small fort and were roundly defeated, a full third of Tecumseh's warriors deserted him.)

Tecumseh had little faith in his British allies. "Our British allies are led by a general who is not only weak but who has now become very much afraid. I fear that when Harrison soon comes knocking on our door that the general will do what is best for him with little regard for us."

When Tecumseh confronted the British general about his intentions, he was told that they were awaiting reinforcements. "My hands," the general confided, "are tied by a lack of troops of my own and the necessity to send those that I do have in support of the British Fleet."

The battlefield, it appeared, had moved onto Lake Erie. Although severely undermanned and lacking in supplies, the British Fleet was still far larger than the tiny fleet of American ships under command of Commodore Oliver Hazard Perry, and they were ready to attack.

Having learned of the critical problems of the British Fleet, Commodore Perry, in conjunction with General Harrison, quickly devised a course of action. Perry was to sail across Lake Erie and try to lure the British Fleet to attack before they were prepared to do so. On September 10, 1813, Perry sailed out in search of the British. Once the fleets sighted each other, they began to prepare for battle. Perry had more ships than the British, but he was seriously outgunned and outweighed.

When all was ready, the American commodore, aboard the *Lawrence*, ordered the fighting flag to be flown. The white letters against deep blue ground proclaimed: "Don't Give Up the Ship." The ships maneuvered into battle lines, facing each other. The lines moved together, and just before noon, the first shot was fired. In short order, the *Lawrence* was hopelessly damaged, and most of her men killed. Perry hauled the flag onto an oar boat and went to take command of the *Niagara*. He sailed into the midst of the British line where the *Niagara* could fire on two British ships at once. Having damaged the first two ships of the enemy, and forced them to haul down their flags and stop fighting, he then took on the next of the majestic British battleships. By 4:00 pm, the battle was over and, unbelievably, the Americans were victorious.

Perry sent the now-famous message to Harrison: "We have met the enemy and they are ours." Without wasting any time, Harrison loaded his troops on Perry's boats and moved at once to invade Canada.

The British general announced his intention to retreat to the Thames River in present-day Ontario, Canada. Tecumseh was furious. He reminded the general of all the promises now broken that had been made to the Indians: how with the aid of the Indians, the British would restore their lands taken by the Americans; how if they brought their families that the British would take care of them while the men fought; how the British had sworn never to take their foot off of British soil. Nevertheless, the general explained that with the Americans in control of Lake Erie, the British and Indian forces would not be receiving necessary provisions. He believed they would stand a better chance against the Americans on unfamiliar ground— land that was better suited to the Indian mode of fighting, and where they could get supplies, but where Harrison could not. So Tecumseh and his Indians reluctantly accompanied the retiring British to the Thames River.

Harrison pursued the British and Indian troops to the Thames River. There, on October 5, 1813, at strength of 1,100 men, Tecumseh knew his warriors were greatly outnumbered by Harrison, who had at least 3,000 troops. Harrison sent in the cavalry first, knowing that they were best prepared to fight in the woods. The British defense lasted barely fifteen minutes, but the Indians fought on stubbornly. Tecumseh was wounded several times, but throughout the fighting, he could be heard shouting: "Be brave! Be strong!" His war club wrenched from him, Tecumseh grabbed up the rifle of a downed warrior and took cover behind a tree. As he took aim at a soldier crawling along the ground towards him, another soldier shot him through the heart.

Tecumseh was dead.

The warriors had been instructed that if Tecumseh was killed, they were to break off all fighting and flee. They did so. The next day, the Americans searched the battlefield for Tecumseh's body. They could not find it. To this day, Tecumseh's grave has not been discovered.

Harrison won a great victory. Tecumseh's death marked the end of the British-Indian alliance and of Indian resistance in the Ohio Valley and in most of the lower Midwest and south. Soon after, the depleted tribes were pushed beyond the Mississippi River.

Following the war, Harrison settled in Ohio, where he quickly became prominent in Whig politics. He served in the U. S. House of Representatives (1816-1819), in the Ohio Senate (1819-1821), the U. S. Senate (1825-1828), and as Minister to Colombia (1828-1829). In 1826, Harrison was one of three candidates for president from the Whig party but lost the election to Martin Van Buren. In 1840, he won the Whig nomination, largely because of his military record.

To attract votes of Southern Democrats, John Tyler of Virginia was chosen as Harrison's running mate. Capitalizing on voter discontent with economic depression, the campaign deliberately avoided discussion of national issues and substituted political songs, slogans, and appealing mementos. Miniature log cabins and jugs of hard cider were liberally distributed to emphasize Harrison's frontier identification, and the cry "Tippecanoe and Tyler Too," rang out throughout the country. It was the first time a presidential campaign had ever been launched. These emotional appeals triumphed. Harrison and Tyler won the election with a huge victory.

President William Henry Harrison penned his lengthy inaugural speech in the bedroom at Berkeley Plantation in which he had been born. Inauguration ceremonies at the capital took place in a cold drizzle on March 4, 1841, and the old campaigner insisted on delivering his long address without a hat or an overcoat. He contracted a cold. At first, doctors were not overly concerned, but his cold developed into pneumonia. On April 4, 1841, he died.

A Curse?

In 1840, Harrison was elected the ninth President of the United States. He was the first President to die in office. But, as we know, he was not the last. Although Tecumseh had accurately predicted his own death, he did not get his wish that he would personally kill William Henry Harrison, whom he saw as the Indians' greatest enemy. Perhaps as he died, he cursed his rival from the grave and set in motion this phenomenon that would fix the destiny of future Presidents for the next 120 years.

Visitor Information: Berkeley Plantation is located halfway between Richmond and Williamsburg, off Scenic Route 5, at 12602 Harrison Landing Road, Charles City, Virginia 23030. Telephone: 804-829-6018/1-888-466-6018.

Tecumseh! is a professionally produced outdoor drama about the legendary Shawnee leader shown every summer from June to September in the Sugarloaf Mountain Amphitheatre near Chillicothe, Ohio. See www.tecumshdrama.com.

THE CLOCK WATCHER

Founded in 1789, the same year the U.S. Constitution took effect, Georgetown University is the nation's oldest Catholic and Jesuit University, and is older than Washington, D.C. itself. The construction of Healy Hall was completed in 1879. It is a magnificent structure, built in the Flemish Renaissance style. Situated high on a hill overlooking all of the city of Washington, its prominence proclaimed that this Roman Catholic college would be a major force in the city and the country.

I was looking over her shoulder as she read my journal. This young woman, whose jeans displayed more of her abdomen than I had ever seen, didn't know I was there, of course. She just thought that the shivery feelings she was experiencing were a result of her discovery of a handwritten history of her ancestors.

This young woman, my great-great niece, had been unpacking an old box of books when she noticed among them my distinctive brown leather one. She set it aside, fixed a cup of herbal tea, and wrapped herself in the warm red tartan blanket that she kept on the back of the couch. She picked up my journal once again. She took her time, tenderly stroking the leather cover, releasing the full, rich scent of the cowhide. At length, she opened it once again and began reading slowly....

August 20, 1891

It is exactly 100 years since the first students entered Georgetown College and, by the Grace of God, the will of my family, and the Jesuit priests under whom I have studied, I have the great good fortune to follow in their footsteps. I have waited for this opportunity for a long time.

As I write, I am in my seat on the Baltimore & Ohio Railway on my way to Washington from my home in Kansas. Just this April, President Benjamin Harrison became the first president to travel across the country by train. As I am covering a large part of that same distance, I feel I am in very good company! On the other hand, I am a bit homesick already as I venture forth into the unknown. I am certain that Jesuit fathers around the world are as caring and wise as those I have known in Kansas and that I will be quite content at Georgetown as I pursue my long-cherished dream of becoming a priest. Nonetheless, I do feel some anxiety. I miss my Jesuit teachers and their confidence in me and wonder when I may ever expect to see my family again. My parents probably felt the same way when they left home.

Maybe that's why my astute mother gave me this lovely journal as a going-away gift. From her own experience, she knew that leaving home was an adventure. But with God's grace, I will be as successful in finding myself in this new world as they were.

I feel quite fortunate to be able to avail myself of a sleeping car, which was only invented some thirty years ago. I also enjoy delicious meals in a "dining car," another new invention. The food is now prepared in the train's own galley. One of my fellow passengers told me that, until recently, the train used to pick up meals at stops along the way. Apparently, by the time they were served on board, they were quite unpalatable. I can only guess at how the first students at Georgetown made this trip. Perhaps in those early days they did not come from as far away as Kansas!

August 21, 1891

I have decided that in order to make this a meaningful history, I must document the circumstances that led to my being in this place at this time. So, I will start at the beginning of what I know.

My parents, Edward Rowan and Miss Helen Callahan, were married in 1859 in Boston. In 1860, they moved to Kansas, where they built our house, started a family, and began farming and raising cattle.

These were the years when New England abolitionists, such as my parents, were pitted against the pro-slavery Southerners. They were lured to Kansas not so much by westward expansion as by the desire of the abolitionist/slavery factions to outdo one another in populating the Kansas and Nebraska Territories.

The Kansas-Nebraska Act of 1854, which created these territories, opened new lands to settlers and allowed the two territories to decide the slavery issue themselves. Of course, this caused a great conflict. The Southerners knew that if Kansas became a free state, their power in Congress would be eroded and their entire political, cultural, and economic existence would be in jeopardy. The abolitionists formed societies to encourage citizens to settle in the new territory. In the process, a chain of events was set off that ultimately led to the Civil War.

Father always told me that the catalyst for their move from Massachusetts to Kansas—a big move in those days—was the caning of Senator Charles Sumner, the leader of the antislavery forces in Massachusetts. In 1856, Sumner criticized the Kansas-Nebraska Act in a fiery speech called "The Crime Against Kansas," and attacked its authors: Stephen Douglas of Illinois and Andrew Butler of South Carolina. In response, Preston Brooks, the nephew of Andrew Butler and a representative from South Carolina, entered the Senate chamber and beat Sumner into unconsciousness by slamming a metal-topped cane onto his head time and time again. Sumner was so badly injured he couldn't attend the Senate for the next three years. The caning of Sumner symbolized Southern brutality to the Northerners. Although Brooks was initially censured for his actions, the South thought that he had defended Southern honor and reelected him.

Meanwhile, my parents moved to Kansas. Like all settlers in the Kansas Territory, they underwent many trials and tribulations. They found the weather to be as arbitrary as that in Massachusetts. But they built their houses and stores, established schools and churches, and raised crops to feed themselves and their livestock.

Father and Mother found a great deal of solace in their faith. Having attended the Jesuit Boston College, Father was pleased that Jesuits had come to Kansas to minister to the fast-increasing tide of immigrants of which my parents were certainly a part. As a child I lived, studied, and prayed under their guidance. From my early years, they and my parents taught me obedience, diligence, and piety, and life on a Kansas farm taught me to be practical and resourceful.

The Jesuits baptized hundreds of Indians, and the missionary priests managed to create Catholic prayer books in the Indian dialect as well as establish manual training schools. Their dedication to their work is a major factor in my being on this journey today. I plan to walk in their footsteps.

August 22, 1891

The emotion of my leave taking combined with the excitement of my journey caught up with me yesterday. Apparently I fell asleep while writing for I awoke with a terrible stiff neck several hours later, still hunched over this journal. I will now pick up where I left off in my story.

I had always known I would become a priest. By the time I was born in 1873, my family had endured much hardship. To be sure, there was a great deal of love and happiness that surrounded my growing up, but Kansas' violent beginnings certainly shaped my future. Lest I digress, I shall recount some of those events as my father told them to me.

My brother Tom, my parent's firstborn child, and the State of Kansas entered the world at almost the same time. On January 29, 1861, Kansas was finally admitted to the Union as a free state. Thomas arrived just two months later. From what I can understand, Tom's birth was far less difficult.

Kansas was born under the slogan "Bleeding Kansas" as a result of the struggle over the still unsettled slavery issue. Although my parents were strictly anti-slavery, my father had managed to avoid the bitter and bloody skirmishes as the abolitionist Jayhawks clashed with pro-slavery Bushwackers, each attempting to sway popular opinion to their favor. People were kidnapped and killed as part of these skirmishes over slavery. The five-year brutal conflict between Kansas and Missouri brought the country, month by month, to the brink of Civil War. When war broke out in April 1861, Father felt compelled to fight for his beliefs, so he joined a Kansas militia unit.

The Civil War ended when General Lee formally surrendered at Appomattox on April 8, 1865, but Kansas had suffered a terrible toll during this conflict. This new state had contributed over 20,000 men to the Union Army, a remarkable record since the population included fewer than 30,000 men of military age. It had suffered the highest mortality rate of any of the Union states. Thank God that Father survived!

The suffering of the nation did not cease with the war's end. On April 14, 1865, John Wilkes Booth shot President Lincoln while he was attending a play at Ford's Theatre. The President had told the nation in his inaugural speech just a month before: "With malice toward none; with charity for all...let us strive on to finish the work we are in...to do all which may achieve and cherish a just, and a lasting peace, among ourselves and with all nations." The President died of his wounds the following day, and was unable to finish his work or enjoy the peace, which eventually did come.

My sister, Mary, was born the next year. My parents and five-year-old Tom hailed her advent with joy. Subsequently, Cornelia and then Caroline arrived, but then tragedy struck the family. My mother was well along into her fifth pregnancy when a fall while horseback riding caused her to miscarry a boy and almost caused her death as well. By the grace of God, Mother did recover. It was considered something of a miracle when, several years later, she carried another pregnancy to term and I was safely delivered in 1873. My parents were so grateful for a second son after my mother's life had been spared that they decided at my birth that I would become a priest. I cannot remember that there was ever a time when I was not directed toward that destiny. It suited me just fine. I am determined to be a good priest. I have the character for such a position and the capability to pursue a sustaining, lifelong commitment to serving God.

August 23, 1891

We will be arriving soon at Point of Rocks, Maryland, where I must change trains to go to Washington. We will pass right by Harper's Ferry, where one of the bloodiest battles of the war was fought. The reality of my father's stories become clear to me as I ponder the enormous number of lives lost in the fields and valleys surrounding me now. I have had my breakfast and cleaned my teeth. My valise is packed and ready for arrival.

(Continued) —Am now on the train from Point of Rocks into Washington. I was able to change trains with little drama. I have little to do until I arrive as I will not open my bag again until I am safely ensconced at Georgetown.

Throughout my life, people talked about my becoming a Jesuit. It was the goal that was dangled before me. If I became a priest, this world of violence that had affected my family would become a world of peace. My life would be lived as the Lord ordained "to the greater glory of God." I would preach or teach or do whatever else that the Church required. Political events or war or my beautiful neighbor, Jane, down the street, wouldn't lead me astray.

Back home, Father Thomas told me that Bishop John Carroll purchased 1.5-acre plot in Georgetown in 1789. It was there that he planned to establish a Catholic school of higher learning and erected the first building. The Catholic Church was undergoing trying times. Father Carroll, a native of Maryland, had studied and been ordained in Europe. But in 1777, Pope Clement XIV dissolved The Society of Jesus, so Father Carroll returned to his home in Maryland. At this time, even in the United States, laws discriminated against Catholics, so Father Carroll became a missionary to Maryland and Virginia. He eventually became a bishop. In 1791, he enrolled the first students in Georgetown College.

In 1805, the Society of Jesus was reestablished in the United States, and the Jesuits took over the administration of the college. By 1815, Congress elevated it to the status of a university, when it was firmly established as a leading Catholic educational institution. I am very proud to be able to study there.

The conductor has just come by to announce that we are approaching Washington, so I will conclude my writing for now.

August 23, 1891

Here I am at the capital of the Nation! I left the train at the station, which is very near the enormous and grandiose Capitol Building, which is built all of white marble. It shines so brightly in the sunlight, I was almost blinded by the sight.

I was able to secure a carriage with little difficulty, and it brought me across town to the university. When I see this beautiful city, I find it easy to understand George Washington's thinking that majestic buildings would reflect the importance of the city. On my ride across town, I could see where new streets were being opened up in all directions and grand residences were being built. We drove past the Washington Monument, the War Department, the Treasury (which is not where the currency is printed), and then the White House. Across the Potomac, sitting high on a hill, was the most beautiful house. Upon questioning, my driver informed me it was once the residence of General Robert E. Lee. The Soldier's Cemetery is there as well. I am a long way from Kansas—almost in a different country altogether, surrounded by all these vast and beautiful structures.

The main gates at Georgetown University open toward Healy Hall. Its clock, which chimes every fifteen minutes, can be seen and heard from much of the surrounding area. Healy Hall is a National Historic Landmark and is considered the flagship building of Georgetown University. *Courtesy of Michael Lodico, Jr.*

August 28, 1891

There is so much to do and learn. I have not been faithful about recording it all here. I have wanted to write my family and give them all my fascinating news, and I find I do not have the time to do it twice. There are some things, however, that I feel compelled to record here, lest I ever forget any of it.

The college is formidable in its own right. It sits high on a hill overlooking the Potomac River and all of Washington. When he first announced his plans for Georgetown, in 1788, Bishop Carroll wrote to his friends, "We shall begin the building of our Academy this summer. In the beginning we shall confine our plans to a house of 63 to 64 feet by 50, on one of the loveliest situations that imagination can frame. Do not forget to give and procure assistance. On this Academy is built all my hope of permanency and success to our holy religion in the United States." When Bishop Carroll founded the university, Catholics had little standing in America. Consequently, the early college buildings mirror the architecture of the surrounding area rather than advertise their religious affiliation.

Healy Hall, on the other hand, is totally different and very impressive. This building was built during the presidency of Father Patrick Healy, known as Georgetown's "second founder." Its architecture reflects its roots in Catholicism and the European influences that Carroll shied away from. Father Healy was the first Negro president of an American university (1874-1882). How a man of color became a college president in a southern city is something marvelous indeed. He is credited with changing Georgetown from a small liberal arts college into a modern university.

Smithmeyer and Pelz, the architects who have since designed the Library of Congress, which is currently under construction near the Capitol Building, designed Healy Hall. It was only completed in 1879, and the 200-foot central clock tower was added three years ago in order to increase ventilation in the building.

September 20, 1891

I am discovering that the characteristics of the Jesuit teachers in Kansas—which made them so effective—are, in fact, a universal feature of this Religious Order. The desires that first drew Ignatius Loyola to serve God led him from the pursuit of worldly fame to a genuine, inner freedom. Jesuits seek to educate the whole person—mind, body, and spirit. Each priest that I have met appears quite genuinely concerned for the success and well being of each individual student. My spiritual formation is advancing quickly.

In general, my fellow students are quite a likeable lot, although there's one from New Jersey who gives me pause. I do believe that my devotional life and emotional balance far outweigh his. Clearly, those who are accepted to study at Georgetown University are carefully chosen and tend to be dedicated, studious, and like-minded individuals. Although we hail from many different parts of the country, we obviously have been educated and prepared similarly for the strenuous academic and spiritual life that we are leading here.

October 23, 1891

Day-to-day life at Georgetown requires integrating the hard classroom work, my conversations and debates with colleagues, and regular intervals of prayer and meditation, along with the necessities of daily life. My New Jersey classmate is obviously vying with me in classroom debates. I am more intelligent than he, however.

Having studied here for several weeks now, I feel I am called to be a forthright messenger of hope. The Jesuit priests who taught my brother and me in Kansas always encouraged us to open our minds and be inquiring. In addition to all the duties that farming entails, my parents would always find time to read to us all manner of literature. As a result, we became avid readers, which I believe promoted our curiosity about the world. I am sure I can manage any task that is put before me and become a spiritual guide for both the lost and the faithful. Already, the other students look up to me.

November 4, 1891

Daily, I learn more about the fascinating history of this university. Apparently, Georgetown was a southern college in the antebellum period. Of its alumni who served in the Civil War, more than four-fifths were Confederates. The war nearly closed the college. The student body fell from 313 in 1859, to 17 in the fall of 1861. Federal troops briefly occupied the campus in the first month of the war. From the heights on which Georgetown is set, the Jesuits were able to hear cannon fire from the war's major battle at Manassas, Virginia, on the banks of Bull Run Creek on July 21, 1861. In the fall of 1862, several of the college buildings were turned into hospitals after the Second Battle of Bull Run.

In the years following the Civil War, Georgetown University adopted blue and gray as its official colors in tribute to the role that the school and its sons played in that conflict and to signify the reunification of the North and the South.

Spiritually and theologically, I feel I am growing swiftly. As I learn more about St. Ignatius Loyola, who founded the Society of Jesus, I am gaining an understanding of what is God's will for me. My calling is evident. I am meant to be a Jesuit father, and I will be an excellent one.

November 13, 1891

Very important news. Father Luke informed me that as a reward for my academic excellence and leadership qualities, the fathers have selected me to become one of those in charge of the magnificent clock in the tower above Healy Hall. The clock is 600 feet above the ground and can be seen and heard in much of the surrounding area. Because it rings on the quarter hour, it regulates college life. If the clock were ever to be off, even by a few minutes, it would disrupt the entire order of the campus. It is a great honor to have been chosen for this duty.

November 15, 1891

Father Luke took me into the bell tower today! We had to climb the stairs to the fourth floor of the building to reach the door to the clock tower. He showed me the keys that I will use to open the various latches. Then I have to climb a ladder, which leads to the next level where there are two wooden boxes. These protect the rock-weighted chains that are connected to the clock and its huge bells. Father tells me that the clock was purchased for $1,188 and came with the three massive bells—Holy Mary Seat of Wisdom, Saint John Berchmans, and Saint Aloysius. I have the honor of ringing these bells, each weighing in excess of 350 pounds!

Another steeper ladder leads to the next level with a small wood-framed room in the middle. Here reside the rare clockworks, gleaming with their gold gears set in a heavy black iron frame. We spent some time admiring this mechanical wonder. I just wanted to get on with the actual bell ringing.

November 17, 1891

Back to the tower! Father Luke instructed me today on the three drums on the clock—one for the time, which is easy to turn; one for the striking of the hours, which is much heavier; and one for the quarter chimes, which is a great deal heavier still. A gray-bearded man, Father Luke was panting after climbing the stairs and ladders leading to the ringing chamber. He told me that winding all three drums without stopping not only measures one's physical strength, but one's sheer stupidity. I am not stupid and I am quite strong. I am certain that I can accomplish this feat and that God will help me do so. That will be my goal once this duty is mine.

******

She has finished reading, but no, there is something stuck among the pages…it is a yellowed newspaper clipping and she is unfolding it carefully…. "Young Jesuit loses life at hands of Georgetown Clock" is the bold headline.

The obituary does not recount my hours of agony before I died, nor the events leading up to the mistake that cost me my life. She will never know about that. Nor does she know that I roam the upper floors of Healy Hall, moaning and wailing.

I had so much work to accomplish on earth. Before the accident, my life had stretched out before me as a beautiful, endless road. But I suffered from the sin of pride. Father Luke had told me not to try to wind all three drums without stopping, but I thought that I could easily wind them all.

All I can do now is try to protect my clock. Sadly, Georgetown students have made a tradition of stealing the hands from the wondrous clock. At least once a year, they risk their lives by climbing up into the tower and crawling outside in their desire to be the victors in this foolhardy competition. I become very noisy when I hear them coming. I hope that my ghostly presence will drive them away, but I have had limited success. The less courageous do leave, but there are always the reckless who, egged on by their peers or the false courage of alcohol, accomplish the deed. And the news people reward them by widely documenting their success.

These pranks have been taking place since an electronic device replaced the human bell ringers and caretakers in the 1930s. The greatest number of thefts of the clock hands took place in the 1960s when students were particularly carefree and foolish.

At times, the Administration has thrown up their hands and not replaced the clock's hands for weeks at a time, with the implied message to the culprits: Steal these hands and you will be late! No one and no thing has prevailed, however. Thefts of the clock's hands continue with each class, and no amount of locks, fines, threats, or vigilance have had the power to end this tradition. I will keep trying, however.

Visitor Information: Founded in 1789, Georgetown University is the nation's oldest Catholic and Jesuit university. Today, Georgetown is a major international research university. Its Main Campus is at 37th and O Street, N.W. , Washington, D.C. 20057

DEMON CAT
IN THE CAPITOL

The United States Capitol is one of the most recognizable symbols of democracy in the world. It serves as the location of the United States Congress, the legislative branch of the U. S. Government. Pierre Charles L'Enfant chose the site for the building on top of what is now known as Capitol Hill at the east end of the National Mall. George Washington laid the cornerstone for the Capitol in 1793, and the building held its first session of Congress in 1800.

John Oakes, Capitol Police force member for over thirty years, arrived for the night shift at his usual 9:40 pm. He quickly pulled his aging red Camaro into one of many empty spaces in the east lot of the United States Capitol Building. He turned off the ignition, sat back in the seat, and closed his eyes for a minute. Discovering a flat tire as he was leaving for work had forced him into frantic action, and the surge of adrenalin and energy that he expended on the tire changing and subsequent dash into the city had left him drained. He was so late that he couldn't stop for his usual coffee from the McDonalds on South Capitol Street. He would rather go without coffee than be late, but the lack of caffeine certainly didn't improve his mood. Not a good beginning to the night shift.

The evening was warm, but the moonlight through the clouds cast flickering shadows across the mammoth building. John loved the Neoclassical style of the Capitol. The sight of it never failed to warm his heart, no matter what his mood. With the majestic and ghostly white marble structures of the Supreme Court and the Library of Congress guarding his back, John made his way to the concealed entrance under the steps on the Senate side of the Capitol.

The light at the very top of the Capitol dome, which would indicate an evening session, was unlit, giving the building a rather forlorn air. Neither the House of Representatives nor the Senate was in session, John thought. Nonetheless, people were always working late, sometimes extremely late. He often saw legislative assistants bent over a desk in a dimly lit office, painstakingly adjusting the language of a bill their boss was to introduce the next day, or aides running massive copying machines reproducing campaign letters to promote the re-election of their congressperson and hopefully to secure their own employment. Sometimes, John even spotted a Congressional member working into the early hours—maybe the member was especially conscientious, or perhaps the office was just preferable to home.

"Well, there you are! Darn! Dave and I were just making book on how late you would be." Tom and Dave grinned as John walked through the door. His co-workers constantly teased John about his punctuality. He was used to this ribbing, but tonight, instead of playing along, John replied sullenly to his friends: "It certainly wouldn't hurt you two to get here a little earlier and be a little less anxious to leave!"

"Who wouldn't be anxious to leave after dealing with tourists all day?" Dave replied.

"I had a flat. I'm really sorry if I kept you a minute or two from the warm comfort of your beds."

John was rarely sarcastic, and Tom and Dave grimaced at each other behind his back. These guys had known each other for years. They might have badgered one of their other friends, but they both respected John and his serious dedication to his job. Tom smiled. "It's been really quiet tonight, John. Almost spooky how empty this place has been."

John nodded. "Yeah, when it's empty, it can be creepy."

"The phones didn't even ring. You should have an easy shift." Tom placed a friendly hand on John's back as he was speaking. He then turned and grabbed his coat off the rack in the corner, winked at Dave, and opened the heavy, highly polished door of the Office of the Capitol Hill Police. Standing in the open doorway, Dave and Tom turned and mock saluted John. "It's all yours."

"Bye guys," he said with a half-hearted smile.

Alone in the office, John felt somewhat ashamed of his ill humor. He fingered his badge. As he slipped his billy club into the loop on his pants, he tried to invoke the feeling of pride that had been a constant since the day the Senator from his home state of Kentucky appointed him to this patronage position. Usually, just the act of putting on his uniform reminded him of the moment of transformation in his life when he pinned on his badge for the first time and became one of the United States Capitol Police. He had been just a kid then, fresh out of college, but completely uncertain of what he wanted to do in life. Through luck and persistence, he had managed to

Many ghosts are associated with the United States Capitol Building, which is among the most architecturally impressive and symbolically important buildings in the world. It houses the Senate and the House of Representatives. Today, it stands as a monument to the American people and their government. *Courtesy of D. Peter Lund*

wangle the appointment. In the early seventies, Congress had terminated the patronage system in the Capitol Police and John had found the force had become even more professional and respected in the years since.

John picked up his flashlight. "Time to get moving," he reminded himself. With his mission and responsibility to protect and support the Congress firmly in hand, he exited the office and headed upstairs to the Rotunda.

The lonely hours of his watch gave John plenty of time for reflection. Usually, he enjoyed the graveyard shift. It gave him time to think, but his wife used to say that sometimes he thought too much. He should have more fun in his life, she would say. When he was on the day shift, he enjoyed interacting with the public and telling them stories about the Capitol. John would point out the painting, *Burning of Washington, 1814,* and explain that as the War of 1812 raged on, invading British troops marched into Washington and set fire to the U. S. Capitol, the President's Mansion, and other local landmarks. Only a torrential rainstorm had saved the Capitol from complete destruction. The blaze did destroy the collection of 3,000 books and manuscripts of the Library of Congress, then located in the Capitol building. Former President Thomas Jefferson offered his own library—the largest personal collection of books in the nation—to replace the loss. Appraisers valued the collection of nearly 6,500 volumes at $23,950, which Congress agreed to pay.

When he led visitors into the Rotunda, John would have them tip their heads way back to look at the Rotunda canopy with its enormous fresco painting depicting George Washington rising into the clouds in glory. *The Apotheosis of Washington,* he would explain, enjoying the feel of the word as it rolled off his tongue. "Apotheosis," he would say, "means literally the raising of a person to the rank of a god, or the glorification of a person as an ideal." He would go on to explain, if his audience showed any interest, that "the female figures on either side of Washington represent Liberty and Victory, and the thirteen maidens around these central figures represent the original thirteen colonies. The artist was Constantino Brumidi, an

Italian who painted murals and frescoes throughout the Capitol from 1855 until his death in 1880."

During his years on the force, John had come to appreciate history to a depth that his lackluster school days never would have presaged. He took tremendous pleasure in his job, his innate patriotism having found its legs the minute he first set foot on the hallowed grounds of the U.S. Capitol. From that moment, his passion for the American way of life made clear his ultimate purpose of "making a difference" and opened an obvious path for him to follow protecting not only this very public building, but the public servants and the public itself as they roamed the hallways.

As he went on his nightly rounds, John often pictured himself as the original "John"—John Golding, the Capitol's first watchman who had been appointed to his post in 1801. That John, and presumably others like him, was solely responsible for the well being of the Capitol until 1827. The Marquis de Lafayette's visit to the Capitol in 1824 and a fire in the building's library the following year heightened concerns about public safety and unattended property and led President John Quincy Adams to appoint a four-man watch in 1827. When President Adams' own son was attacked and beaten in the Rotunda a year later, the city of Washington extended police regulations to the Capitol and its grounds, founding the U. S. Capitol Police Force in 1828.

By now, John knew his beat like the back of his hand. He took the stairs back down to the first floor and walked south down what are known as the "Brumidi Corridors," with their intricate Minton tile floors. He passed the closed doors of committee rooms and spaces for congressional officers. Initially, the ornate wall painting style, based on Raphael's *Loggia* in the Vatican, had not appealed to John. However, as he had learned more about the history of the paintings and the ancient Roman, Renaissance, and Baroque techniques and explained it again and again to the Capitol's thousands of annual visitors, he had come to admire it more. He was particularly fond of pointing out, among the portraits and historical and allegorical scenes on the intricately decorated and brightly colored walls, the artist's use of American flowers and birds and animals. Among the symmetrical designs of scrolling vines, mythological figures, and classical gods and goddesses, Brumidi and his assistants would integrate the figures of a chipmunk or a mouse. John's revelation of one of these perfectly detailed little creatures was always a sure way to delight the children on tour. Tonight, however, his mood continued to get in the way of his pleasure in his surroundings. The next time he would stop for coffee even if he were going to be five minutes late.

Walking more slowly than usual down the corridor, John occasionally paused to open one of the committee room doors just to reassure himself that all was well on the other side. When he arrived at the Old Supreme Court Chamber, he scrutinized it carefully. The shadows seemed immense tonight. To forget his dour mood, he explained aloud to a nonexistent audience of happy, baseball-capped tourists and crying babies, that this semicircular room with its dramatic umbrella vault ceiling, the plaster relief sculpture of *Justice* and the busts of the first four justices, was laid out as it had been when it served the Supreme Court from 1810 until 1860.

"At other times, it has been used for a committee room, a law library, a meeting room, and even a storeroom," John finished, giving a quick nod to the empty room and walking out.

The lights were dim. As John continued walking his rounds, he was certain that the shadows that played in the corners, in the ceiling vaults, and around the columns were exactly as they were every night, but they were making him slightly ill at ease on this entirely unremarkable Tuesday night. *Stop being ridiculous, John!* he told himself. *You know this place as well as your own home!* He felt better after this chastisement, the truth behind the statement relaxing him. "I could make this tour blindfolded," he would joke with his assembled "guests," as he often regarded the tourists, "but that would sort of defeat the purpose." Proceeding with a lighter step, smiling at his absurdity, John approached what was known as "the Crypt," a large circular area with forty Doric columns and sandstone arches which supported the floor of the Rotunda and the Capitol's nine-ton iron dome. Housed inside were the display cases that chronicle architectural and historical events of the Capitol, as well as a sandstone Corinthian column from the original East Front. The center star on the floor represented the point from which the streets in Washington D.C. were laid out and numbered, making this exact spot the true physical heart of the nation's capital.

Suddenly, John sensed movement out of the corner of his eye. Often, he would catch his reflection in the glass display cases, which would startle him until he realized the cause. Nonetheless, he flicked off his flashlight. He needed to be invisible. He stood stock still for a moment and held his breath, listening for the slightest sound. He peered into the darkness, straining to adjust his eyes so he could distinguish the reflections on the display cases from anything unusual.

There was no sound and John shook his head, upset with himself for acting like such a novice—dramatic and skittish. As he took a deep breath to calm himself, a painfully loud screech split the quiet like a shard of glass falling to shatter on marble. John's head snapped up. Crouching, he flicked his flashlight on, flashing it right and left into the recesses of the room. He was unable to identify the source of the sound, which seemed to have come from every direction at once. As if in a dream, the noise registered in his mind as being completely and sickeningly inhuman.

But this was not a dream.

John knew that he was very much awake and that he was not alone. Rivulets of sweat began winding their way down his temples. His damp shirt was clinging uncomfortably to his torso, and he was shivering, the cold completely at odds with his own sweat and the warmth of the evening. Another alarm sounded deep inside his head, a discomfort he had never felt before. Something was here in the darkness with him, and he couldn't find it. Fighting the fear that was now in control of his body and mind, he slowly, quietly began to circumnavigate the room, his back to the center, ears searching for any sound.

John heard another unidentifiable noise, but this one was as quiet as a breath—though as terrifying as the earlier screech. Fear pricked sharp, hot needles through his neck. He was all alone with this thing!

Again, something as infinitesimal as a lash swept across his eye, and as he reached up to clear it, a more definitive motion drew his eyes to the floor. He blinked, and then blinked again, gradually able to make out a small black cat crouched in the shadows. Relief wrapped her warm arms around him as John tried to recover from the terror he had felt a moment before. The cat was the most beautiful sight John thought he had ever seen. To think that he had feared for his life, trapped in that moment as he was. "Well, I'll be damned! How the hell did you get in here?" John could hardly believe his eyes, but the reprieve that he was experiencing was enormous. "Here kitty," he coaxed, as he squatted down to get a better look, "Here, kitty." Very slowly, the little black cat began to move towards John.

As the kitten drew nearer, John was mesmerized by the strange, opaque quality of the cat's eyes. They were like silver marbles—lifeless, with no pupils, just silver balls encased in black. He couldn't stop staring into their metallic depths. As the cat came closer, it hissed and arched its back. Its black fur stood straight up, making the creature appear double in size. It again screeched its unearthly cry and approached more swiftly, growing bigger and bigger.

Horrified, John began moving backward, but he couldn't take his eyes off this strange creature before him. Now it was enormous and John found himself rooted to the ground. His mind was telling him to turn and run, but he was paralyzed from fright. He could only stand motionless while, with dagger-like outstretched claws, the demon sprang in hideous slow motion towards John's throat. The last thing he registered was the warm, sickening taste of his own blood in his mouth as he bit his lip, muffling a scream. Then darkness took over.

Authors' Note

A stream of myth, folklore, and legend is attached to the cat. There are European tales of "earth spirits," which are not good enough to be angels, nor bad enough to be devils, but are mischievous to humans. Such spirits most often appear as cats with blazing eyes. Did this particular "legend" result from an attempt to cover up an embarrassing situation? Or does a cat really "haunt" the Capitol, and if so, who is this cat?

Thirteenth century belief was that witches would turn themselves into a hare or a cat in order to transport themselves to midnight meetings with the devil (Sabbat). Did the night watchman interrupt a witches' Sabbat about to take place? Or, as was also believed, could the cat have been the devil in feline form, creeping among the faithful to defile a soul?

As it has been told in the past, only a few details are attached to the story of the "Demon Cat in the Capitol." The same cat has supposedly been sighted in the White House. One further part of the tale insists that sightings of the Demon Cat presaged disaster, such as a presidential assassination, but research has not been able to substantiate this claim.

Visitor Information: Capitol Hill is at the east end of the Mall. The Capitol is open to the public for free guided tours only, which are conducted from 9 am to 4:30 pm, Monday through Saturday. Telephone: 202-225-6827. Tickets are available on a first-come, first-served basis at the Capitol Guide Service kiosk, near the intersections of First Street, S.W. and Independence Avenue.

GHOST HUNTING 101

The Dwight D. Eisenhower Executive Office Building (EEOB) is located next to the White House at 17th Street and Pennsylvania Avenue, N.W. It stands with the Capitol, the White House, and the Treasury building as a symbol of the U.S. Government and the strength and power of the United States. In contrast to many of the classical revival buildings in Washington, the EEOB's flamboyant style illustrates the optimism of the post-Civil War period.

Wow, is he ADORABLE! Polly thought, eyeing the guy sitting in front of her in the auditorium of the Eisenhower Executive Office Building. She loved the way his dark brown hair curled up in the back and around his ears, and he had *such* broad shoulders. From where she sat, he looked very attractive.

Their "jolly tour leader" is what her Grandmother would have called the thirty-something guy who was in charge of Intern Orientation. He had introduced himself as "Mike" and had been telling them about rules and regulations, security, and various other issues pertaining to their summer's employment. Now, he announced, "You all need to go to Room 125 where you will have your pictures taken for your badges, and then on to the room next to that to fill out all the necessary forms. People are down there to direct you, so that this process doesn't take any longer than necessary. From there, you can go to the cafeteria for lunch, and we will all meet back here at 2 pm to finish your orientation. Good luck and welcome aboard!"

One hour later, with her pictures taken and papers completed, Polly spied Mr. Broad Shoulders in the cafeteria line. She grabbed a salad and followed him to a table where a few others of their group were already seated. "I'm sure glad that job's over," she said to no one in particular, "I have never signed my name so many times! I'm Polly Webb, by the way, and I'm from Richmond, Virginia." The group began exchanging names and hometowns. Polly caught most of them, but paid particular attention when Broad Shoulders introduced himself as Sam Campbell of Indianapolis.

Now that Polly could see him head on, she found Sam had lovely green eyes framed by black lashes and heavy brows, an aristocratic nose, and full lips all set in a long slender face. Her heart beat faster when he smiled. *He is sure to have a girlfriend back home,* she thought, and her mood plummeted at the idea. *Oh, well, he's here for the summer and so am I, so we might as well enjoy it.*

After lunch, the twenty-five interns assembled back in the meeting room for the afternoon orientation session. "I will be happy to answer any questions you have about the topics discussed this morning," Mike said, "and then I will take you on a tour of the building before sending you off to the offices you will be working in for the next two and one-half months!" Mike answered several questions and then added, "Now since you guys are going to be working here, you need to know that this building is commonly referred to as the EEOB. That's what the staff calls it, and you're now staff."

Polly was eager for the tour to begin. She had been looking forward to this moment for almost a year. She had been so excited last year when she had first seen the gray granite exterior of the Eisenhower Building that she couldn't wait to tell her friend, Sarah. "You won't believe it when you see it!" she had exclaimed. "It has tiers of porticoes and paired Doric and Ionic colonnades—just like we studied in Art History." She and Sarah had come to Washington together last summer to examine the possibility of an internship for the current year. They were both thrilled when they were accepted and rented an apartment together for the summer. Sarah was interning for a Senator on "The Hill." Polly had realized her dream of working on the staff of the Vice President, whose office was housed in the EEOB. "It is soooo ornate. It's the spookiest building I've ever seen. I wonder if it has any ghosts!"

Sarah had laughed at her friend. "All right, Miss Nancy Drew wannabe...don't start looking for ghosts everywhere. You'd better focus on getting a job there before you start playing detective." Sarah was quite practical. Probably a good thing or Polly might not have gotten this job.

Mike was speaking, "Let me give you some background on this building and its history before I show you around. The Dwight D. Eisenhower Executive Office Building was built between 1871 and 1888 as the 'State, War, and Navy Department Building.' Under one roof, these three Executive Branch departments conducted the nation's foreign policy during the last quarter of the nineteenth century and the first quarter of the twentieth century."

"Isn't that the period when the United States emerged as an international power?" Sam asked.

"Yes, and many historic events occurred here."

"Like what?" someone shouted out.

"Well, it was here that a conference established the International Dateline and Greenwich Mean Time. To get back to where I was, when the building was completed, it was the largest office building in Washington."

"Who designed it?"

"An English architect, Alfred Mullett, designed it in a style known as French Second Empire. You might guess that it is a French style because of the slate-covered mansard roofs. The Pavillon Denon, an addition to the Louvre, inspired him. Mullett was so taken with it that he went on to design one hundred different buildings in this style, but only fourteen or so survive."

"All in Washington?"

"No," Mike answered, "some of his other well-known designs are the San Francisco and Carson City Mints, the Old Post Office in St. Louis, and the Pioneer Courthouse in Portland. But he also designed the Sun Building here in Washington. This one building replaced two existing executive office buildings west of the White House. It was built in four stages over seventeen years, and by 1949, all three departments had outgrown it and moved out. Then, this building became known as the Executive Office Building, and its occupants were the White House staff and the Bureau of the Budget."

"So when did it become the EEOB?" The girl sitting next to Polly asked.

"In 1999, President Clinton renamed the building in honor of President Eisenhower for his years of military and presidential service in the building. President Bush formally rededicated the building in 2002. A little point of interest here is the irony of naming the building for President Eisenhower because it was his Commission on Office Space that recommended in 1957 that this building be demolished!"

"Demolished? Why would anyone want to demolish this?" called out a voice from the back of the room.

Mike smiled. "Actually I know of three movements aimed at significantly altering the EEOB, if not actually demolishing it. The first was in the 1870s, shortly after construction began. Some Members of Congress did not like the French style and wanted it torn down in favor of the Greek style. The second push occurred in 1930 when Congress appropriated three million dollars to replace the granite facade with marble to replicate the Greek facade of the Treasury Building. The final movement occurred between 1957 and 1960 when more office space was needed. That is when Eisenhower's Presidential Commission recommended tearing the building down to build a modern steel and glass high-rise office building."

Mike was beginning to appreciate the interest shown by this group of interns. He had been conducting these orientations for ten years, and this appeared to be the most intelligent, curious, and mature group that he had yet encountered. Inspired by being treated as an authority on the subject matter and by his ability to hold their attention, he suggested, "Let's take a walk through the building now so that I can point out some of the more fascinating aspects."

Polly was more than ready to get on with the program. As they started to leave the meeting room, she maneuvered her position so she was standing next to Sam. He had addressed several remarks directly to her at lunch, and afterwards she had stopped in the Ladies' Room to check that her long blond hair was brushed and shining. She already had a nice tan and had carefully applied dark mascara and liner to give definition to her blue eyes and fair lashes. Reasonably satisfied, she had gone back to the meeting.

After Mike led them into the corridor, he gestured towards the ceiling. "These ceilings are eighteen feet high!" Pointing down the hall, "And there are nearly two miles of corridors constructed from white Vermont marble and New York black limestone. There are eight monumental circular stairwells with over four thousand solid bronze balusters."

As he turned and started walking forward again, he spoke over his shoulder: "The granite walls are nearly four feet thick. The window frames, exterior roof sculpture, cornices, and roof trim are cast iron. As you can see, this building was built to withstand the ravages of time! But as you have also undoubtedly noticed, renovation is going on throughout the building. Notice the beautiful robin's egg blue walls." Mike was gesturing to his right and left. "They were painted white around World War II and have recently been restored to their original color, along with the pale lavender columns. This renovation is not expected to be totally complete until 2010.

"The EEOB was designed just a few years after the completion of the Treasury Building. You all do know the Treasury Building, right? Just on the other side of the White House at 15th and Hamilton?" Mike looked around at his group for verification. Noting a variety of reactions from nods to blank stares, Mike went on: "Well, if you are not familiar with that building, look for it when you leave this evening. It is one of the most important and historical buildings in the government."

"How many people work here and how many rooms are there?" asked a female voice from behind Polly.

Oh, for heaven's sake, thought Polly in exasperation. Although she found the building awesome, the statistics were so boring. She glanced at Sam to see how he was reacting and smiled when she saw him check his watch.

"I'm not certain exactly how many people work here today, but I do know that it is a fraction of the 4,500 people who worked here during World War I. When the building was constructed, it had 553 rooms. As I think most of you already know, the EEOB houses the offices of the Executive Branch that support the President, the Vice President, and the White House. Several of you will be working in the Vice President's office this summer, which has had space here since 1960. Lots of the President's staff are also here, although the West Wing of the White House has been the traditional 'home' for the President and his staff since 1902."

"Does the President have an office here?"

"Three presidents have had offices in the EEOB," Mike responded. "President Hoover worked in an office here for three months in 1929 after a fire damaged the West Wing. President Johnson used his EEOB office for day-to-day business and reserved the Oval Office of the White House for ceremonial purposes. President Nixon had a private hide-away office in which he recorded most of the famous Watergate tapes that got him into trouble."

Polly thought, *It's time to change the subject.* She raised her hand, "I've heard that there are ghosts in this building. Can you tell us any stories?"

"Actually, ghosts *are* purported to be here. There have been some mysterious deaths in the EEOB. It would take more time than we have to tell you those stories though." Polly was elated to hear about the presence of ghosts here, but sorry that Mike stopped short. Ghosts were much more interesting than the number of stairways.

The group stopped in front of the two-story Indian Treaty Room with its rich marble wall panels and gold-leaf ornamentation. Mike pointed out the many nautical motifs such as the shells over the Italian and French marble panels, seahorses and dolphins in the cast iron railing at the second floor balcony, stars for navigation in the ceiling, and the compass in the center of the floor. The floor was constructed of colorful English Minton tiles, resembling mosaic. "This room contains the only surviving original lighting fixtures in the building," Mike said, "The name—The Indian Treaty Room—remains a mystery. It has been said that that was because treaties with the Indians were signed in this room, but that isn't true. Originally the Department of the Navy's Library and Reception Room, this room has hosted the signings of many international peace treaties, the first televised Presidential press conference, and other presidential ceremonies. Can everyone see the huge bronze lamps in the corners? Those represent Peace and War, Liberty, Arts and Sciences, and Industry, and each weighs 800 pounds!"

"Is it true that Thomas Edison worked here?"

"Great question. Someone has done their homework; not many people know that. Yes, Edison and his staff worked for two and a half years in what was once Admiral Dewey's office— Room 270. They were researching ways to solve the U-boat terrorism threat to the Allied fleet during World War I. Edison felt the final report was his best work ever.

"Okay," Mike said, at last, "You all have been a great audience, and I know you are probably tired and eager to get on with your jobs. We'll just go by what was the State Department's Library. It is the largest of the three libraries in the building and is now used as the Executive Office of the President Library."

"Wow, this room is so tall!" exclaimed one intern.

"Four stories," Mike responded. "Completed in 1876, it is constructed entirely of cast iron." Leading the group to the double staircase in the west wing, Mike pointed out the stained-glass rotunda above. "There is a matching staircase and rotunda in the east wing," he told them.

Polly yawned and smiled at Sam. "Now, it is time for you to report to your offices. You have your room numbers. You all have been a great group, and I wish you a wonderful summer with us here in the EEOB. You know where my office is; don't hesitate to come by if you need anything."

Midterms

"I absolutely adore my job!" Polly proclaimed one evening to Sarah.

"Me, too," Sarah replied. "Can you believe we are this lucky? Look at us…college students in the big city working for the most important people in the world! And it is so much fun!"

"Yeah," Polly replied. "The days go by so fast, I can't even believe it. Mary, the Veep's Personal Secretary seems to think I am reasonably competent. She seems satisfied with my responses to his mail. I even enjoy answering the phones."

"Well, that's no surprise! Nobody loves to talk as much as you do, Pol." They both giggled.

A few days later, Polly called Sarah during lunch. "Hey, Sam, Jeff, and Julie want to go hear the Marine Band on the lawn of the Capitol this evening. Do you want to join us?"

"Sure, Pol, I'll ask around here to see who else might want to come. Seven-thirty, right? I'll see you there."

And this was how the summer would go. This group of young adults who had been thrown together for a brief period of their lives was evolving into fast friends who enjoyed nothing more than sharing a constant round of activities in their summer residence. They took full advantage of the many free events and admissions available to them in the nation's capital. They attended the various military band concerts, where they would sit on a blanket on the grass; they visited the Smithsonian, the National Gallery of Art, the Botanic Garden, and the Zoo. Occasionally, one of the embassies would have a function, and they all dressed up and marveled at the embassy's opulence and the interesting food of whatever culture they were celebrating. They knew this was an eighty-day experience, and they loved sharing the joy of the moment, the exuberance of their youth, their freedom, the warm sunny days of July, and the birth of memories that they would carry with them for life.

For the first few weeks, Polly was so busy in the Vice President's office, learning the complicated telephone and intercom system, running errands for everyone in the office, and trying to juggle all the different requests that were made of her, that she had little time to pursue her passion…ghosts!

Probably her interest had begun when she was about nine. Her second cousin, Anna, had died that year while playing in the house that was being built next door to her own. Polly's mom had taken her to the funeral home. They stood in the back, and Polly never forgot the vision of the small open white casket containing the tiny white face and silky blond hair—all she could see from where they stood—with clouds of white tulle draped all around. Polly felt connected to this dead child, felt a relationship with her beyond having known her alive. She would imagine how the accident had happened. How could Anna have been off playing in such a dangerous place without her mother knowing? But Polly knew Anna's mother. She knew that the little girl had been very much adored and very well taken care of. Her family lived in a safe neighborhood, and the children were allowed go out and play with their friends without fear of any evil befalling them. She was unable to make any sense of it.

Polly dreamed about Anna. This was her cousin. She had played with her, spent time at her house, and now she had ceased to exist. Poof! Gone! So quickly, she was just erased. Polly began having secret fears that she could disappear just that fast.

After Anna's death, life, as it has a way of doing, went on. Gradually, the adults ceased going around with their sad looks and speaking in hushed tones. Polly regained her equilibrium, occupied as she was with the business of growing up and taking part in all the usual childhood activities. But she did not forget Anna. The initial horror of her death turned, for Polly, into a fascination with death and what happened thereafter and, ultimately, with ghosts.

As she was growing up, Polly retained a certain preoccupation with ghosts. She loved to watch movies or television shows or read any new book that came out that dealt with the supernatural. She told herself she wasn't obsessed. After all, she had lots of other interests. But she continued to dream about Anna even after she came to Washington. One Sunday afternoon she was taking a nap, and there was Anna. These dreams further fueled her interest in the ghosts in the EEOB.

The first day that Polly had time on her lunch hour, she headed off to see Mike. "Hi, Mike, do you remember me? Polly Webb…I'm an intern in the Vice President's office…" she trailed off, looking for a sign of recognition.

She had interrupted him, and his initial blank look confirmed that. Then, he smiled. "Oh hi, Polly. How are you getting along? They're not working you too hard, I hope."

"No, no, I love it! Everyone is really nice and I don't think I've made too many irreparable mistakes yet. The reason I'm here though is…" Polly paused, realizing that Mike might not have time for her, and, if he did, he might think her questions really frivolous.

"What is it, Polly?"

"Well, I wondered if you had time to tell me about the ghosts that you said inhabit this building?"

Mike laughed, shook his head, and then leaned back in his chair smiling. Polly noticed that he looked tired, but his expression was friendly. She waited for him to respond.

"That's right. You were the one who asked about the ghosts. I do have some information that I have learned since I came here, but I am awfully busy right now. If you could come by after work today though, I will hopefully have finished this project and we can talk. How about 6ish?"

"Great! Thanks, Mike. I really look forward to this." Polly made a quick wave and retreated back into the hall. *Super,* she thought. *Finally, I am going to get the real story.* She had talked to a number of people who she thought might know about ghosts in the EEOB. Someone had told her that they had heard that the architect of the building had killed himself and that his ghost lurked in the building. Most people she questioned, however, didn't seem to know anything, and many of them seemed to think she was just silly.

Polly showed up at Mike's office on the dot of 6 pm. "Are you always this prompt?" Mike glanced up at her from over his computer. He didn't look quite as happy as he had earlier. *Oh, dear,* thought Polly, *please don't let him tell me he doesn't have time now.*

"If you aren't finished, I can come back later," Polly offered quickly.

"No," Mike responded with a sigh. "I know you have been eager to pick my brain about the ghostly inhabitants here. If you don't mind just sitting down for a minute, I should be finished soon."

"Sure," she answered, gracefully alighting on the nearest chair. Polly tried to keep her eyes off Mike, hoping he didn't feel too pressured. If he was in a bad mood or very tired, she knew she wouldn't get all that she was looking for.

After about fifteen minutes, Mike reached up, turned off his desk lamp, arose from his chair and grabbed his jacket off the back of it. "Shall we go?"

Polly was surprised. She had expected that they would just sit here in his office and chat.

"Go?" Polly asked.

"Yeah," Mike responded. "It's been a long day, and I'd like to get a drink. Let's go across the street."

Mike made pleasant small talk as they exited the building and walked out to the scorching sidewalk. Without moving to the crosswalk, Mike started across the street, grabbing her hand, and zigzagging their way through traffic. Polly had to hustle in her high heels; she certainly didn't want to be run over. Mike led her into a small café. Polly noticed that he seemed to be well known, because the hostess in her obligatory black skirt and white shirt, smiled and spoke to him in a familiar way.

"What would you like?" he asked Polly now.

"Mmmm, Virgin Daiquiri, please." Polly was slightly mortified that Mike had to know she wasn't yet twenty-one. Polly had gotten the funniest tingle inside when Mike had grabbed her hand to cross the street. He must be at least thirty-five or so, and he was attractive. Polly knew he was married and that his wife was in Maine with their two young sons. She certainly wasn't interested in Mike, but she had felt very grown up and important walking by his side and being taken out for a drink... until she had to order the drink, that is. Now, Polly was feeling about twelve years old, and she hated it.

Mike took no notice of her discomfort nor did he bat an eye as he ordered their drinks and an appetizer. He turned from their waitress back to her, "So, now I am going to let you in on a little secret. I am quite fascinated by the ghosts in our building, too!"

"You are?!" This did surprise Polly.

"Yes, I am!" he affirmed with a grin. The waitress brought their drinks and a plate of mini quesadillas. Mike swigged his vodka tonic. "I've discovered that several people died in the building. Supposedly, seven died between 1880 and 1888, during the last phases of construction. Two people committed suicide in the building. Eight died in accidents or from heart attacks. I believe the EEOB could be the most haunted office building in Washington."

"Really? That's great. I just knew it had ghosts!"

"At least one person fell down the stairs and broke his back. It has been rumored that when he was Secretary of War, William Howard Taft fell down the stairs but suffered no worse injury than a bruised ego. He saw to it that new brass railings were installed for safety. And, Polly," Mike paused for emphasis, "allegedly three persons have fallen *over* the railing to their deaths."

"How did those people fall OVER the rail? Do you think they were pushed?" Polly's leap to a conclusion of murder and intrigue amused Mike. He was finding her quite adorable, but he had dealt with cute interns before and his defenses were in place. When the waitress reappeared to ask if they would like another drink or perhaps dinner, Mike declined.

"I really don't know anything about those falls. As with all of the fatalities, most of what I know is hearsay."

"So the architect was one of the suicides?" Polly asked.

"How did you know about that?" Mike quizzed her.

"Oh, I have other sources, you know," Polly announced proudly.

"Yes, actually he is the only one I have any real intel about."

Polly was disappointed by this admission. She was sure Mike was a treasure trove of information. "Will you tell me what you know about him, then?"

"Well, the story goes that in 1874, the Secretary of the Treasury, Benjamin Bristow, was questioning the added costs and time to completion of the building. Mullett, the architect, who felt his honor was in question, threatened to resign until the Secretaries of State, War and Navy assured him that he was not being accused of 'skimming'. However, he eventually determined that he was unable to work with Bristow and resigned at the end of 1874.

"When the building was completed in 1888, Mullett sued the U.S. government for payment of his fee for designing the building as that work was above and beyond his regular duties. A lower court ruled in favor of Mullett. However, the U.S. government sought a higher court's ruling. Their decision was that while Mullett was indeed the designer and was entitled to a fee, the statute of limitations had expired. Therefore, on a technicality, Mullett lost the suit and was never paid a fee for his largest design ever. Poor old Mullett had worked seventeen years on that project. He shot himself, and supposedly his ghost wanders the two miles of corridors."

"Oh, that's awful!" exclaimed Polly. "First there were people who wanted to tear his building down before it was even finished and then he wasn't even paid for it? I can see why he might have shot himself. But, did he kill himself in the building?"

"Well, I don't know actually. But, since the building was the source of all of his problems, if Alfred Mullett's ghost is roaming about, that would be the logical place for him to be."

"Have you ever seen any of these ghosts, Mike?"

"No, but I have experienced some unexplained phenomena." Mike drew this sentence out.

"Oh tell me! What?" Polly almost shrieked, but quickly put her hand over her mouth, then whispered again, "Tell me!"

Mike leaned across the table towards Polly and looked intently into her eyes. "Sometimes," he spoke very softly, "when I work very late, and the building is almost deserted, I hear doors slamming—one right after another. *BANG, BANG, BANG.* I look out into the hallway, and I can even see a door open and then close, and no one's there." He stopped for effect. Polly's eyes had grown huge. "One time, when I had gone back into the library for a short while, I returned to find every drawer and cabinet in my office *open*."

"Was anything missing?"

"No, nothing. But I am convinced it wasn't a burglar. Security is way too tight."

Polly was speechless. When she finally regained her tongue, she asked, "Whose ghost do you suppose did that?"

"I haven't been able to figure that out. I have little information to go on. Now listen, Polly, will you please be discreet about this conversation?" Mike appeared somewhat embarrassed that he had confided these secrets to her. He signaled to his waitress for the check.

On the sidewalk, Mike hailed Polly a cab and wished her a good night. Polly thanked Mike profusely for the information, assuring him that she wouldn't say a word to anyone. When she arrived home, Polly called out to Sarah. "Anybody home?"

"Hey, where have YOU been?" Sarah asked accusingly. They did so many things together, that either of them could get a little jealous when the other went out somewhere on their own.

Ignoring Sarah's tone, Polly flopped down on the nearest chair and started quickly, "Oh, Sarah, you will not believe what I have found out." Although she had promised Mike not to tell anyone about their conversation, she didn't consider her roommate just 'anyone'. She related the events of the evening, telling her roommate almost word for word what Mike had told her about the ghosts. "Do you believe that about the drawers? Isn't that incredible? Oh, Sarah, we have to go there some night and see if we can see them."

"I don't know who this 'we' is…you can have your ghosts. I don't believe in them, and if I did, this would scare the wits out of me! Now, there's this show on TV I really want to watch…."

Finals

Disappointed by Sarah's lack of enthusiasm, Polly went off to bed. Polly had vivid dreams that night. When she awoke, her bed was a mess, the sheets untucked, the pillows on the floor. She felt drained, not refreshed. She lay for a minute, staring at the ceiling, knowing she had to get up and get ready for work, but her body felt leaden. As she lay staring at the ceiling, wisps of dreams surfaced. She saw Anna's face as clearly as if they had just been playing. Now if she could just pull the dream back....

"POLLY!" She woke with a start and that hideous realization that she had overslept. "Polly, get up, it's seven-thirty...you're going to be late! I'm out the door...see you later."

As Polly scrambled out of bed, she heard the door close behind Sarah. Turning on the shower, Polly stood under the soothing water. Although her eyes were closed against the shampoo, those dreamed images floated once again behind her eyelids. Anna was standing in front of her, looking sad and pitiful, staring at her, but saying nothing. Polly opened her eyes and sputtered under the spray. It was so real. Anna had been right there, but the bathroom was empty.

Polly wondered if she was hallucinating, but she wasn't even sure what hallucinating was. *What is going on?* she asked, directing her question to a higher power. Somehow, without realizing it, she stumbled through her morning ritual, blow-drying her hair, getting dressed, and dabbing on the important eyeliner.

By the time she was in her car and on the road to work, Polly realized that she couldn't even remember how she got there. Trying to clear her head, she rolled down all the windows and let the warm summer air, the traffic noises, and the bustle of the capital's morning come into the car with her. Bit by bit, she recalled the evening before. She could still feel the protected feeling she got when Mike held her hand, but that gave way to the revelations he had made about the EEOB spirits. As she stopped at a red light, she thought she saw Anna again, but she knew that was impossible. Anna had died a long time ago.

"Morning, Polly." It was Mary, and she was looking quizzically at her.

"Oh, good morning, Mary."

"You okay?" Her boss asked, looking concerned.

"Yes, I'm sorry. I overslept. I'm sorry I'm late."

"You're only a few minutes late; don't worry about it. Don't you hate to oversleep? Puts you out of sorts for the entire day! Well, dear, here are some letters I would like you to work on this morning. Maybe you should get some coffee, it'll make you feel better." Mary was not the type of woman you would expect to be the Vice President's right hand person; she was quite motherly.

Polly did feel 'out of sorts' for the entire day. Her brain was foggy; the weight of the world on her shoulders. She worked more or less by rote, but Mary did have to return some of the letters to her so that she could fix her typos…mistakes she didn't generally make. Polly turned down an invitation to join her friends at the local pub. She felt so strange and she was tired from not having slept well the night before. She went immediately home from work, changed into shorts, and flicked on a "Friends" repeat. The next thing she was aware of was Sarah shaking her.

"Hey, Pol, don't you want to get in bed?" Sarah smiled down at her on the couch.

"Mmmmm, what time is it?"

"It's eleven-thirty. Mr. Smith's was really fun; why didn't you come?"

Sitting up, Polly tried to clear her head. "I just had a wretched day…I overslept, and then I couldn't get anything right all day. I just wanted to do nothing this evening; I was really tired."

"Well, you were missed. Sam looked really sad all evening. He barely said a word. Then, he left early. I think he really is hooked on you, Pol."

"Really?" Polly responded vaguely as she wandered toward her bedroom. "'Night, Sar. Please, if I'm not up when you get up in the morning, wake me," and she closed the door. All night Polly tossed and turned and dreamed of Anna who just stood looking at her. The construction site was in the background. Finally, Anna spoke, "Help me, Polly."

Polly sat straight up in bed and switched on the light. She was perspiring and panting as though she had just gone on a long run. Anna was so real to Polly that she expected to see her standing right next to her bed.

Wide awake and heart fluttering, Polly went into the kitchenette and poured herself a glass of milk. She leaned against the counter as she drank it slowly, contemplating her dream. The milk and the comfort and familiarity of her surroundings soothed her. She came to me, Polly thought calmly. Anna came to ME. Why does she want help? Why has she come to me for help? Polly really wanted to call Mike, but she looked at her watch and saw it was 3:45 am. She would have to wait until morning. She decided to go into the office extra early hoping that he might be there early as well. With her mind settled on this plan, Polly went back to her bed and quickly fell back to sleep.

At 5:30, Polly was awake again. It was light outside. Springing into action, she was on the way to the office by 6:15 am. Mike's office door was still firmly locked. Polly swore under her breath and went back to her office where she completed some work so she could have more free time to work on this problem.

Sam came in about quarter of eight. His eyes lit up at the sight of her. "Where have you been? You haven't been avoiding me, have you?"

Oh yea, thought Polly, *I can talk to Sam!* She jumped up from her desk and gave him a big hug. "No, silly, there's just been some crazy stuff going on. Look, let's go down to the cafeteria and get some coffee. We have about half an hour before anyone else will be in. I really need to talk to you."

Polly knew that Sam had been trying to figure her out during the summer and suspected that at times he thought her a bit ditzy, but she knew that he'd found out the hard way that she was not to be trifled with. There was a lot more to her than her blonde hair. "Sure," was his only response to her, however.

Once seated at a table in the cafeteria, Polly sipped on her latte while Sam attacked eggs and sausage. "Listen, Sam, the most amazing things have been happening. I have been asking

Mike about ghosts here and the other night...." Polly related the events of the evening with Mike to her friend. She omitted nothing, except her promise to Mike not to tell about their conversation.

"I know you probably think I'm crazy, but I really feel that maybe I have some connection to the world of the supernatural."

"What!? Why?" Sam obviously saw no connection between Mike's tales of ghosts in the Eisenhower Building and Polly's relationship with the spirit world.

Polly felt a little hesitant about telling Sam of her dreams of Anna. That was so intensely personal to her that she didn't know if she could tell someone who might be at all skeptical. "Well, I don't know," she lied. "I just do. I really want to stay here some night and see for myself what might be roaming the halls."

"Are you crazy?"

"And I want you to stay with me."

"We could lose our internships."

"We can find a ghost, too." She retorted. "Think how you would feel then."

"Jobless."

She laughed. "Please, Sam." Although she could tell he was intrigued by the idea of ghosts, she could also see that he'd never given much thought to the subject of the supernatural until now. It might be a curiosity about her that interested him more than any ghost she could conjure.

"Okay," he said, "but I can think of a better way to spend my time."

She smiled. "Great, how about tonight?"

"Tonight we're supposed to go the party at the Austrian Embassy."

"Oh, I forgot about that. What if we came here afterwards?"

"Polly, I seriously doubt that we can get in this building in the middle of the night. We can probably stay late, so many people do, but they are going to want to know why we are coming here in the middle of the night!"

"I guess you're right. How about tomorrow night?"

"I suppose that's okay. Look, we've got to get to work. People will be showing up, and you've already been late this week."

Back in the office, Polly had a hard time keeping her mind on her work. She did run out to Mike's office during the morning, only to find that he had someone with him. She really did want to talk to him because she sensed that he felt a connection to the supernatural like she did, and she felt like she could trust him with her dreams of Anna. She went by again later in the afternoon.

"Hi Polly. Please don't tell me you have a problem? I have been dealing with intern problems all day! Everything from parking tickets to complaints about overtime."

"No, Mike, I don't have a problem. I was just hoping you had a minute to talk."

"If it can wait, I'd appreciate it. I am up to my eyeballs, and my wife and kids get back tonight from visiting her parents, so I'd like to get out of here early."

"Oh, no problem. Sure, it can wait." Polly was disappointed. She had counted on Mike to be interested and to help her interpret what had happened. He didn't even seem curious as to what she wanted to talk about. As she walked back to her office, she decided that Sam would just have to do. She knew he wasn't that interested, but she also knew that he was a willing participant in any endeavor that she presented to him. He was always a good sport.

The following evening, Polly was prepared. She had brought with her a small duffle packed with shorts and a t-shirt to change into after work, as well clothes that she could wear the next day in case she didn't go home. She also had a bag of trail mix, two apples, and two bottles of water.

She had gone by Sam's desk in the morning to be sure he was still planning to join in the adventure. "We're on for tonight, right?"

Sam looked up and over at the other desks in his office. The other three people who worked in this room appeared not to have heard Polly. She immediately picked up on Sam's concern. "You're still going to the ghost movie with me, aren't you?" she said a little louder. Sam was relieved and nodded.

Their plan was to go out and grab a quick bite of dinner, returning early enough so that they wouldn't raise any suspicions. Polly had analyzed the watching post possibilities. Because something had visited Mike's office, she thought that a site at the end of his corridor where they could see for a good distance, would be the place for the most probable sighting.

When they had eaten dinner and had walked the halls on the third floor to get a feel for any people there who might be working late, they sat down at the end of the hall, their backs against the wall. It was almost dark outside, and little light filtered into these interior corridors. The regular electric lighting in the halls was quite dim. It was very quiet compared to the normal activity of the workday. The dimness and the quietness made it feel quite spooky. Sam thought about Polly's warm body sitting next to him. Polly thought about the possibility of actually seeing the ghost of one of the people whose life had been lost here.

"Sam," Polly said softly, "just think about those poor people who died here. Some of them were undoubtedly workers here. They probably fell off a ladder or scaffolding...."

"Or they could have been electrocuted, if they were working with the building's wiring," Sam offered.

"Mike said there were a lot of heart attacks. Wouldn't you guess that those were people who were employed here, maybe when it was still the Army, Navy Building? Just think, someone's husband went off to work one morning, kissed his wife and children good-bye, and then never came home again. Isn't that just awful?" Polly twisted around to look at Sam in the near darkness. His face was very close to hers and she could feel his warm breath. Her soft, sentimental side was one she hadn't shown him before. Sam leaned towards her and kissed her gently.

"Yes, it is awful, very sad..." Sam agreed. Polly didn't resist but rather curled herself into his arms, tucking her head against his chest. He seemed to like this soft and tender side of her. He'd only really seen the energetic, quick-moving, fast-talking girl, and he was obviously relishing this moment with her. He was hanging on to it. Polly was content.

Sam woke first. The arm he had wrapped around Polly's shoulder had gone to sleep, and he was sore from sitting so long on the marble floor. He shifted his weight slowly, trying not to disturb her, but Polly moaned and stretched. Suddenly, she was wide awake and out of his arms.

"We fell asleep!" she said accusingly. "What time is it; can you see your watch? I can't believe it! We can't make contact with ghosts if we're asleep. Damn! I can't believe this happened." Polly was whining now.

"It's almost four o'clock," Sam answered. "No wonder I'm so stiff. How could we sleep for six hours on these hard floors?" Sam got to his feet, stretched, and twisted. Then he pulled Polly up. "Hey, I've got an idea…let's go watch the sun come up!" Sam was a romantic, Polly thought.

"Okay, where shall we go?" Polly realized that their chance, as she envisioned it, had passed them by. Feeling romantic herself, having just spent the better part of the night in Sam's arms, she mentally put the ghost quest away for the moment, knowing she would try again another day.

"We could go to the Capitol. That would be the best place because it's so high. With our passes, we shouldn't have any trouble getting in to sit on the steps."

They left the EEOB, drawing a sidewise glance from the guard on duty, which they ignored. They drove through the nearly deserted streets, parked in the free Botanic Garden lot, and walked up the hill to the Capitol. They sat on the steps on the East Front and talked and laughed and hugged and kissed until the first red glimmer appeared over the Library of Congress. The sky was cloudless; as it got lighter, the blue became brighter, streaked with the gold and red of a hot summer sun. Sam and Polly looked at each other and broke into the joyful laughter of celebration. They knew instinctively that this was a rare moment in life, one to rejoice in and commit to eternal memory.

Polly had to wait until the next week before she could stay late again in the EEOB in search of the unknown inhabitants of this historical building. She decided that this time she must stay alone. She didn't want to be distracted. Time was growing short. The summer would soon come to an end, and she had a goal to accomplish before it did.

She prepared as before and sat in the east stairwell, at the end of the long corridor. The hours before midnight dragged interminably. She had brought her iPod for entertainment, but even the music didn't keep her from feeling tired and somewhat lonely. She walked up and down the hall several times to wake herself up before she finally settled down to watch in earnest.

Polly didn't have to wait long. Down the long corridor, she could just make out two hazy forms approaching. Fog swirled around them, impeding her view of them. As they drew nearer, she could see that one was small, like a child, the other much taller. Finally, she realized that the child was Anna. She was holding the hand of a dark-bearded man, who was unknown to Polly.

"I've brought someone you've wanted to meet, Polly." The little girl spoke.

Polly was speechless and just stared. The man spoke, "I

The Eisenhower Executive Office Building (EEOB) is located next to the West Wing, and houses a majority of offices for White House staff. Originally built for the State, War and Navy Departments between 1871 and 1888, the EEOB is an impressive building that commands a unique position in both our national history and architectural heritage. It too has its ghosts. *Courtesy of Michael Lodico, Jr.*

believe you have been looking for me…what do you want? Can't you leave us in peace? This is our home, and we have just as much right to be here as you do."

"Of course you do." Amazingly, Polly, though initially quite startled, felt right at home with this ghost. She had been right about there being ghosts, and now she was actually meeting one! "I didn't mean to disturb you. I am just very interested in your story. WHY do you stay here?"

"Because this is MY building! I put all of my best ideas into building it and then received nothing but ridicule. I wasn't even paid for my work. I will never leave here. I have many friends here, many who have also given their lives to this building and now have chosen to stay here with me. We keep waiting for people to recognize what we sacrificed our lives for—what we did for our government, for this city, for our country. Until we receive the recognition we deserve, we will make a nuisance of ourselves. We will slam doors and open drawers; we will brush by you in the halls, giving you a chill; we will move things around so that they can't be found."

"Oh, please, will you do some mischief now…something that I can point to so that I can try to convince people that you are here and explain why you are here?"

The ghost gave her a scornful glance and walked away.

"Wait! Please don't go! Anna, will you tell me why *you* are here?"

"I idolized you, Polly. I always wanted to be just like you. I was so mad when I died, that I couldn't be doing all the things you were doing. And Polly," Anna said shyly, "I really didn't want you to forget me…that is why I keep coming to you."

"Oh, Anna! I could never forget you."

"Really, Polly? If that is true, then I think I can pass over peacefully now."

"Of course it's true, trust me."

"Polly," Anna said slowly, "I am sure Mike trusted you when you told him you wouldn't tell anyone else his ghost stories."

When Polly opened her eyes, her watch said 5:40. She looked up and down the corridor, jumping up and going down a few stairs to look into the hallway below. There was nothing. The building was dead silent. She recalled her encounter. The dark, bearded man had to be the architect... Mullett was his name. Anna had brought her Mullett. She had actually, really and truly, talked to a ghost. She had made contact with a spirit. She was jubilant.

When Mike walked in his office at 8:30 sharp, Polly was waiting for him. "I HAVE to talk to you, Mike!" Her tone made him laugh. Nothing was as urgent to a young woman as her immediate needs.

He slipped out of his jacket and hung it on the back of his chair all with one smooth movement. Sitting down at his desk, he looked over at her. "Okay, shoot."

"Mike, I SAW Mullett! I stayed here all night last night and I saw him!!" Polly anticipated his reaction.

But he didn't seem entirely skeptical. "Really? Tell me about it."

Polly recounted her encounter with every minute detail. Mike was watching her closely as she told her story. When she finished, breathlessly, he said, "Polly," he asked gently. "Do you think you might have been dreaming?"

"Of course not! How could I have been dreaming? I talked to them, it was so real."

Mike nodded in assent.

"Mike," Polly said hesitantly, recalling only too poignantly Anna's words. "I have something to tell you." Mike said nothing, waiting for her to continue. "I told you," her lip trembling, she finished quickly, "I told you I wouldn't tell anyone what you told me about ghosts and I broke that promise."

"I'm sorry to hear that, Polly. The ability to keep your mouth shut is important, especially in a city like Washington. Knowing how to keep things confidential is critical; you're only as good as your word."

Polly was embarrassed. He was right. She had told not just one person but two. And probably each of those people had told another, which is how rumors get spread according to her Grandmother.

That night Anna came to her again. Polly wasn't surprised. She had been expecting her. Anna took her hands, and Polly looked into her little face. Anna asked, "How are you, Polly?"

"Well, I'm so pleased to have met Mullett. One day I might even write a book about ghosts, I think."

Anna nodded. "Anything else?"

Polly thought Anna sounded more adult than her boss Mary.

"Yes, Anna, you taught me something very important about myself. I hurt someone who had been good to me by not keeping his secret. I won't EVER make that mistake again."

"I'm sure you won't, Polly. Now I think I am ready to go. Good-bye, Polly." As Polly watched, Anna drifted slowly away, and Polly knew she wouldn't be back to see her again.

The last few weeks of their internships passed too quickly for the young group of friends. They celebrated a few birthdays, went to concerts at Wolf Trap, a weekend at Rehobeth Beach, and continued to enjoy life and their friendships. When the summer was over, they promised to stay in contact and meet each other in Washington next year. But, as we know, promises are often broken.

Visitor Information: 17th Street and Pennsylvania Avenue, Washington, D.C. 20001

LORE

Then there are those tales that are part of our history. They are ones we all know—that we have heard growing up—and where the spirits from the past remain with us today.

QUEEN DOLLEY

For over two hundred years, the White House has symbolized the United States government and the American people. In December 1790, President George Washington signed an Act of Congress declaring that the federal government would reside in a district "not exceeding ten miles square…on the river Potomac." Then city planner Pierre L'Enfant selected the site for the President's House, which is now 1600 Pennsylvania Avenue. On July 16, 1792, Washington chose an Irish-born architect's design of white-painted Aquia sandstone in the late Georgian style.

Construction began in October 1792. President John Adams and his wife, Abigail, were the first residents of the unfurnished mansion in November 1800. The roof leaked; the grand stairway wasn't built; and Mrs. Adams hung her laundry in the unfinished East Room because the residence lacked an exterior fence.

President Jefferson turned the south end of the unfinished East Room into an office and bedchamber for his aide, Meriwether Lewis. Jefferson's successor, President James Madison used the room as his Cabinet Room. Finally, during President Andrew Jackson's tenure, the East Room was decorated. Since that time, each President has made his own changes and additions.

Dolley Madison, the turbaned grande dame of Washington society, made many changes. A legendary heroine for many Americans, she remained in the President's House during in the War of 1812, packing up presidential belongings, including the portrait of George Washington. In books depicting the lives of great American women, she is included as a matter of course. Although she did not have the advantages of wealth or rank, she had such great personal charm, abundant warmth, and generosity that she had a host of friends and admirers.

By the 1920s, her name was linked to many products, ranging from bed linens, to food, to tobacco products. Dolley is famous; she also is a ghost haunting the gardens of the White House.

Dolley Madison, was the second of six children. Born in 1768, she was named Dorothy for her mother's aunt, Mrs. Patrick Henry. Both of her parents were members of the Society of Friends or the Quakers. A favorite with all, she was especially close to her grandmother who often gave her jewelry, which Quakers weren't supposed to wear. Dolley carried these gifts in a bag around her neck. One day, she lost that bag—which was never found again. Perhaps that is why she was so careful with the nation's treasures later on in her life.

Her father was one of the first Quakers in Virginia to question slavery. He sold his Virginia plantation, freed all his slaves, and moved to Philadelphia with his family in 1786. There he became an Elder and was known as a Quaker preacher. Unfortunately, his transition from plantation owner to urban life led to financial difficulties. Meanwhile, Dolley was growing in grace and stature. When John Todd, a lawyer and a member of the Society of Friends, asked her to marry him, her father told her to do so. An obedient daughter, she followed his dictate and bore John two children.

In 1793, yellow fever broke out. Although Dolley, with her children, moved to Gray's Ferry to avoid the epidemic, her husband went back to the city to assist his dying parents and other friends and to close his office. When his task was completed, he returned to Gray's Ferry, saying, "I feel the fever in my veins, but I must see her once more." Dolley rushed downstairs, throwing herself into his arms. He died within a few hours. In turn, Dolley developed the fever. Her second child died, but Dolley survived. Although Dolley had lost her husband and child within a few days of each other, she was alive, only twenty-six years old, attractive, and wealthy.

When James Madison, seventeen years her senior, met her, he immediately fell in love. Dolley supplied all the social graces that he, a brilliant but retiring bachelor, lacked. By September 1794, Mrs. Todd had become Mrs. Madison; by December, she had cast aside her Quaker ways for the joys of society. No longer would she conceal any gifts of jewelry. Although she was not a learned woman, she possessed significant charm and was so warm hearted that even her early Quaker friends condoned her for what they feared was an "undue fondness for the things of this world." Dolley created a glittering social life for the shy Madison, who was President Jefferson's Secretary of State.

A widower, President Jefferson often asked Dolley to act as his hostess at dinner parties and receptions. Mr. Jefferson's code of etiquette, which focused on republican principles, often outraged royal representatives. He didn't follow the orders of precedence, irritating the British minister and his wife. With Dolley acting as his unofficial first lady, his social events were more successful.

Dolley set her own standards, preferring generous Virginian hospitality with occasional portions of snuff to European stylishness. When her husband was elected president, she initiated her social leadership as First Lady by agreeing to the first presidential "inaugural ball" with four hundred guests in attendance. Dolley Madison knew exactly what she wanted to do as First Lady—she wanted to set a tone for the presidency.

Although Dolley had not been educated in music, dancing, painting, or foreign languages, she had immense charm. She had not been raised with advantages of wealth or rank, but historians say that Dolley never forgot a name she heard or a person she met.

Mrs. Madison's Crushes

In March 1809, as Jefferson left the capital to return to Virginia, Dolley and James Madison moved into the unfinished President's House. During the ensuing years, Dolley forged a role as the President's adviser and hostess and developed a much-envied social style for the Executive Mansion.

Working with Benjamin Henry Latrobe, Jefferson's architect, Dolley set out to make the Presidential House a national symbol. After persuading congressional members to give her some money to spend on the house, she created large sophisticated public rooms that impressed foreign diplomats and met the Republican desires of the new nation. Together, they brought a Greek theme to the oval drawing room, site of her Wednesday evenings. They rearranged space to create a state dining room and set the table with newly purchased silver and china. In the dining room, which acted also as a portrait gallery of presidents, they hung the Stuart portrait of George Washington.

Dolley understood the power of clothes and jewelry. She dressed magnificently, wearing richly colored satins, silks, and velvets trimmed with luxurious braids and other accents. She often wore a plumed turban to give her additional height during evenings of refreshments, music, and lively conversation. She used rouge and other cosmetics, but it was her personal radiance and her ability to make every guest feel valuable that were memorable.

The President's House became the sophisticated center of the Washington social scene. Drawing on her considerable charm, she introduced local community, foreign ministers, cabinet secretaries, the social elite, and members of Congress at her "Wednesday drawing rooms," or "Mrs. Madison's crush or squeeze." With no invitation required, these weekly parties sometimes attracted four hundred guests. At dinner parties, Dolley sat at the head of the table directing the flow of conversation, expressing her opinions to Congressional members, and introducing her husband's opinion. She captivated her guests with unusual menu items, such as ice cream in warm pastry, and her extraordinary conversational skills, while her husband, who was often called "Father of the Constitution," sat quietly.

The Madison's partnership resulted in the establishment of a working political culture for the fledgling federal government. At her events, people could gather information, make connections, and secure offices. Whenever the cabinet met, Dolley held parties for the cabinet wives to implement projects of interest to the local community. Through her charismatic warmth and hospitality, she helped make the President's House the home of the American people.

The Burning of Washington City

Between 1793 and 1815, Britain and France, the great European powers, were almost constantly at war. President Jefferson, who began his second term in 1805, declared American neutrality. To prevent American trade with France, Britain seized American merchant ships and cargoes and impressed American seamen into British service, claiming that they were either British deserters or subjects, regardless of whether they had

For over two hundred years, the White House with its 132 rooms has symbolized the United States government, and the American people. *Courtesy of D. Peter Lund*

become American citizens. The United States stood by its right to naturalize foreigners. When the HMS *Leopard* fired on the USS *Chesapeake* inside American territorial waters and removed four of its crew members in June 1807, the two countries teetered on the brink of war. President Jefferson and his Secretary of State, James Madison, tried economic coercion and negotiation but were not successful. During the next several years, Great Britain's continuing impressments of American citizens, its blockade of the European coast, thus hampering neutral trade, and its support for the Indians defending their native lands against encroaching American settlements continued to frustrate the Americans.

On June 18, 1812, the United States declared war on Great Britain, which was engaged in the Napoleonic Wars. Many thought that an American invasion of Canada would make Britain concede to the American demands. Instead, the British refused to give into American demands, and British General Isaac Brock, commanding local militias and Native American allies, skillfully repulsed the American invasion. Once France's Napoleon surrendered to the British, the United States stood alone against the great British Empire. Britain sent Major General Robert Ross with 4,000 British soldiers to the mouth of the Patuxent River in Maryland with Washington City as his objective.

Back in the federal city, James Monroe, the Secretary of State, ordered the public papers and records to be removed and taken to safety. One of the clerks bought coarse, durable linen and had it made up into book bags. Together with other clerks, he filled the bags with historic documents, such as the Declaration of Independence, the Constitution, and the correspondence of George Washington, including the historic letter resigning his commission. He then loaded the bags on to a wagon and sent it out of the city. As the wagon crossed the wooden bridge over the Potomac, Washington's citizens swarmed on the bridge, attempting to escape the enemy. James Madison left the President's House to join his troops in defending the city.

Until the British soldiers were marching on Washington, Dolley Madison had continued entertaining. Even the day she left the White House, the dinner table was set for forty guests. Although the government officials had already fled, she and a few servants had remained at the White House, packing up valuable documents, the silver service, the blue and gold Lowestoft china, and other items of importance. In between selecting what to take, she would run to the roof with her spyglass to watch the approaching British.

She particularly wished to save Gilbert Stuart's portrait of George Washington, which hung on the west wall of the large dining room at that time. The federal government had acquired it for the President's House in 1800 at a cost of $800. The picture was screwed into the wall. "Save that picture if possible!" cried the First Lady. "Under no circumstances allow it to fall into the hands of the British!" When she saw that her slave, Paul Jennings, and another servant were taking too long to unscrew the giant frame from the wall, she told them to break the wood and remove the linen canvas. At that moment, her steward, Jean Pierre Sioussat, known as French John, entered the room and took out his penknife and cut the heavyweight English twill fabric from its frame. They hid the famous portrait in a farmhouse. By rescuing it, Dolley guaranteed her place in the history books.

About 3 pm, James Smith, who had accompanied the President to Bladensburg, galloped up to the Presidential

House, waving his hat, crying, "Clear out, clear out. General Armstrong has ordered a retreat." Dolley ordered her carriage, and on the way through the dining room, grabbed whatever silver she could crowd into her reticule. She jumped into the chariot with two servants. French John took her parrot in its cage over to the residence of the French minister for protection under the French flag.

By the time the British soldiers appeared on Capitol Hill on the evening of Wednesday, August 24, about ninety percent of Washington's residents had left the city. Every responsible official had fled, so no one was available to formally surrender the city. The advance guard of British troops was too small to occupy the city, so Major General Ross sent a party down the quiet streets under a flag of truce. A volley of sniper fire from a house at the junction of Maryland Avenue, Constitution Avenue, and Second Street, N.E. felled the horse ridden by Ross, killed at least one enemy soldier, and wounded another. The invaders retaliated by quickly torching the house, although the anonymous snipers had run off.

The Capitol was a prime objective of the British. At this time, the Capitol consisted of two white square buildings housing the Senate and House of Representatives linked by a covered 100-foot-long wooden walkway. William Thornton had designed the Capitol originally, and English-born Benjamin Henry Latrobe was hired to work on it with Thornton's plans. Together, they'd created a national capitol that was as magnificent as many of its overseas counterparts. The grand staircases led into rooms adorned with fluted columns and vaulted ceilings. A grand American eagle, with a wingspan of more than twelve feet hung high above the Speaker's chair in the House of Representatives.

The British soldiers lit fires made from piles of furniture spread with the combustible content of their Congreve rockets. The ravaging fire melted one hundred panes of English plate glass and consumed the grand American eagle and many other pieces of art. Its heat was so intense that the outer stone of the columns expanded and fell off, leaving the deformed shafts wobbly and grotesque.

Approximately one hundred British troops advanced down Pennsylvania Avenue toward the President's House. When they entered it, they were tired, hot, thirsty, and hungry. Once inside, the British soldiers supposedly found the dining hall set for a dinner for forty people. One of the Britons is said to have toasted the health of their Prince Regent. Another raised his glass to the success of His Majesty's land and naval forces. Then they drank "to peace with America and down with Madison." Someone found one of James Madison's three-cornered hats and, raising it by the tip of his bayonet, declared that if they could not capture "the little president" they would parade his hat in England.

By 11 pm, the President's House was ablaze. British crewmen aboard warships in the Patuxent River and anxious Americans in Baltimore, Maryland, and in Leesburg, Virginia, could see the flames in the night from fifty miles away. Supposedly, the British added fuel to the fires that night to ensure they would continue burning into the next day. By dawn, the President's House was a blackened shell. Fortunately the day after the fire, a tremendous hurricane hit Washington, tearing off roofs of houses and extinguishing the fires.

The British set fire to the Library of Congress, destroying 3,000 rare books. They burned the offices of the War and Treasury Departments. Other troops marched south to burn more of the Navy Yard, already roaring with flames set earlier by the Americans to prevent capture of stores and ammunition. William Thornton, the architect of the Capitol and then superintendent of patents, convinced the British that The United States Patent Office should be saved.

The next day Admiral Cockburn entered the building of the D.C. newspaper, *National Intelligencer*, intending to burn it down; however, neighborhood women convinced him otherwise. Legend tells us that Cockburn wanted to destroy the newspaper because it had branded him as "The Ruffian," and the *National Intelligencer* had written many derogatory articles about him. He ordered his troops to tear the building down brick by brick, making sure that they destroyed all the "C" typefaces so that no more pieces mentioning his name could be printed.

The following day, the victorious British left for their ships in the Chesapeake and headed toward Baltimore, the third largest U.S. city at that time and an important harbor. On September 13, 1814, the British ships began firing on Fort McHenry in Baltimore harbor. They fired into the night, and Francis Scott Key witnessed one of the most important battles of the war. When daylight appeared the next morning, the American flag with its fifteen stars and stripes was still flying. The city was still American.

Although the occupation of Washington by British troops lasted just twenty-six hours, evidence of their vandalism survives to this day. Some of the blocks of Virginia sandstone that make up the original walls of the White House are clearly defaced with black scorch marks. They are the indelible stains from the fires of 1814.

After days of wandering around the Virginia countryside, the Madisons reunited and returned to the blackened ruins of the federal city. With the White House in ruins, the Madisons moved into the Octagon House at the invitation of its owners on September 8, 1814. They had vacated it before the British entered Washington and induced the French minister to occupy it with a view to its protection. The distinguished mansion became the temporary Executive Mansion until the following March.

James Madison established his office in the circular study on the second floor. Dolley personified the effort to restore and revitalize the city. After replenishing her wardrobe, Dolley held many receptions and parties in the Octagon drawing room. On New Year's Day 1815, Dolley wore a robe of rose-colored satin with ermine trim, gold chains around her waist and arms, and a white satin turban. She knew she had to look the part of a triumphal presidency.

The Aftermath

By that winter, both sides wanted the conflict to end. On December 24, 1814, they signed the Treaty of Ghent (also known as the Peace of Christmas Eve) in Belgium. It provided for ending the war, returning all conquered territory, and restoring the pre-war status quo. Because of the uncertainty of sea travel, American officials sent home three separate copies of the treaty to ensure the safe arrival of at least one. Henry Carroll, secretary to peace commissioner Henry Clay, was the first to arrive with the treaty, carrying it in his personal brass-studded document box, now known as the Ghent Treaty Box. On February 17, 1815, Madison signed the Treaty of Ghent in the Round Room of the Octagon House, with Dolley welcoming visitors and congressional members on this happy occasion. A large party presided over by Dolley in her feathered satin turban and gold chains followed this solemn occasion.

The signing took place two weeks before the Battle of New Orleans, a further example of the difficulty of communications during this era. This treaty set the stage for the Anglo-American cooperation that has persisted to this day.

Only two objects of art that were in the President's House before August 1814 remain in the White House today. One is Gilbert Stuart's full-length portrait of George Washington, which now hangs in the East Room. The other is a small wooden medicine chest in the downstairs Map Room. Archibald Kains, a Canadian, returned the medicine chest to the White House in 1939. In a cover letter to President Franklin D. Roosevelt, he wrote that it was, "looted or

The White House has survived fires, leaky roofs, laundry being hung in the unfinished East Room, sheep grazing on its lawns, and various presidential ghosts. *Courtesy of D. Peter Lund*

pillaged from the White House by my grandfather, who was paymaster of the *Devastation*, one of the boats that sailed up the Patuscent [sic] at that time... I hope you will find an appropriate resting place for this little relic and should be very pleased if you gave it shelter in your own home."

James and Dolley Madison planted the lovely Rose Garden, where many press conferences and important meetings occur. When Woodrow Wilson took office in 1912, his wife decided that the Rose Garden needed to be replanted. It wasn't the thorns, but Dolley's spirit that prevented the gardeners from touching her roses. Today, it continues to bloom as it has for the last two hundred years. People often smell Dolley's lilac-scented perfume and hear the sound of horse-drawn carriages arriving for one of her famous crushes. Her ghost, wearing her elegant clothes and a feathered turban, is also said to have roamed the Octagon House after her death.

Thomas Jefferson later sold his library to the government to restock the Library of Congress. (In July 2003, British Prime Minister Tony Blair jokingly apologized for the burning of the Library of Congress.)

Mr. Gales, the publisher of the *National Intelligencer* borrowed type and printed his newspaper again in one week. Admiral Cockburn was mentioned.

The thick sandstone walls of the President's House survived, although scarred with smoke and scorch marks. President and Mrs. Monroe reopened it with a New Year's reception in 1818. Although commonly called the President's House, the building had always been whitewashed. When the building was given a coat of oil-based white paint during its rebuilding, the term White House came into more general use. Incidentally, the house has survived two fires, the Truman renovation, and the original exterior walls still remain. President Theodore Roosevelt established the term "White House," when he had it engraved on the stationery in 1901.

Known as "Old Hickory," Andrew Jackson was the seventh President of the United States (1829–1837). He was also military governor of Florida (1821), commander of the American forces at the Battle of New Orleans (1815), and a founder of the modern Democratic Party. *Courtesy of D. Peter Lund*

Visitor Information: 1600 Pennsylvania Avenue NW Washington, D.C. 20500. To request a self-guided public tour for groups of 10 or more, write your Member of Congress. These free tours are available from 7:30 am to 12:30 pm Tuesday through Saturday (not federal holidays) For the most current tour information, please call the 24-hour line at 202-456-7041.

Located at the southeast corner of 15th and E Streets, The White House Visitor Center is open seven days a week from 7:30 am until 4 pm.

State Song of Maryland

A Maryland native, James Ryder Randall, wrote "Maryland, My Maryland," in April 1861 when he learned that Union troops were marching through Baltimore. The song is set to the tune that many associate with "O Tannenbaum" or "Lauriger Horatius." Maryland adopted it as the state song in 1939.

The despot's heel is on thy shore,
Maryland!
His torch is at thy temple door,
Maryland!
Avenge the patriotic gore
That flecked the streets of Baltimore,
And be the battle queen of yore,
Maryland! My Maryland!

Hark to an exiled son's appeal,
Maryland!
My mother State! to thee I kneel,
Maryland!
For life and death, for woe and
     weal,
Thy peerless chivalry reveal,
And gird they beauteous limbs with
     steel,
Maryland! My Maryland!

Thou wilt not cower in the dust,
Maryland!
Thy beaming sword shall never
     rust,
Maryland!
Remember Carroll's sacred trust,
Remember Howard's warlike
     thrust,
And all thy slumberers with the
     just,
Maryland! My Maryland!

Come! 'tis the red dawn of the day,
Maryland!
Come with thy panoplied array,
Maryland!
With Ringgold's spirit for the fray,
With Watson's blood at Monterey,
With fearless Lowe and dashing
     May,
Maryland! My Maryland!

Come! for thy shield is bright and
    strong,
Maryland!
Come! for thy dalliance does thee
    wrong,
Maryland!
Come to thine own anointed
    throng,
Stalking with Liberty along,
And chaunt thy dauntless slogan
    song,
Maryland! My Maryland!

I see the blush upon thy cheek,
Maryland!
For thou wast ever bravely meek,
Maryland!
But lo! there surges forth a
    shriek,
From hill to hill, from creek to
    creek-
Potomac calls to Chesapeake,
Maryland! My Maryland!

Dear Mother! burst the tyrant's
    chain,
Maryland!
Virginia should not call in vain,
Maryland!
She meets her sisters on the plain-
"Sic semper!" 'tis the proud
    refrain
That baffles minions back again,
Maryland!
Arise in majesty again,
Maryland! My Maryland!

Thou wilt not yield the Vandal
    toll,
Maryland!
Thou wilt not crook to his control,
Maryland!
Better the fire upon thee roll,
Better the blade, the shot, the
    bowl,
Than crucifixion of the soul,
Maryland! My Maryland!

I hear the distant thunder-hum,
Maryland!
The Old Line's bugle, fife, and drum,
Maryland!
She is not dead, nor deaf, nor dumb-
Huzza! she spurns the Northern scum!
She breathes! She burns! She'll come! She'll come!
Maryland! My Maryland!

BELLE BOYD, GIRL SPY

Today, the United States Supreme Court Building designed by noted architect Cass Gilbert and constructed by 1935, stands proudly at its site on One First Street Northeast, immediately east of the United States Capitol. Previously, a large brick building built in 1800 as a tavern and boarding house occupied this site. Known as the Old Capitol Building, it temporarily housed the Capitol employees while the current building was being repaired from a fire. When the Civil War broke out, the building was sixty-one years old, abandoned, and had fallen into disrepair. In other words, it was a perfect place for Civil War prisoners. Bars were added to windows, and prisoners were brought in.

The well-known Confederate spy, Belle Boyd, was incarcerated in this building. Some say that they can still hear her singing "Maryland, My Maryland." Although she didn't die there, she was such a charismatic presence, she left her mark there.

After the war, the pioneers of the Woman's Suffrage Movement assumed control of the building. Ghostly screams, swearing, and banging often interrupted the women's meetings. Today, many Washington residents will tell you that if you walk past this site before the sun rises you can hear the screams, crying, and pleas for justice.

Today's generation would consider my sister, Belle Boyd, truly something. Although she wasn't even beautiful—she had this big nose and teeth that stuck out—she always got her way, especially with men. They said they found her bravado charming. Of course, she did have a great figure, and that counts for something. But let me start at the beginning.

Family is really important if you are a Southerner. It's how people know who you are. When you visit in the South, you don't

A cloudy skyline.

get asked about where you went to school or where you work, but about your family. "Who's your family, girl?" Belle and I and our other sisters and brothers grew up in beautiful green rolling hills of the Shenandoah Valley in a nice house.

Like a lot of things in the South, our home appeared perfect in the classic sense, but our parents were generally short of cash. Our brothers' clothes were twice-turned, and Mother would remake her white muslin dresses to hand them down to Belle. But Belle wouldn't tolerate these muslin hand-me-downs. She would stomp her foot and demand something new, something bright and colorful. Somehow she made my parents listen, and she would get her new dress. And I, number two sister, would get the hand-me-down. The same thing happened with our shoes. Our shoes were often filled with holes and lined with paper, but Mother said no one could see them. But Belle said she could feel them, and she wasn't wearing "any old holey shoes." So guess who got new shoes? Not I.

Our parents traced themselves back to the kilts and bagpipes of Bonnie Prince Charlie and some ancient Scottish clan. But our daddy was nothing but a storekeeper and a tobacco farmer, who hadn't done as well as some of our distant relations. We were reminded frequently—when we complained about our lack of new dresses—that we had highly-placed kin in New Orleans and Kentucky and a family connection with George Randolph, later Confederate Secretary of War. That still didn't mean we had new dresses.

Belle was the boss of all of us children. She was the reckless tomboy, who dove into running streams, raced her horse through the woods, and climbed the tallest trees. She was the one who could hang upside down the longest, who figured out how we could sneak out at night, who sassed Ma and Pa. I was her sidekick and the second in command. Our brothers and sisters were our messengers and definite projects for improvement. Our parents—they were her doormats.

They had this rule about no children at dinner parties for example. Belle really protested, but Mother stuck by her guns. "She would draw herself up and announce, "Maria Isabella Boyd. You are not coming to our dinner party." The day of one party, Belle declared, "It's not right. I'm nearly an adult, and I want to attend." When Mother said no, Belle stomped upstairs, slamming her door. Later that evening when the guests were still there, enjoying their whiskey, Belle rode her horse right into the front hall. With her best scowl, she announced, "My horse is old enough to attend, even if I'm not." One of the men burst into laughter. "Now that gal has spirit!" he cried. "I'm glad to meet your little rebel." Mother couldn't do anything but smile sweetly, although her eyes were dagger points. After all, she didn't want that brown and white horse in her front hall.

Our parents never scolded her. She would say exactly what she was thinking, and Mother would just blink dumbly at her and then pick up her latest copy of Godey's Lady's Book. Father would laugh and give in. If any of the rest of us had acted that way, we would be sent to our rooms, made to stand in corners, or get our legs switched. They never touched her. Perhaps it was because she would just laugh at them.

In many ways, I hated Belle. Tall and graceful, she was always the center of the crowd. More importantly, she had a way of tilting her head, sashaying her long hair over her back, and looking at a man through her long eyelashes. And in an era when a lady wasn't supposed to show her legs, she was know to have the best pair of legs in the area. Sometimes, if I watched her carefully, I would catch her flourishing her skirts so gawking young men could just glimpse her slender ankles clad in lace-like clock stockings and French slippers. Of course, my ankles were ugly extensions of my short and plump legs. I was never the center of the crowd—unless I was with Belle.

When Belle was twelve, our mother said we needed to be "finished" and learn some manners to deal with society. The race for the "American Dream" was on! After all, Mother said if we were to better ourselves, we had to know how to behave. She arranged for our wealthy kin to pay for Mount Washington Female College at Baltimore, where we studied math, government, and literature along with music, dancing, and needlepoint. There we were taught how to pour tea, arrange flowers, make the perfect soufflé, fold napkins—basically we were learning how to keep our tiara sparkling along with other essential qualities for a proper social existence. Once we were properly refined, we could attend family dinner parties. We also could go to more formal functions in the city.

At age sixteen, Belle was ready to be launched on society at a debutante ball in Washington, D.C. Mother told our cousins to introduce us to the proper hostesses so we could receive invitations to the best affairs. The point of a debut is to start meeting possible suitors for marriage. I was considered too young—thank the lord. But if Belle married well, life would be more pleasant for our family. There would be more money for all those luxuries, like new promenade dresses in plain and figured fabrics, lace shawls, and hats. A favorable marital alliance would enhance our family's honor and prestige. It might even facilitate the development of some beneficial personal and business allegiances for father.

To be proper ladies, we were supposed to be modest, circumspect, kind, and considerate. A well-bred lady, according to mother, is never vain, conceited, haughty, or proud. Of course, a lady is always polite and never dresses so as to attract undue attention. Belle certainly didn't fit this image. She was what they call flamboyant. Rich shining taffetas in great rustling reds and greens graced her willowy figure. Her dresses were just a bit tight, and she flashed her ankles just a little too much.

At her debut ball, Belle waltzed her way into the capital's high society. She entered into conversations with uniformed officers, judges, and senators. I would be quietly talking to one of the gray-haired chaperones, and I could hear her laughter clear across the room. "How dare those Yankees tell us how to run the South," she would proclaim. "We know how to run homes, our plantations." I had to laugh when I heard her say that. Our pretty little home certainly wasn't any plantation. "Our people are happy living with us. We take care of them. We doctor them, we feed them, and they work in our fields and our kitchens," she would pronounce. She made sweeping gestures and loudly declaimed her opinions. "The great nation. Bravo!" she would exclaim. "You Yankees like to tell us how to live our lives, but we know how to live—with honor." Rather than being scorned for her outspoken ways, she became even more popular. And I dutifully followed in her tracks because I knew I was rising in social rank—not because of anything that I had done, but because I was Belle's sister. I hated that fact, but she got me to places I never could get to otherwise.

We went to the best parties, dances, and cotillions. Our Washington hostesses had lavish standards for entertaining and the staff to carry them out. Their opulent dining rooms were filled with an astonishing assortment of elegant china, glassware, and flowing linens. They liked to show off their compotes; oval, round, and shell-like bowls; epergnes; oval, rectangular, and even fish-shape platters; butter servers; gravy boats; jelly dishes; candy bowls; powdered sugar dispensers; biscuit boxes; pitchers; and decanters. We were served such feasts on all this china and silver. One meal had seventeen courses, beginning with turtle soup and ending with beautiful pyramids of iced fruits. Five wine glasses marked each place setting. After dinner, coffee was served to women in the parlor while the men gathered in the study to enjoy after-dinner liqueurs and large fat cigars.

Belle found life to be a continuous carnival, crowded with people, gay with parties, and echoing with music. She engaged in long conversations with some and gave wanton glances to others. Groups of men surrounded her, asking her to dance, to go horseback riding. She wore her shining bright taffetas while I dressed in soft blues and grays over my hooped crinolines. She was in her element, talking easily with some of the most important men in Washington. Her head tilted slightly upward, she often engaged in enthusiastic debates. "That Mr. Lincoln doesn't understand us Southerners. We may just have to secede, you know." She tried to educate the Northerners about life in the South. "You all just understand factories and businesses," she would proclaim. "We're the land of fruit and honey. We grow things like cotton. The slaves help us with all that labor."

Belle began seeing a wealthy young Union officer. He started taking her for carriage rides and calling on her. But her Southern leanings became evident after Mr. Lincoln won the election. One day, I heard her say to some Yankee boys, "I am sure I feel no hostility to you all. You know I wish you well, but I also know that you do not understand the great Southern states of this country." As the decision to secede began snowballing through the Deep South, her statements became more and more inflammatory. Certainly, her talk wasn't appropriate for a young woman living in Washington City who grew up in Martinsburg, Virginia—a town, which couldn't decide whether it was pro-Yankee or pro-Confederacy.

Washington City was an exciting place to be. Before the war, it was filled with Southerners. Many slaves lived in the city, which had been a slave-trading center where Negroes were sold to be shipped farther south. More than a third of the 66 Senators and 237 members of the House of Representatives were proslavery. By the time of Mr. Lincoln's inauguration, Army and Navy officers from the south began to resign in order to join the Confederacy's fighting force. One damp March day, we stood on Pennsylvania Avenue and watched tall Mr. Lincoln in his open carriage go to his inauguration. He wore a shiny new ill-fitting black suit and stovepipe hat, and the crowds cheered. Hundreds of soldiers were about because there had been rumors of attempted assassinations. Sharpshooters looked down from roofs. Then on April 11, the Southerners attacked Fort Sumter in South Carolina, and our country was at war. President Lincoln called for 75,000 volunteers, and Belle's young officer disappeared. With many other Southerners, we fled back home to what Belle called "our country, the South."

The Yankees Are Coming

The loyalties of the good citizens of Martinsburg, Virginia, were deeply divided. Many were pro-Union, but there were ardent Southern sympathizers, and our family was one. Father had decided to get out of his comfortable chair and go to fight for our way of life with General Stonewall Jackson. Although he was offered "that grade in the army to which his social position entitled him," he insisted on enlisting as a private. Mother was beside herself. "He's too old to fight against all those young strong men," she cried, but Belle was so proud of him. "Look at what my daddy is doing," she crowed. "He's going to protect our way of life." We said goodbye to Father as bands played, crowds cheered, and long boring speeches were made. Cannons were sounding as we tearfully shouted hurrah, hurrah.

As our men folk answered the call to arms, we had to redefine our roles. No longer were we flirting on the porch, rather we were attempting to sew soldier's uniforms and knit socks. Wherever I went, I always had a sock that I was working on. Knitting and sewing for our troops gave me a sense of participation in their efforts. Belle's talents ran more to organizing cotillions and fairs and raising money for Father's regiment, the 2nd Virginia. When Father went to the camp, Belle and I organized a festive visit to General Jackson's camp in nearby Harper's Ferry. I worried about refreshments, and she worried about getting enough officers and men to attend. Not yet seventeen, Belle really wanted to sing in a concert to raise money, but Mother said that would be highly improper—as if impropriety ever stopped Belle!

By this time, Belle was wearing a rebel soldier's belt around her waist and a velvet band across her forehead adorned with seven stars representing the Confederacy. She really admired old "Stonewall." She saw him to be "that undaunted hero, that true apostle of Freedom." She didn't care about who she said that to either. Gray or blue uniform, she told them just how she felt. That was Belle. She would not be tied or bound or confined or guilted into anything. She did as she wished when she wished. While the rest of us waited, saved, stored, prepared, she acted on what she felt at the moment. It was as if she lived to be totally reckless.

Now, Martinsburg, where we lived, was in northeastern Virginia, which was right in the middle of the war. When the war was over, we heard that the town changed hands almost thirty times! In July 1861, Stonewall Jackson retreated through Martinsburg. The Union soldiers quickly followed and occupied Martinsburg.

To celebrate the Fourth of July, the Yankees began enjoying the local liquor supply. The more they drank, the worse their behavior became. They began to loot houses, insult the local Southern sympathizers, shoot through windows, and make general nuisances of themselves. Belle describes it this way: "The doors of our houses were dashed in; our rooms were forcibly entered by solders…glass and fragile property of all kinds was wantonly destroyed; chairs and tables were hurled into the street." One squad came to our house because they had heard that Belle had decorated her room with Confederate flags. Luckily, one of the Negro maids rushed upstairs and burned the flags before the soldiers got to Belle's room.

One Yankee sergeant, who had obviously had too much liquor, was determined to raise the Union flag over our house in token of our submission to their authority. He was hollering and screaming. Trying to shut the front door, Mother yelled, "Every member of this household will die before that flag is raised." Cursing, the sergeant pushed mother. So Belle, who had come down stairs, drew out her pistol and shot the man who was threatening mother. As he fell to the floor, Belle declared, "Don't you ever push my mother around again." There was this dead silence. The other soldiers picked up the mortally wounded belligerent and left. And we all gave a great sigh of relief. Belle muttered about "the blue devils."

But it wasn't over. One of the servants ran in, crying, "Oh, missus, missus, dere gwine to burn de house down; dere piling de stuff a'gin it. Oh if Massa were back!" As a last resort, Belle sent a servant to headquarters to get help. Her tears and flashing ankles stalled the arsonists until a Federal officer in command arrived. The mob was stopped; the shooting declared self defense. Our Belle knew how to smile, bat her eyes, and seemingly promise all sorts of things that she shouldn't have been promising as a good Southern woman, and the authorities would always let her go.

But she didn't fool the Union authorities. They posted sentries around the house and kept close track of her activities. Towards the end of 1861, she made her first big mistake. She didn't know any codes and didn't worry about disguising her handwriting. One of her notes reached Union headquarters, and the balding colonel in command had her arrested. Mother was horrified. They took her to headquarters and read her the Articles of War. Belle yawned, stretched, and batted her eyes at several attractive Union soldiers who were watching with interest. The colonel asked sternly if she knew she could be sentenced to death? She smiled, murmured her thanks for his time, and swept out. Underneath all her bravado, she knew she had to be more careful. For a time she used as helper an old Negro, who carried messages inside a big watch from which the insides had been removed.

Many Union soldiers wanted to meet our Belle because she had quite a reputation—and not just for carrying messages. Leaning into them, she would bat her eyes, rub her hand up and down their sleeves, and ask another leading question. Soon they'd tell her everything they knew. A *New York Tribune* reporter who stayed at our house got daily briefings from the Union officers. Belle would manage to be in earshot of these reports and pass the information on to the Confederate officers. She went to dinners and dances, acting like a flirtatious ninny, but learning all she could about Union military plans and movements. Late at night, she would write notes, pack them in the old watch, and send Eliza to General Jeb Stuart and Stonewall Jackson. Much to my horror, she would also take the Union officers' sabers and pistols and pass them on to the Confederacy.

In the spring of 1862, the authorities arrested her in the town of Front Royal and sent her to Baltimore by train. Although we were worried, Belle just laughed. Nothing was going to happen to *her!* They would see and nothing did—even though she waved her small Confederate flag out the window the entire trip. When she arrived, General Dix didn't know what to do with her, so he put her up in the Eutaw Hotel, one of the nicest hotels in the city, for a week and then sent her home.

Belle the Spy

Belle loved performing acts of heroic daring, while I'd rather sit and sew. She was a woman of action. As the Union authorities became more aware of her, she loved outwitting them, charming them into conversations that they shouldn't have been having with a Confederate. When she got bored, she would visit the camps, call on generals and colonels in their tents, and accept carriage rides on lazy summer afternoons. She danced and flirted with Northerners as well as Southerners because she said she had to be on good terms with both sides. I think she liked all the danger involved.

In Front Royal, she began spying away, compromising a young Captain who gave her flowers, wrote her poems, and passed her information. She discovered that Union General James Shields and his staff met in the parlor of the local hotel so she hid in a closet, eavesdropping on their meeting through a knothole in the floor. For hours she knelt in that closet, trying to catch every word. Once she knew their plans, she scrambled through meadows and woods to reach the Confederates, trying to avoid being caught by the Union sentries. When she came to a clearing, the Union soldiers spied her and shot at her as she ran, waving her white bonnet, to the Confederate lines. Several bullets actually hit her clothing, but none hit her body. Thanks to her keen ears, General Jackson took Martinsburg and Fort Royal and advanced towards Washington, D.C. In a note to her, Jackson said, "I thank you, for myself and for the army, for the immense service that you have rendered your country today." For her contributions, she was awarded the Southern Cross of Honor and made an honorary member of Jackson's staff.

Although Belle wasn't beautiful, she could beguile most men. A charming, witty conversationalist, she talked easily with anyone she met, while I remained tongue-tied. Perhaps the difference between the two of us was the minute she saw a good-looking man, her adrenalin started pumping—and they knew it! When Federal commanders accused her of acting as a courier, she would look very demure and let her eyes tell them how good looking they were. Few men could resist her.

The Yankees decided that the time had come to trap her. A handsome and experienced Union spy named C. W. Smitley posing as a paroled Confederate officer set about to charm her. She invited him to dine with our family. We all liked him. Later he accompanied her to a party, and the two of them sang "The Bonnie Blue Flag," looking deeply into each other's eyes.

> We are a band of brothers,
> natives of the soil,
> Fighting for our property
> we gained by honest toil;
> But when our rights were threatened
> the cry rose near and far,
> Hurrah for the Bonnie Blue Flag
> that bears a single star.

Our brothers teased Belle because she turned all sorts of color when anyone mentioned Smitley's name. The two of them rode horses, took long moonlight walks hand in hand, and sang duets. Although she was warned that he was a Yankee scout, he denied it, and she believed him. Finally,

Belle asked him to take a dispatch to Stonewall for her. The trap was sprung.

The Union detectives stormed into our house. They lined us up against a wall, while they went through Belle's closets and desk looking for contraband and messages. Our wonderful Eliza had run off with some papers and burned them, but they found enough to lead Belle away through the mob standing outside the house. My sister who could laugh at everything told me later she wept on the way to Washington—not because she was arrested—she figured she could handle that, but because she had fallen for the wrong man.

When she arrived in Washington, she was sent to the Old Capitol Building in Washington, D.C. She told me later that this vast brick building reeked of unwashed bodies, wet woolen uniforms, and gas jets. She waited only several minutes before she was brought into the inquisition room. There, Superintendent Wood, greeted her most affably, "And so this is the celebrated rebel spy...I am glad to have so distinguished a personage."

"Well, I'm not glad to be here," she retorted.

Mr. Wood told her that she could ask for anything she wished, so she requested a rocking chair and a fire. During the month that she was imprisoned, the authorities pressured her to sign an oath of allegiance to the United States. "I hope when I commence that oath, my tongue may cleave to the roof of my mouth," she declared. "I hope before I swear allegiance that my arm falls paralyzed to my side." Realizing that she wouldn't give in, the prison authorities let her alone. The Washington Southerners provided her with good food. Her fellow prisoners gave her tokens of their affection, and she often sang well-known Confederate songs for her fellow inmates.

> Maryland!
> She is not dead, nor deaf, nor dumb.
> Huzza! She spurns the Northern scum!

As one prisoner said later, "She would sing that song as if her very soul was in every word she uttered. It used to bring a lump up in my throat every time I heard it." Known for her lively spirits, she could influence both Union and Confederate soldiers. People talked about her more risqué behavior, saying that she teased Union solders with lewd remarks and dressed in an unseemly fashion. But her fellow prisoners always swept their hats off when she passed. Never brought to trial, she was paroled to Richmond with about 200 prisoners. As they drove off, the Confederate prisoners cheered her loudly.

One story Belle omitted from her own recollections was her involvement with another prisoner, Lieutenant McVay. A good-looking young man, he had known Belle when they were younger. Never one to miss an opportunity, Belle announced her engagement to McVay. They planned a wedding as soon as they won their freedom, and Belle asked permission to buy her trousseau in Washington. The War Department coldly denied the request, which was just as well, because McVay remained in prison.

But my sister managed to convince Superintendent Wood of the Old Capitol Prison to purchase her trousseau and send it after her, under a flag of truce! When her trousseau arrived in Richmond, Belle permitted the ladies to see and feel her Washington finery. Once upon a time, these ladies had been the proud owners of many beautiful day outfits and evening gowns. Their wardrobes also contained a healthy supply of elegant slippers, stockings, corsets, and hoops. These days we haven't had any new dresses since before the war. Instead, we were dying and remodeling our dresses, or making clothes out of homespun. When it became tired, we would unravel it and weave it into a new garment.

Life was hard. We were using parched wheat to make coffee and sassafras for tea. We had food because the woods were full of animals that could be killed and streams full of fish. But we didn't have the luxury of a nice dress. Long ago, we had torn up our silk dresses to make flags and banners. We had made socks and mittens from unraveled wool blankets or tattered clothing and shoes from old felt hats or bits of canvas. We had learned how to spin, weave, and knit, but we certainly didn't have any fine new dresses!

Richmond citizens were thrilled to see Belle. Crowds lined the streets, calling her name. The celebrated Richmond Light Infantry Blues presented arms in her honor. Generals visited her; women stopped her on the streets to praise her. Wearing the gray riding costume of an "honorary captain" of the Confederacy, she was on horseback at troop reviews.

By July 1863, Belle was back in Martinsburg, helping us devise ingenious ways of making coffee and bread in the Virginia climate of scarcity, when the Union captured the town again. Not wanting her mischief on his turf, Secretary Stanton ordered her arrested and sent to Washington's Carroll Prison, which houses prisoners of state, hostages, smugglers, spies, and criminals. Using India rubber balls to throw messages out her window, she communicated with her many admirers. When a fellow inmate, a Southern mail runner, planned an escape, she asked the superintendent to come to her cell. Several prisoners cried, "Murder, murder!" In the ensuing excitement, the mail runner crawled to the roof, slid down, and escaped.

After three months of imprisonment, our Belle became ill with typhoid. Our father managed to have her sentence commuted, and she was banished "to the South—never to return North again during the war." By this time, my sister Belle was a celebrity.

Leaving Home

When our father died, Belle decided to carry Southern dispatches to England. On the night of May 8, 1864, under the name of Mrs. Lewis, Belle sailed on the three-masted blockade runner, *Greyhound*, which carried tons of cotton bales, to England. To reach open water, the *Greyhound* had to sail past Union warships that lined the coast. When the darkness lifted, there was a shout: "Sail ho!" The *Greyhound's* frantic captain increased her steam pressure and set more sails, but the pursuing Union gunboat drew closer and began firing. As the crew threw valuable cotton overboard to make the ship sail faster, the *U.S.S. Connecticut* moved in. Belle burned the messages she was carrying from the Confederate secretary of state and tossed $25,000 in gold and Confederate bills overboard.

When a young Ensign, Samuel Hardinge, boarded the ship to sail the captured crew and the *Greyhound* to Boston, Belle decided to charm him. She said to me:

> I saw at a glance he was made of other stuff than his comrades . . . . His dark brown hair hung down on his shoulders; his eyes were large and bright. Those who judge of beauty by regularity of feature only, could not have pronounced him strictly handsome . . . but the fascination of his manner was such, his every movement was so much that of a refined gentleman, that my "Southern proclivities," strong as they were, yielded for a moment to the impulses of my heart, and I said to myself, *Oh, what a good fellow that must be.*

When Ensign Hardinge asked permission to enter her cabin, Belle replied pertly: "Certainly. I know I am a prisoner." Although he was now in command, he said, "I beg you will consider yourself a passenger, not a prisoner." As the *Greyhound* started north, Ensign Hardinge sang, read poems, and told stories to a fascinated Belle while the Confederate captain pondered about escaping. Soon Ensign Hardinge was asking her to marry him, but Belle hesitated. He was a Yankee after all. When she sent Hardinge on an errand, she helped the Confederate captain to escape. At the official inquiry into the escape, Sam Hardinge was arrested, tried, and dismissed from the Navy for neglect of duty. Union officials took Belle prisoner but released her to Canada with the admonition that if she were caught in the United States, she would be shot. After several months in Canada, she traveled to London, where she told the Confederacy's agent that she had destroyed the messages she carried in the *Greyhound*. That ended her role as Belle Boyd, Girl Spy.

After his court martial, Ensign Hardinge followed Belle to London. Their marriage on August 25, 1864, was a great event for Southern representatives in London, the newspapers, and a delighted American, British, and French public. She was considered a great heroine with amazing charisma. One excited correspondent revealed that, thanks to Belle's charms, Sam intended to leave England with his bride, run the blockade, and join the Confederacy! Belle had demonstrated indeed that women can sometimes work wonders.

Hardinge returned alone to the United States. It is unclear whether he carried Confederate dispatches. He was arrested by the Union and jailed in Old Capitol Building for desertion. Meanwhile, alone in London but with many admirers, Belle had to sell first her jewelry, then her wedding presents. To win sympathy for Hardinge and earn more money, she wrote her memoirs, *Belle Boyd in Camp and Prison*, which appeared at the war's end. Before she published them, however, she wrote President Abraham Lincoln offering not to publish the book if Sam was set free. The President ignored her letter.

Upon his release from Old Capitol Prison in February 1865, Hardinge returned to England, but only for a few months. The young man who had given up so much for her is said to have died a few months later, and Belle was a pregnant widow at twenty-one.

Belle began appearing in theatrical performances and lectured about her deeds as a Confederate spy. In 1866, President Johnson signed his Proclamation of Amnesty, allowing Belle to return home. She and her baby returned to United States, where she continued her stage career as Nina Benjamin. On March 17, 1869, she married an Englishman and former Union officer, John S. Hammond. Four children later, they divorced in 1884. Only six weeks after their divorce, she married Nathaniel High, Jr., a handsome actor from Toledo, Ohio. When her husband's income could not support them, Belle went on tour again, giving dramatic speeches about her experiences during the war. She began to emphasize the union of the North and South and ended her speeches with "One God, One Flag, One People forever." She died at age fifty-six. Four Union veterans lowered her coffin into the grave. One former Confederate soldier erected a tombstone that read: "Belle Boyd. Confederate Spy."

MARYS STORY

The site appears to be doomed. In the beginning, French-born American architect and urban planner, Pierre C. L'Enfant included Fort Lesley J. McNair as a major site for the defense of Washington, D.C. when he designed the street plan for the city. The fort was established in 1791 on Greenleaf Point where the Potomac meets the Anacostia River.

Unfortunately, the fort did not halt the invading British in 1814. Instead, the Americans abandoned the fort, carrying away as much gunpowder as possible. They hid the rest in a well. As the British soldiers stood in the empty fort, someone threw a match into the well, causing a tremendous explosion. Nearby officers and soldiers were killed. Perhaps this was an ominous sign for the future. The remaining soldiers destroyed the arsenal buildings, but the facilities were rebuilt after the war.

In 1826, the government purchased land north of the arsenal for the first federal penitentiary. During the Civil War, the Army took over the penitentiary; in 1864, an explosion killed twenty-one woman laborers in the arsenal room. President Lincoln attended their funeral and led the procession to Congressional Cemetery.

An ardent Southerner, Mary Surratt probably did not realize that the charming actor who sat at her boardinghouse table would assassinate the President. She surely did not realize that her son would abandon her to the authorities and that she and the conspirators accused of assassinating President Abraham Lincoln would be imprisoned here. She certainly did not know that she, along with three other conspirators, would be hung "by the neck 'till she be dead" for her part in the plot on July 9, 1865. A tennis court now occupies the site of the scaffold, but Mary Surratt in her black bonnet still roams the grounds of Fort McNair woefully proclaiming her innocence.

I was only seventeen when I married twenty-eight-year-old John Harrison Surratt of the District of Columbia. I married well, even though I was young. John was a successful man

Mary Surratt's boarding house is still standing at 541 H Street in the Chinatown area of Washington D.C. It is now a Chinese restaurant called *Wok n Roll*. *Courtesy of Michael Lodico, Jr.*

and he treated me kindly. Of course, when I gave him two sons and one dutiful daughter, he treated me even better. In 1852, he purchased 287 acres of farmland at the intersection of the Marlboro-Piscataway and New Cut roads in Prince George's County. By April 23, 1852, we had built and were living in the brand new Surratt House and Tavern. When John got a license for the tavern, it became a favorite meeting place for townsfolk and farmers bringing their herds or loads of produce to market. Teams of horses waited outside as their drivers in open vests and black-peaked caps sipped some Holland gin and ate a ham or turkey dinner. The community was now known as Surrattsville. I would make my famous pies—apple, lemon, and blueberry—and everyone would eat at least one slice and order another cup of coffee.

Local farmers, politicians, lawyers, and laborers came to eat, drink, and talk about the problems that were dividing the country in the 1850s. The North wanted the South to give up their farms, build factories, and abolish slavery. The South needed to keep its slaves to maintain its fields of cotton and tobacco and to live the way we did. Our lives were much more laborious than the Yankees. They didn't center on factories but on agriculture, tobacco, and cotton. John and I believed in the South, and that's what we taught our children.

On December 6, 1853, we bought another piece of property on H Street in Washington. I felt so fortunate. I had a husband who was doing well, three children, and two properties. I got a new hat. I was on my way up in the world.

When the Civil War broke out in 1861, my son, Isaac, was a Confederate soldier; Anna was at home; and our third child, Johnny, was still studying at St. Charles College. But in August 1862, his father suddenly died. Abruptly, I was a miserable thirty-nine-year-old widow who had inherited debts and two properties. There was a war on, and money was scarce for everyone. Everything went downhill—even the Surrattsville tavern and farm.

Widowhood

Johnny or John, Jr., who was home at the time, did not return to school. He became the Surratsville postmaster on September 1, 1862, which was better than having him help out in the tavern. He didn't mind serving the drinks, but he kept disappearing, saying he was too busy to be involved in the humdrum life of a landlord. By 1863, he was working as a Confederate secret agent, carrying messages to Confederate boats on the Potomac River and sending messages about Union troop movements south to Richmond in the Washington area. He didn't realize how dangerous the spy business was. He was like a little boy playing a grown man's game.

Meanwhile, people didn't consider it proper for a woman to run a tavern, and I wasn't making enough money anyway. So I rented Surrattsville Tavern to John Lloyd. Then October 1, 1864, my seventeen-year-old daughter, Anna, and I moved to our Washington property on 541 H Street and turned it into a boardinghouse—a much more respectable occupation than running a tavern. Washington was a city of high stoops and brick houses; teams of horses pulled heavy wagons; and from almost any point in the city, you could see the Capitol and the Washington Monument. But the city had changed a great deal since I had last been there. A citywide water system had replaced the corner pumps; taverns had replaced private residences; and there were many more Whites from the North and Negroes from the South. Spies and sympathizers from both sides filled Washington.

I kept a nice middle-class home with a family atmosphere. I accepted my guests on the basis of referrals, recommendations, or interviews. It wasn't the world's best job, but offering space in my home to young people who left farms and villages behind was considered a decent job for a widow. After all, as a mother of three, I knew how to guide these young people in the ways of the city and shelter them from undesirable influences. I offered them simple, but ample, meals of roasted meats and fresh vegetables in the dining room and on the side porch when it was really hot.

As I said, my main concern was my son, Johnny. He thought it was exciting to carry dispatches to Confederate boats on the Potomac River or to send information regarding Union troop movements to the Confederate generals. He enjoyed this reckless lifestyle and often carried the messages in his boots or in the planks of his buggy. Outfoxing the federal detectives gave him a thrill, but then he was so young. He often stayed at the boardinghouse and brought his friends to visit. I found it odd that while other men fought and maybe died on the battlefields for the Confederacy, Johnny and his friends just talked about it.

One of his new friends was a handsome actor—another John with jet-black hair and the most striking eyes. Oh, he was a charmer, and he knew it. Of course, the likeable John Wilkes Booth came from a famous family of actors. He kept us all amused by his ability to suddenly declaim Shakespeare's lines or to take on the role of Marc Anthony or Romeo. We had some wonderful charades with him, and dinners became more exciting when he was around. I would sit with them longer than usual, enjoying the fun. The smoke from their big black cheroots would swirl around the ceiling; they would drink their corn liquor; and they would talk about how the world could be different. It was "if only" time.

When Booth wasn't reciting some Shakespeare, he would talk about Mr. Lincoln and how he hated him. He said he had promised his mother not to become a soldier and that's why he wasn't in uniform. At one point, he had been a member of the Know-Nothing Party, which believed in preserving the country for native-born white citizens. He also said that he had been so excited about the Southern cause that he had attended John Brown's execution at Harper's Ferry. He and my Johnny became good friends. They would attend the theater and then go out for drinks and oysters.

When Lincoln was elected for a second term, Booth said he had to make the world a better place. I fed them roast pork and blueberry pie as he cast his spell. My son,

Johnny, some other men, and he began to talk about kidnapping President Abraham Lincoln and taking him to Richmond. "The South wants justice. She will wait no longer." Booth declared. By capturing Lincoln, they expected to force the federal government to return Confederate prisoners of war who were confined in Union prisons. I rolled out my pie dough in the kitchen and listened to them plot. They thought England would support the gallant Southerners who had outwitted the Union and captured their president. The South and they would gain so much. His dark eyes sparkling, Booth declared that they would be famous forever for this heroic deed. In this way, they would swell the dwindling ranks of the Confederate army and help the South win the war. Such dreams of glory. Didn't they know that life doesn't work that way?

Within several months, Booth had recruited Michael O'Laughlin, Samuel Arnold, Lewis Powell (Paine), David Herold, and George Atzerodt. They would visit and converse in whispered tones upstairs. Johnny would ride off on mysterious errands. In early 1865, he and Booth, along with their friends, awaited the carriage of Lincoln as he left the Campbell General Hospital traveling back to Washington. They hoped to kidnap him that night, but Lincoln changed his mind. He stayed in Washington to meet with the 140th Indiana Regiment and to present a captured Confederate flag to the governor.

Our country was divided and unhappy. By January, Southern schoolboys had left their homes and classes to follow their older brothers to war. Barefoot and hatless, they would feel the pangs of hunger as they shivered with cold, hoping that something would happen to rescue them from their plight. Booth became more determined to take action. "Our country owes all her troubles to him," he declared.

When the Union siege of the Confederate capital of Richmond, Virginia, finally ended, we all knew that the war was coming to an end. The Union Army marched in, and Confederate forces under General Lee moved west. In Washington, people began to celebrate: strangers hugged strangers, church bells tolled; cannons fired. People were dancing in the streets, while we were sitting behind closed shades. On Tuesday, April 4, the State Department ordered that all federal buildings be illuminated. At twilight, an army band played "The Star Spangled Banner," and the War Department buildings burst into light.

One week later, on April 9, 1865, Lee surrendered to Grant, and all the celebrating began again. Old or young, rich or poor, white or Negro, people filled Pennsylvania Avenue; the Marine band played marches; the crowd shouted for Lincoln. Booth and his friend, Lewis Paine, went to hear. The rest of us stayed home. We could hear the music and the raucous laughter of the Yankees. The war was almost over.

The Assassination

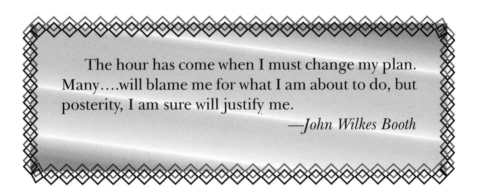

The hour has come when I must change my plan. Many....will blame me for what I am about to do, but posterity, I am sure will justify me.

—*John Wilkes Booth*

The day was Good Friday. Deciding that kidnapping Mr. Lincoln was a formidable task, Booth opted to kill him instead. He planned that some of his friends would kill Secretary of State Seward and Vice-President Johnson. Everyone knows what happened that night at Ford's Theater. Afterwards, Booth fled eleven miles south with David Herold to Maryland and my tavern there. He drank some whiskey, and the two fugitives collected supplies, including field glasses and a Spencer rifle. They didn't know that Paine failed to kill Seward, and Atzerodt had made no attempt to kill Johnson. From the tavern, they went to Dr. Samuel Mudd, who treated Booth's leg, injured from his fall.

As the President lay dying, investigators paid a visit to our boardinghouse. They came looking for Johnny because they knew that he was one of Booth's friends. But I hadn't seen Johnny for almost two weeks. He had gone to Canada. By midday, the city was draped in black and flags were lowered. The celebration was over; only the crowds remained. Meanwhile, spurred on by a $100,000 reward, federal soldiers, policemen, and private detectives hunted for Booth, David Herold, and my son, but the three men were quite successful at eluding their pursuers. The government had better luck at arresting some of the accomplices; Edman Spangler, who had held the reins of Booth's horse, was a stagehand at Ford's theater. On April 17, the authorities came again to my boardinghouse to investigate Johnny's disappearance. While there, a man claiming to be a laborer called. An officer asked me if I knew the man. When I swore I didn't, the authorities arrested everyone in the house and the mystery man, who was Lewis Paine, the would-be assassin of Secretary of State Seward. They charged me with conspiracy. They said I had aided the assassins and assisted in their escape, but all I had really done was feed and house them.

They put me in Old Capitol Prison with its dank wet smell. My dirty room had an iron bed covered with a straw mattress and a pillow, but no clean white sheets—just brown blankets, which probably had covered many other prisoners. It also contained a filthy wooden bucket and a small table with a tin cup. I spread my handkerchief over the pillow, wrapped myself in my cloak, and fell asleep that first night. I kept telling myself that this was all a bad dream. But the next morning, when I saw the gray flour bread and gray liquid called coffee, I knew that it wasn't a dream. My strength failed me, and I sank into a stupor interrupted only by my grief or by my jailers.

One of the jailers told me that Mr. Lincoln's body was taken to the Capitol to lie in state. Eight gray horses pulled the funeral hearse. The coffin was black and silver—odd for a man who was so simple. The church bells tolled; the guns boomed; the bands played softly; and everyone marched alongside him. Even the horses' hoofs were muffled. People filed past the bier in the Capitol. The crowds milled in the street in front of my prison windows. I could feel their hate coming through the walls.

David Herold gave himself up, but Booth refused to be taken alive. Federal troops shot him on April 26, 1865, in a burning barn on the Virginia countryside. As the nation mourned and Mr. Lincoln's body was carried home to Springfield, Illinois, the prosecution prepared its case against the eight remaining accused conspirators. On May 1, President Andrew Johnson ordered that a military commission try the case.

The Conspiracy Trial

We were moved to Arsenal Prison in the old fort with its swarms of mosquitoes, rattling chains, half-stifled moans, and dank chillness—even in the heat of a Washington spring. Fortunately, my hands were left free. Only my ankles were in chains.

My trial began on May 12. As a forty-two-year-old widow, I wore black and covered my head with a black bonnet and veil. So many things went against me. The tribunal knew that Booth used to visit my son at the boardinghouse, just a few blocks from Ford's Theater. They knew that Lewis Paine, David Herold, and George Atzerodt also frequented the boardinghouse. I shouldn't have said that I didn't know Lewis Paine that time when the officers came back. Now they thought me a liar. They knew that Booth visited me the afternoon of the assassination. My Surrattsville tenant, John M. Lloyd, became a state's witness just prior to the trial. They say he placed the rope around my neck. He testified that I had requested that he have field glasses and carbines ready for Booth and Herold when they arrived at the Surratt House late on the night of the assassination.

I knew nothing of Booth's plans, and my trips to Surrattsville had to do solely with collecting money I was owed. Just because those men came to my boardinghouse doesn't mean I knew what was going on. I was too busy taking care of the house, and cooking for all those people.

I kept expecting that Johnny would return home. He certainly wouldn't abandon me to the authorities. Once he did return, I knew I would be released.

The Execution

After seven weeks, the military commission found all eight of us guilty. They gave Samuel Arnold, Samuel Mudd, and Michael O'Laughlin hard labor for life at Dry Tortugas Prison, off the Florida coast. The court found Lewis Payne, David Herold, George Atzerodt, and me guilty of conspiring with Booth in Mr. Lincoln's assassination and the attempted assassination of Secretary of State Seward. They sentenced us to be "hanged by the neck 'till they be dead for treason, conspiracy, and plotting murder" the very next day, July 7, 1865, between the "hours of ten o'clock am and two o'clock pm." *The Daily Morning Chronicle* reported that, "Mrs. Surratt was completely unnerved and begged for a reprieve."

As the authorities informed us of our sentences, workmen were constructing a scaffold in the yard of the Old Arsenal Prison. Someone told me that the high scaffold was strong enough to support three men and one woman. Besides the scaffold, the authorities had ordered four graves to be dug. A coarse pine box used for packing guns stood besides each grave.

The newsboys were shouting that we would be hung. Reporters spied on us through cell windows. The hangman prepared four nooses from Boston hemp supplied by the Navy Yard.

On a clear hot July 7 morning, the four of us were led out for execution. I am glad I wasn't alone. I could feel the sun on my body, but it no longer warmed me. They bound my arms and legs with strips of linen. I complained I was being bound too tightly. "It hurts," I said.

"Well," was the consoling reply, "it won't last long."

Many people believed that I would not be hanged. No woman had ever been executed under federal orders. Until the moment when I stood on the gallows, just before the noose was put about my neck, I thought I might be saved, but I wasn't. My last words on the scaffold were, "Don't let me fall."

Maybe it was my son, Johnny, who kicked the blocks from underneath me. If he had returned, I might be living still.

At 1:26 pm, the signal was given, the large blocks supporting the uprights were knocked out, the drops fell heavily, and the four bodies hung suspended. The bodies were allowed to hang about twenty minutes before they were pronounced dead. The four conspirators were buried in unmarked graves beside the gallows.

The Political Fallout

Whether Mary was completely innocent will never be truly known, but her trial was a low point in our legal system. If she had been tried a year later by a civil court, events might have gone differently. After her hanging, the Supreme Court confirmed the Constitutional principle that a military court had no jurisdiction over civilians.

A majority of the military tribunal sent a written request to President Johnson recommending that because of Mary's "sex and age" that the penalty be changed to life in prison. That clemency plea for Mary Surratt is immersed in murky political dealings. Many believe Secretary of War, Edwin Stanton, a rival of Johnson's, withheld the plea from the President. When Johnson learned later that the written appeal had been concealed, he fired Secretary Stanton, who opposed Johnson's actions. Once Stanton was fired, the Radical Republicans moved to impeach President Johnson. He was acquitted by one vote, but the Democrats refused to nominate him for a second term. Discredited, Johnson returned to Tennessee and ran for State Senator but was defeated.

The Postlude

Four years later Anna Surratt made a successful plea to the government for her mother's remains. Today, Mary Surratt is buried in Mount Olivet Cemetery in Washington, D.C. Her headstone reads simply "MRS. SURRATT."

Michael O'Laughlin died in prison in 1867; Edman Spangler, Dr. Samuel Mudd, and Samuel Arnold died after their release. The one conspirator remaining alive, Johnny Surratt joined the Papal Zouaves at the Vatican after fleeing to Canada. In 1866, a fellow Zouave denounced him, and he was ultimately sent back to Washington for trial by a civil criminal court.

After a two-month trial, a mistrial was declared. He was a free man who had left his mother to be hung and who was known to be a participant in the plot to kidnap President Lincoln. In a publicity stunt worthy of the twenty-first century, John Surratt got on the lecture circuit by December 1870, where he boasted about his role as Confederate agent and a member of Booth's plot to kidnap Abraham Lincoln. Daringly, he decided to lecture in Washington a few blocks from Ford's Theater. But his intended lecture was seen as an outrageous attempt to profit from the assassination just five years after Lincoln's death. The event was canceled, and he never lectured again.

Mary Surratt was the first woman executed by the United States Government. To this day, her execution comes under considerable criticism. If you listen carefully in Washington's misty dawn, you might hear her voice crying over the ramparts of that ancient prison, "I am innocent."

The Smithsonian Institution is the world's largest museum complex. *Courtesy of D. Peter Lund*

BIBLIOGRAPHY

Allgor, Catherine. *Parlor Politics*. Charlottesville, VA: University, Press of Virginia, 2000

"American Indians." The New Encyclopedia Britannica. 1986. Macropaedia Volume 13, p. 310-400

"The Architect of the Capitol." 2007. Http://www.aoc.gov/ (March 12, 2007)

Arnebeck, Bob. "The Seat of Empire – a history of Washington, D.C. 1790-1961." Http://www.geocities.com/bobarnebeck/swamp1800. html (June 6, 2007)

Axelrod, Alan. *The War between the Spies*. New York, NY: Atlantic Monthly Press, 1992

Bachman, Susie. Pawprints and Purrs, Inc. July 2007. Http://sniksnak. com/lore.html

Balz, Chrissy A. "Healy Clock Theft Has Roots in GU History." The Hoya. Nov. 8, 2005. http://thehoya.com/news/110805/news10. cfm (April 2, 2007)

"Battle of Tippecanoe." *The New Encyclopedia Britannica*. 1986. Micropaedia Volume 11, p. 792

Berg, Scott W. *George Washington's Rules of Civility and Decent Behaviour.* Cambridge, MA: The Riverside Press, 1926

"Bleeding Kansas." 2007. Http://www.legendsofamerica.com/OZ-bleedingkansas.html (April 20, 2007)

Caughman, H. Shirah. "A Light at the End of the Tunnel." The Hoya. March 1999. Http://thehoya.com/news/032399/features1. htm (April 5, 2007)

Caravantes, Peggy. *Petticoat Spies*. Greensboro, NC: Morgan Reynolds, 2002

Campbell, Helen Jones. *The Case for Mrs. Surratt*. New York: G.P. Putnam's Sons, 1943

Carson, Barbara. *Ambitious Appetites*. Washington, D.C.: The American Institute of Architects Press, 1990

Cooper, Thaddeus. "Places to Tour—Old Stone House." 2004. Http://www.toursofdc.org/tours/oldstonehouse (July 16, 2007)

Curran, Robert Emmett, S.J. "A Documentary History of Georgetown University: A Bicentennial Exhibition, 1989." Http://www.library.georgetown.edu/dept/speccoll/briefhis.htm (April 23, 2007)

Davis, Carroll Curtis. *Belle Boyd in Camp and Prison*. South Brunswick, NJ: Thomas Yoseloff, 1968.

Davis, David Brion and Mintz, Steven. *The Boisterous Sea Of Liberty*. New York: Oxford University Press, 1998

De Kay, James T. *A Rage for Glory*. New York, NY: Free Press, 2004

Duane, O. B. *African Myths & Legends*. London, Brockhampton Press, 1998

Dunbar, Janet. *The Early Victorian Woman*. Westport, CT: Hyperion Press, Inc., 1953

Dunmore, John Murray, 4th Earl of. *The New Encyclopedia Britannica*. 1986. Micropaedia Volume 4, p. 277

Dwyer, Ed. "D.C. Confidential." Nov-Dec, 2003 Http://www.aarpmagazine.org/travel/articles/a2003-10-28-dconfidential.html

Eberlein, Harold Donaldson & Cortlandt Van Dyke Hubbard, *Historic Houses of George-town & Washington City*. Richmond, VA: The Dietz Press, Inc., 1958

Eckert, Allan W. *A Sorrow In Our Heart: The Life of Tecumseh*. New York: Bantam Books, 1992

Fitz-Gerald, Christine Maloney. *Encyclopedia of Presidents: William Henry Harrison, Ninth President of the United States*. Chicago: Children's Press, 1987

Furbee, Mary Rodd. *Outrageous Women of Civil War Times*. Hoboken, NJ: John Wiley, 2003

Georgetown University. 2007. http://www.georgetown.edu/home/about.html (April 5, 2007)
Http://jesuits.georgetown.edu/index.html (April 5, 2007)
Http://library.georgetown.edu/department/speccoll/pfhealy.htm (April 5, 2007)

Georgetown University. 2007 "Ignatius Loyola's Inspiration and John Carroll's Imagination." http://jesuits.georgetown.edu/heritage10.html (April 5, 2007)

German Embassy, Washington D.C.. 2007. Http://www.germany.info/relaunch/culture/ger_americans/paper, html (June 3, 2007)

Goodwin, Doris Kearns. *Team of Rivals*. New York: Simon & Schuster Paperbacks, 2005

Guttridge, Leonard F. *Our Country, Right Or Wrong*. New York: A Tom Doherty Associates Book, 2006

Haley, Alex. *Roots*. New York: Double Day, 1976

Hartman, Saidiya V. *Lose Your Mother: A Journey Along The Atlantic Slave Route*. New York, NY: Farrar, Strauss and Giroux, 2007

Heberle, Robert. "Pilfering a GU Landmark." The Hoya. October 2005. Http://www.thehoya.com/news/100705/news4.cfm (April 2, 2007)

Hickey, Donald R. *Don't Give Up The Ship*! Urbana, IL: University of Illinois Press, 2006

Holzer, Hans. *Ghosts: True Encounters with the World Beyond*. New York: Black Dog And Leventhal Publishers, Inc. 2004

Hong, Michele. "Vandals Strike Clock Tower." The Hoya. October 2006. Http://www.thehoya.com/news/101706/news7.cfm (April 2, 2007)

Hovey, Lonnie. "Ask the White House." August 5, 2004. Www. whitehouse.gov/ask/20040805.html (July 12, 2007)

Jesuit Secondary Education Association. Http://www.jsea.org/ (April 3, 2007)

Johnson, Walter. *Soul By Soul*. Cambridge, MA: Harvard University Press, 1999

Kachur, Matthew. *The Slave Trade*. New York: Chelsea House Publishers, 2006

Kelly, Martin. "Chart of Presidents." About.com: American History. 2007

Knight, Kevin. "The Society of Jesus." Http://www.newadvent.org/ cathen/14081a.htm (April 11, 2007)

Lewis, Charles Lee. *The Romantic Decatur*. Freeport: Books for Libraries Press, 1937

Mccue, George. *The Octagon*. Washington, D.C. American Institute of Architects Foundation, 1976

Mikkelson, Barbara. "The Curse of Tecumseh." November 2004. Http://www.snopes.com/history/american/curse.asp (May 18, 2007)

Moore, Charles, *Washington, Past And Present*. New York: The Century Co., 1929

O'Toole, Patricia. *The Five Of Hearts*. New York, NY: Clarkson Potter, 1990

Norton, Mary Beth. *Liberty's Daughters*. Boston, MA: Little, Brown and Company, 1980

Nagel, Paul C. *Descent from Glory*. New York, NY: Oxford University Press, 1983

Pike, John. (maintained by Steve Aftergood). October 2, 2000. Http://www.fas.org/nuke/guide/usa?C3i/peoc.htm (July 20, 2007)

Progenealogists: The Palatine Project. 2007. Http://www.progenealogists.com/palproject/ (June 3, 2007)

Radi, David A. "Intelligence Inside the White House: The Influence of Executive Style And Technology." March 1997. Http://www.pirp.harvard.edu/pubs-pdf/radi/radi-i97-3.pdf (July 20, 2007)

Reps, John W. *Monumental Washington*. Princeton, NJ: Princeton University Press, 1967

Roberts, Giselle. *The Confederate Belle*. Columbia, MO: University of Missouri Press, 2003

Sage, Henry. "Sage History: An American Experience." 2006. Http://www.sagehistory.net/civilwar/cwdates.html (April 3, 2007)

Simonds, Katherine. "The Tragedy of Mrs. Henry Adams." *The New England Quarterly*, Vol. 9, No. 4. (Dec., 1936), pp. 564-582

Spruill, Julia Cherry. *Women's Life And Work In The Southern Colonies*. New York, NY: The Norton Library, 1972

Steers, Edward. *Blood on the Moon*. Lexington, KY: The University Press of Kentucky, 2001

Sugden, John. *Tecumseh, A Life*. New York: Henry Holt and Company, 1998

Swanson, James L. & Daniel Weinberg. *Lincoln's Assassins: Their Trial And Execution; An Illustrated History*. Santa Fe, NM: Arena Editions, 2001

"Tecumseh." *The New Encyclopedia Britannica*. 1986. Micropaedia, Volume 11, p. 601-2

"The Battle of Tippecanoe." Http://www.rootsweb.com/~usgenweb/ky/tippecanoe/preface.html (May 7, 2007)

The Old Stone House, 1765. Washington, DC: National Park Service. Undated.

"The Old West." January 2007. Http://www.theoutlaws.com/indians1. htm (May 1, 2007)

"The White House." Http://www.whitehouse.gov/history/eeobtour/ mullett-bio_nonflash.html (July 6, 2007)

Thom, James Alexander. *Panther in the Sky.* New York: Ballantine Books, 1989

"2007 Jesuit Conference of the United States." Http://www.jesuit. org/ (March 16, 2007)

Truman, Margaret, *First Ladies.* New York: Random House, 1995

U.S. Capitol Police Http://www.uscapitolpolice.gov/home.php (March 12, 2007)

"William Henry Harrison." *The New Encyclopedia Britannica.* 1986. Micropaedia Volume 5, pp. 723-4

"Words of Tecumseh." Http://www.ilhawaii.net/~stony/shawnee.html (May 7, 2007)

Washington, George. *Rules of Civility and Decent Behavior in Company and Conversation.* Ed. Charles Moore. Boston, MA, Riverside Press, 1926.

Research Notations

The following specific resources have been used to enhance and illustrate story lines.

Pursuit of Glory—Guttridge, p 263
Father Abraham—Lamon, p. 111; Lamon 1895, pp 115-116
The Haunted Hay-Adams Hotel—Moore, 12/5/1885, p. 239
The Clock Watcher—http://jesuits.georgetown.edu
Queen Dolley—Memories and Letters, p.130, p. 71
Belle Boyd, Girl Spy—Davis, p. 132, p. 750;Furbee, p. 84
Mary's Story—Swanson, James L. & Daniel Weinberg, p. 31

INDEX

Washington, D.C. is a city of ghosts. Many heroes lie in Arlington Cemetery. *Courtesy of D. Peter Lund*